ELECTRIC INTERURBANS
AND THE
AMERICAN PEOPLE

RAILROADS PAST & PRESENT

GEORGE M. SMERK AND H. ROGER GRANT, EDITORS

A list of books in the series appears at the end of this volume.

ELECTRIC INTERURBANS AND THE AMERICAN PEOPLE

H. ROGER GRANT

INDIANA UNIVERSITY PRESS

Bloomington & Indianapolis

This book is a publication of

Indiana University Press
Office of Scholarly Publishing
Herman B Wells Library 350
1320 East Tenth Street
Bloomington, Indiana 47405 USA

iupress.indiana.edu

© 2016 by H. Roger Grant

All rights reserved

No part of this book may be reproduced or utilized in any form or by any means, electronic or mechanical, including photocopying and recording, or by any information storage and retrieval system, without permission in writing from the publisher. The Association of American University Presses' Resolution on Permissions constitutes the only exception to this prohibition.

The paper used in this publication meets the minimum requirements of the American National Standard for Information Sciences–Permanence of Paper for Printed Library Materials, ANSI Z39.48-1992.

Manufactured in the
United States of America

Library of Congress
Cataloging-in-Publication Data

Names: Grant, H. Roger, [date] author.
Title: Electric interurbans and the American people / H. Roger Grant.
Description: Bloomington : Indiana University Press, [2016] | Series: Railroads past and present | Includes bibliographical references and index.
Identifiers: LCCN 2016013593 (print) | LCCN 2016022115 (ebook) | ISBN 9780253022721 (cl : alk. paper) | ISBN 9780253023209 (ebook)
Subjects: LCSH: Street-railroads–United States–History.
Classification: LCC HE4471 .G73 2016 (print) | LCC HE4471 (ebook) | DDC 388.4/60973–dc23
LC record available at https://lccn.loc.gov/2016013593

1 2 3 4 5   21 20 19 18 17 16

For my grandmother

KATHARINE BEERKLE DINSMORE (1876–1952)

*who wrecked her automobile while chasing a car of the
Albia Interurban Railway and never drove again*

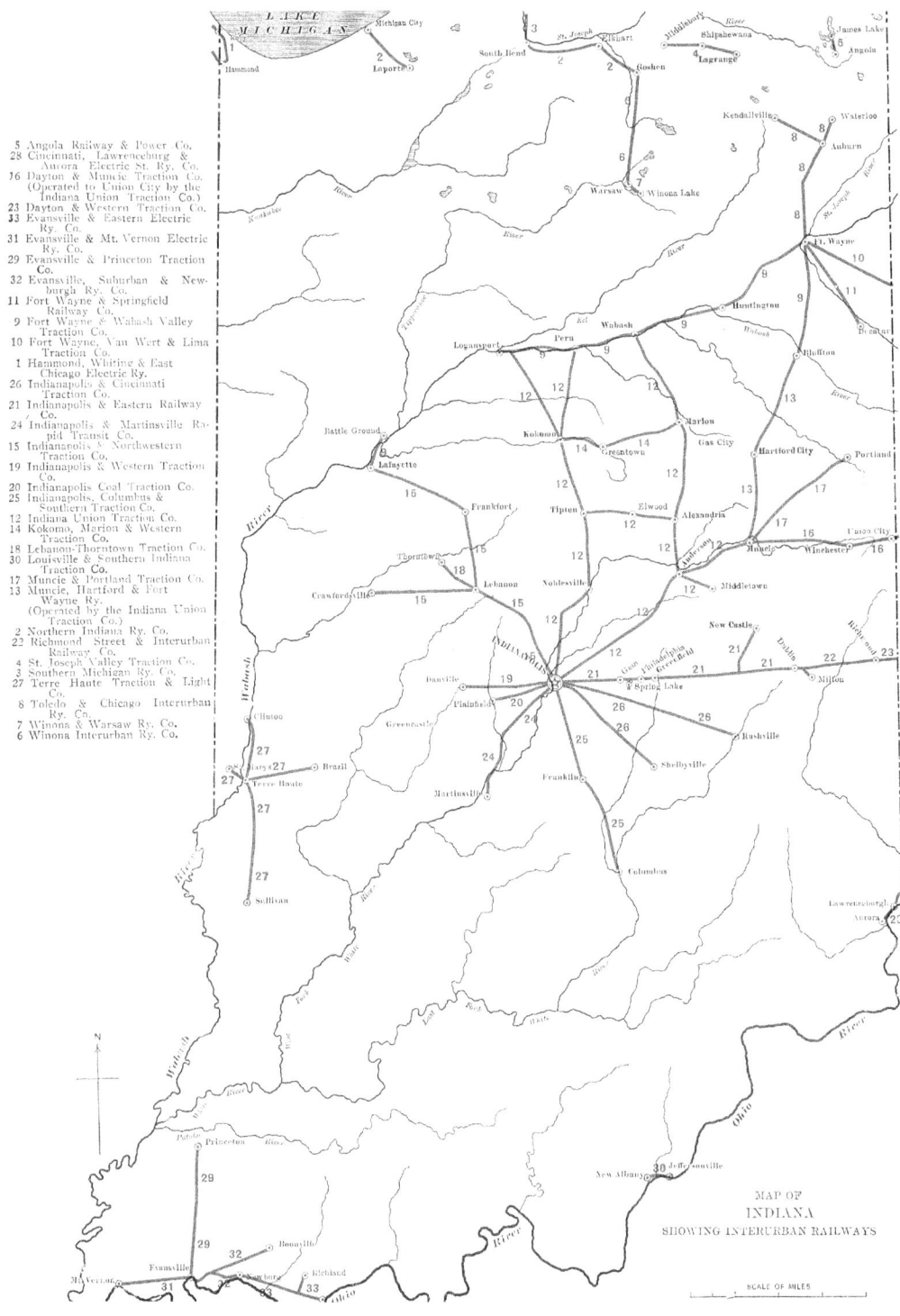

Indiana was second only to Ohio in the size of its interurban network. This map reveals the gestating Hoosier State network. Not until 1910 did the completion of the Winona Interurban Railway make possible a continuous route between Louisville, Indianapolis, and Chicago, albeit over several independent roads.

Author's collection

CONTENTS

FOREWORD *by Norman Carlson*   ix

PREFACE   xi

ACKNOWLEDGMENTS   xiii

1   ENTHUSIASM   2

2   INTERURBANS IN DAILY LIFE   56

3   SAYING GOODBYE   126

NOTES   153

INDEX   165

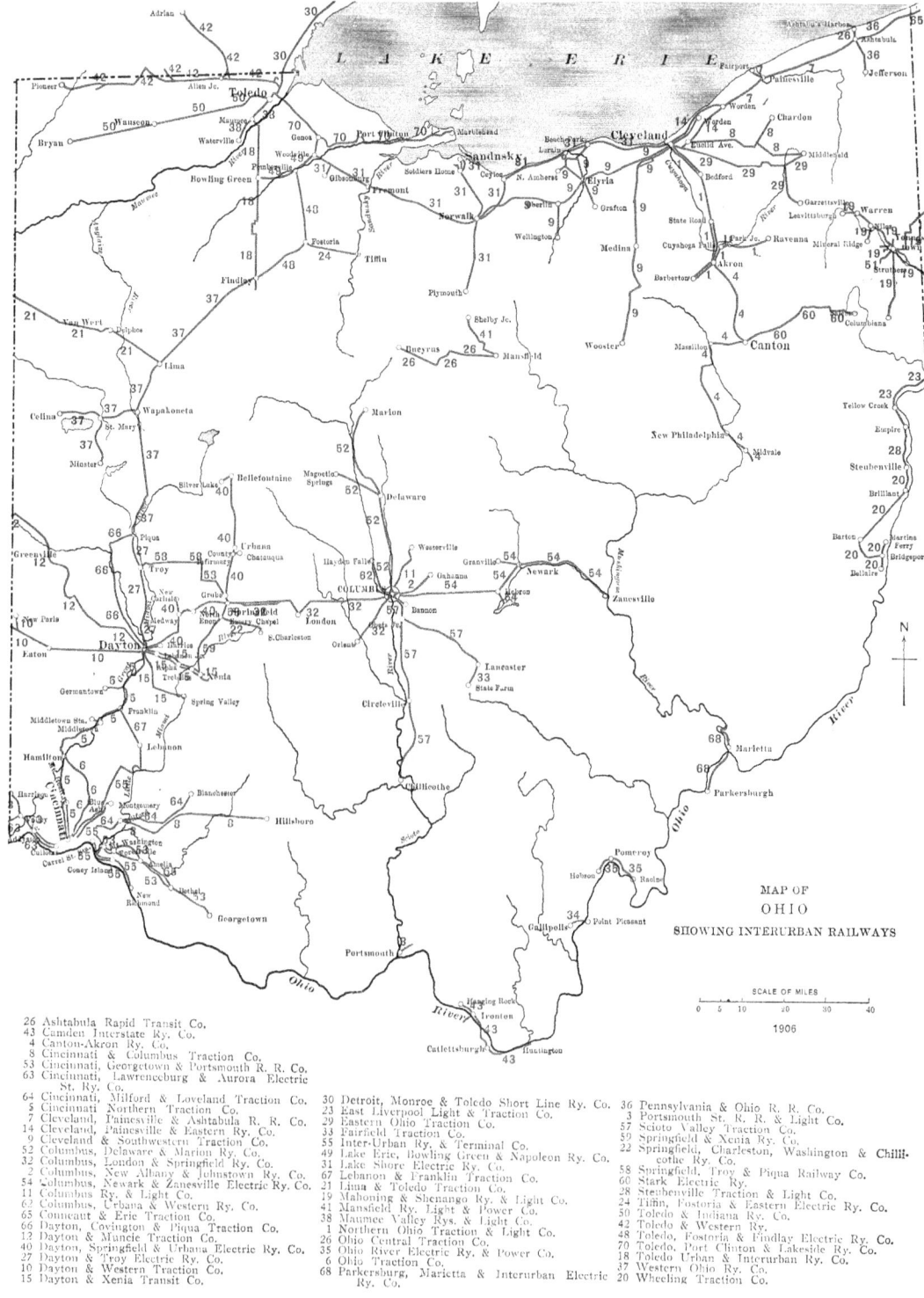

By 1910 Ohio rightly claimed to be the heartland for the electric intercity railway. Mileage exceeded 2,500 miles, and more routes were either being planned or built.

Author's collection

FOREWORD

TODAY, MANY OF US ARE FAMILIAR WITH THE DOT-COM BOOM OF the 1990s followed by the economic collapse of 2007–2008. A century before, in the 1890s and the first decade of the twentieth century, another industry burst into American life, the electric railway interurbans. Expansion of this industry was first affected by the financial impact of 1907's panic, and the building of paved roads sealed the interurbans' doom. Essentially the industry was born, matured, and died within a human life span.

Interurbans were the transition between horse-drawn and motor-powered vehicles, passenger and freight. Their very name, evoking the thought of something running between cities, reflects their profound effect on urban and rural life. Perhaps the most lasting legacy of the interurbans is the genesis of rural electrification.

Especially in midwestern states, the industry was largely owned and promoted by electric utility interests. A power distribution system was needed to provide electric energy for the trains. The investment in these distribution systems was, in part, economically justified by selling power to towns, villages, hamlets, and even individual farms along the way. Electricity changed farm life forever.

Due to their local focus, interurbans created linkages, economic and social, between their terminal cities and the clusters of businesses and population along the way. Markets were created where before none existed. Mobility was provided beyond the range of a horse for both business and pleasure. While the financial and technical aspects of the interurbans have been well documented, the profound sociological impacts of this industry have been rarely addressed. Into this breach H. Roger Grant has stepped.

Grant has nailed it in the work that follows. We now have a definitive study of the impacts of the electric railway industry on life a century ago. Why is this important? Slowly but surely the lines that were abandoned decades ago are being rebuilt at huge capital costs. Where, you ask? Would you believe California and Texas? "Light-rail" and commuter rail lines have become the interurbans of the twenty-first century. In some cases they are being built on the abandoned interurban rights-of-way. Such is the case in the Los Angeles Basin, the Bay Area, and the Dallas–Fort Worth metroplex.

While over a century ago people forsook the horse for motorized vehicles, today there is increasing evidence that young people are forsaking the automobile for mass transit. What was old and forgotten has become new and appealing. We noted that the "hard side" of the business – corporate, equipment, and technical history – has been well documented. Grant is addressing the largely ignored "soft side," namely the social history and its impact. He is addressing such questions as: How did the interurban affect individuals who sought, invested in, and used this flash-in-the-pan transportation phenomenon? How did the rapid collapse of interurbans impact patrons, employees, investors, and the public generally? How have interurbans been remembered?

The approach Grant has taken captures the wide-ranging relationships between people and electric railway interurbans. Still, the content of the three units that make up this book – "Enthusiasm" "Interurbans in Daily Life," and "Saying Goodbye" – while not encyclopedic, brings new knowledge, even for an industry whose component companies mostly lasted for only a generation.

Electric Interurban Railways and the American People is designed to be a companion work to Grant's *Railroads and the American People*, published in 2012 by Indiana University Press. This one is admittedly less complex than that study's vast, complicated story of Americans and their steam railroads. Nevertheless, the social history of electric interurbans is significant, being much more than a footnote to the nation's rich transportation heritage. It helps you to understand the human dimensions of an industry that served as the transition between the "Age of the Horse" and the "Automobile Age" and changed social behavior. These lessons learned over a century ago bring context and understanding to what is happening in public transit today. At least in large urban areas, the automobile is losing some of its glamor for both environmental and sociological reasons.

Norman Carlson
Lake Forest, Illinois
October 17, 2015

PREFACE

FOR DECADES THE RAGS-TO-RICHES SAGA OF ELECTRIC INTER-urbans in the United States has attracted popular interest. Yet, unlike their durable steam railroad counterparts, this transportation form has received only modest publishing attention, likely because it emerged and largely disappeared so rapidly. Those who have written about intercity traction have been primarily amateur historians or "juice" enthusiasts, and they have commonly focused on a single company. Professional scholars have been less active, although several have made major contributions. The standard study of the industry, *The Electric Interurban Railways in America*, by George W. Hilton and John F. Due, late economists at the University of California at Los Angeles and the University of Illinois at Urbana, appeared from Stanford University Press in 1960 and was reprinted with minor revisions four years later. Their work contains a skilled analysis of the rise and fall of interurbans and thumbnail sketches of individual companies and systems. Said one traction authority, "Hilton and Due wrote the interurban Bible." And this is not a farfetched statement.

Nevertheless there is a discernable weakness in the existing literature, whether written by amateurs or by professionals. While writers have produced what veteran interurban historian Norman Carlson has called "the hard side of the corporate, equipment, and technical history," they have largely ignored the "soft side," namely social history. The approach that I have taken is intended to capture the wide-ranging relationships between people and electric interurbans. This human dimension is something that is much more significant than being merely an interesting footnote to the nation's rich transportation past. It underscores Americans' constant desire to have the best possible mobility.

ACKNOWLEDGMENTS

NO SCHOLAR CREATES A BOOK ALONE, AND IN THE COURSE OF MY work on the social history of America's electric interurbans, I have incurred multiple debts. There are obvious and not-so-obvious acknowledgments to be made.

Those individuals who have assisted me include (in alphabetical order): Sally Bates, Gary Dillon, the late Art Dubin, the late Donald Duke, Tom Fetters, Nick Fry, Dick George, the late Louis Goodwin, Linda Graybeal, John Gruber, Herb Harwood, Tom Hoback, Don Hofsommer, Barb Lamphier, Dave and Roxanne McFarland, the late Jim McFarlane, Barney Olsen, Art Peterson, Carlos Schwantes, and John Spychalski. And interurban historian Norm Carlson kindly read a draft of this manuscript, making corrections and suggestions.

Archives and related institutions also need to be thanked. They include the Indiana Historical Society, Indianapolis; John W. Barriger III National Railroad Library, St. Louis, Missouri; Library of Congress, Washington, D.C.; and R. M. Cooper Library, Clemson University.

Upon reflection, there were those family members and others in my home community of Albia, Iowa, a county-seat town once served by two interurban companies, who sparked a childhood interest in electric traction. After more than fifty years I vividly recall stories that they told and retold. These individuals include my grandmother Katharine Dinsmore; my mother, Marcella Grant Dearinger; my stepfather, Tom Dearinger; my uncle John Griffin; and my great-uncle Joe Heinman, who served as roadmaster and lineman for the Albia Light & Railway Company (previously Albia Interurban Railway). And there were additional Albians who remembered the past Interurban Era.

As with my more than thirty earlier book publications, my wife, Martha Farrington Grant, painstakingly read drafts of the manuscript. As always, she has been my guiding star. I also appreciate the financial commitment that members of the Lemon family have made to my Kathryn and Calhoun Lemon Professorship. Their generosity has led to a more productive professional life, providing travel, equipment support, and summers without the need to teach.

H. Roger Grant
Clemson University
Clemson, South Carolina

ELECTRIC INTERURBANS AND THE AMERICAN PEOPLE

ENTHUSIASM 1

INVENTION

Just as the steam locomotive lacked a single inventor, the same holds true for the electric interurban. The roles played in perfecting the iron horse by such Englishmen as William Hedley, George Stephenson, and William Symington had their American counterparts in Horatio Allen, Mathias Baldwin, and Peter Cooper. A combination of Americans and Europeans also blazed the way for the electric interurban to become commercially viable toward the end of the nineteenth century. The creative works of Thomas Davenport, Robert Davidson, Ernst Werner von Siemens, Leo Daft, Charles Van Depoele, and Frank Julian Sprague fostered electric traction. A stream of inventors tinkered with harnessing electricity to some form of flanged-wheel vehicle. In the 1830s Thomas Davenport, a Brandon, Vermont, blacksmith, built a small electric motor that propelled a miniature railway train. He proudly demonstrated his creation in Boston, Springfield, and other New England locations. Somewhat later Robert Davidson, a Scottish engineer, used a wet-cell battery to operate an electric locomotive between Edinburgh and Glasgow, albeit at only a crawl. In 1857 Charles Page of the Smithsonian Institution constructed a more powerful battery car that reached a top speed of 19 miles per hour on a trial run between Washington, D.C., and Bladensburg, Maryland, a distance of slightly more than 5 miles. Yet his invention was far from practical, prompting some to call it the "electromagnetic humbug." Other experiments followed, but before the era of the Civil War electric transport was really only a visionary concept. Motors were curiosities, being not much better than toys.[1]

A sea change began in the 1870s. Electric motors and dynamos of greater sophistication made their debut. Electric power coming from a dynamo (or generator), which fed electric transit from a battery, offered real possibilities. Likely it was the German Ernst Werner von Siemens who fashioned the first successful electric locomotive, one that he exhibited in

1879 at the Berlin Industrial Exhibition. Not long afterward he supervised construction of a commercial electric line in suburban Berlin. Another Siemens breakthrough came in 1883 with the opening of what was the first electric road to have the general characteristics of an interurban, the 9-mile Giant's Causeway Portrush & Bush Valley Railway & Tramway that ran along the coast of Country Antrim in (Northern) Ireland and took its power from a third rail. That year also witnessed the experimental locomotives of Leo Daft, a British-born inventor, and Charles Van Depoele, a Belgian who later moved to America. Daft fashioned a low-voltage third-rail line about 3 miles long in Baltimore, but it was deemed impractical because of dangers created by the exposed current. Soon, though, he perfected a power-distribution system that came from a dual overhead wire where cars received power from a four-wheeled device called a troller. (This mechanism reminded some of a fisherman trolling, and troller became corrupted into "trolley.") In 1888 Daft took pride in his overhead system when the 2.25-mile Pennsylvania Motor Company began operations in Easton, Pennsylvania. Van Depoele likewise favored an overhead wire and conceived of an under-running brass wheel at the end of a weighted pole. Springs at the base kept the pole firmly in contact with the conducting overhead wire. These trolley poles promoted some wags to call electric cars "broomstick trains." And Van Depoele would achieve commercial success in several U.S. and Canadian cities. Yet both Daft and Van Depoele confronted technical difficulties, including current collection, electric motor mountings, and imperfections with the motors themselves.[2]

Then came the breakthrough contributions made by Frank Julian Sprague. This graduate of the U.S. Naval Academy and later problem-solving associate of Thomas Edison developed a reliable direct current (DC) motor and found a way to mount it on a car that resolved the shortcomings that Daft, Van Depoele, and others had encountered. In 1888 Sprague, who had formed the Sprague Electric Railway & Motor Company and attracted a talented staff, successfully electrified the 12-mile Richmond Union Passenger Railway. After much trial-and-error work, he and his assistants took great joy when they determined that by placing motors under the car and gearing them directly to the axle with supporting springs, this equipment was not damaged by the jarring caused by rough street tracks. In addition to these "wheelbarrow" mountings, other vexing problems were solved, including poor-quality trolley wire and flawed motor components. The Virginia capital had an electric-powered transit system that was reasonably trouble free. Almost overnight Sprague's Richmond triumph set in motion a wholesale conversion of street railways from animal, cable, and steam to electricity. By 1890 one-sixth of American street railways had come under wire. Fifteen years after the first trolleys rolled

At the dawn of the twentieth century car No. 6 of the Cleveland & Chagrin Falls Electric Railway rests on a Cleveland, Ohio, street. This pioneer piece of interurban equipment, which contains space for passengers, baggage, and express, is largely of wood construction and comparable to contemporary city and rural trolleys.

Author's collection.

along the streets of Richmond, nearly every transit operation relied on electricity.[3]

Additional advancements followed, and collectively they made *long-distance* electric car operations practical. Yet initially the application of electricity for such projects remained experimental. Noted the *Electric Railway Journal* in 1909, "Apparently no one foresaw the great commercial results that would follow the adaptation of the new power for a railway service that should combine the advantages of good urban street railway service with the functions of short-haul traffic previously discharged by the steam railroads."[4]

Improvement to the electric supply revealed this change. As the nineteenth century closed, pioneer interurban builders had the choice between low-voltage (500- to 600-volt) DC and high-voltage single-phase alternating current (AC) for their power systems. With refinements DC and AC were both used. In the early twentieth century interurban companies might increase DC electrification to 1,200 volts or more, or they transmitted power at high-voltage AC to reduce voltage loss. At substations, which were commonly spaced at 15- to 20-mile intervals, AC was converted to lower DC voltage that then was fed into the overhead lines. A rotary converter, introduced in the early 1890s and subsequently perfected, allowed this change in current. After 1905 or so an increasing number of interurbans selected a single-phase 6,600-volt, 25-cycle AC system, which the Westinghouse Electric and Manufacturing Company promoted to compete with the DC alternative championed by the General Electric Company. Although this AC technology had the advantage of reducing "line drop," requiring less copper wire and needing fewer substations, it

One of America's first interurbans, Sandusky, Milan & Norwalk Electric Railway, which began operations in 1893, met the public definition of an interurban. This 19.5-mile Ohio road served the three communities found in its corporate name.

Krambles-Peterson Archive.

substantially increased equipment weight and maintenance costs for the electrical components. There was another disadvantage: cars accelerated slowly. And some communities, for reasons of safety, required reduction from high-voltage AC to lower AC or DC voltage within their corporate limits.[5]

Improvements were made in electric generation and how rolling stock drew this power. Interurbans frequently produced their own electricity by constructing coal-fired steam-generating plants and sold excess electricity to business and residential customers, including rural residents. In fact, after the Interurban Era faded away, a former traction company often continued as an investor-owned electric utility. Other electric railways relied on commercial sources. (Unlike the majority of Canadian interurbans, only a few American roads, mostly in the West, used cheaper hydroelectric power; it was often impossible to do so.) Most interurbans supplied energy to their rolling stock by overhead grooved copper wire suspended over the tracks from bracket arms or transverse span wires strung from poles alongside the right-of-way. There were instances where a company opted for catenary construction, having the trolley wire suspended from a steel cable. A limited number of roads employed a third-rail system. While this power source reduced maintenance and offered greater conductivity than copper wire, it was dangerous to trespassers, especially animals and children. In 1903 the *San Francisco Chronicle* commented on the third

This quintessential wooden car belonged to the Oneonta & Mohawk Valley Railway, later Southern New York Railway. Pictured in April 1907 near Richfield Springs, New York, this handsome car, which features a clerestory roof and arched windows, likely was a recent acquisition from the Jewett Car Company of Newark, Ohio.

Author's collection.

rail used by the North Shore Railroad (later Northwestern Pacific). "The new electric system has been making a wholesale slaughter of dogs and other animals. Within the last 24 hours, eight dogs have come in contact with the live rail and have been burned to death. Hogs and chickens have likewise met the same fate." Added the *Chronicle*, "The current is not sufficiently strong to kill a human, unless delicate." As the Age of Electricity matured, mostly refinements in technologies of electric supply were debated and discussed, commonly at meetings of street railway and interurban personnel and in trade publications.[6]

Interurban rolling stock also advanced steadily from the 1890s into the 1930s. Paralleling the evolution of steam road equipment, passenger and freight cars went from small and wooden to large and steel. The earliest trolleys (and interurbans) were made largely of wood, employing so-called house-upon-a-flatcar construction, and resembled the prosaic animal and cable cars of the day. By the formative years of the twentieth century, interurban cars had become much longer, commonly 50 to 60 feet in length, and frequently featured smoking and nonsmoking sections, a forward baggage and express compartment, and perhaps a toilet room. They were also more elaborate, often having Gothic-arched windows with upper panels fitted with colored art glass and posh interiors with hardwood paneling, carpeted aisles, and cushioned seats. Cars might have bodies that were of semi-steel or composite construction, although by World War I manufacturers had mostly adopted all-steel components. Then in the 1920s lightweight metal (steel and aluminum) interurban cars appeared, some with aerodynamic styling, roller bearings, and shatter-resistant glass. And electric fans made clerestory roofs obsolete as a source

By the era of World War I state-of-the-art, all-steel cars commonly served passengers, especially on major interurbans. In the early 1920s the Akron-Cleveland Limited, a three-car train of the Northern Ohio Light & Traction Company, speeds along a well-maintained double track near the Cuyahoga-Summit County line.

Author's collection.

of ventilation. During the twilight years the few new cars sported the latest mechanical components and that Art Deco look, resembling contemporary diesel-powered streamliners that raced along the main lines of America's most innovative railroads.[7]

Freight locomotives experienced the same evolutionary development—wood to steel. For the early decades builders constructed either wood or wood-steel "box motors" (so named for their boxlike appearance) or sometimes called "express motors." What were essentially motorized baggage cars, these pieces of rolling stock handled express and light freight shipments. A related freight type was the "trap" car, a motorized flatcar with a small enclosed cab at one end. Larger, more powerful box motors could handle a short train of custom trailers or perhaps several conventional freight cars. By the 1910s steeple-cab freight locomotives had appeared. These units were characterized by their low hoods, which sloped away from their center cabs and provided greater pulling power and better visibility, especially for switching chores. Another contemporary freight type was the box cab that extended the full length of the locomotive. It, too, had more muscle than a box motor and was geared for pulling strength rather than speed. In time some interurbans required more powerful units, acquiring locomotives that resembled those used by steam roads on their electrified lines.[8]

There were interurbans that employed custom-built freight cars or trailers. If an electric road could not interchange standard freight

One example of the popular box motor is seen ca. 1925 at the Bowling Green, Ohio, yards of the Toledo, Bowling Green & Southern Traction Company. The unit is coupled to a freight trailer belonging to the connecting Western Ohio Railway. TBG&S maintenance men are on duty.

Krambles-Peterson Archive.

equipment with a steam carrier, such cars became essential either for the electric road's own on-line usage or for interchange with connecting interurbans. In the 1920s a consortium of Ohio, Indiana, and Michigan electrics gained recognition for introducing these special cars, often required because their city operations involved sharp curves and steep grades. Double-jointed couplers, for example, helped to facilitate safe, dependable operations. Midwestern interurbans also introduced groundbreaking innovations, notably container equipment, "truck-ferry" (trailer-on-flatcar or "piggyback"), and mechanical refrigerator cars.[9]

WHAT'S AN INTERURBAN?

The word *interurban* means what its Latin origin says: "between cities." It is believed that in the 1890s Charles Henry, an Anderson, Indiana, lawyer, politician, and traction entrepreneur, coined the term. Some, in fact, consider Henry (incorrectly) to be the "father of the interurban," having been involved with construction of the first intercity electric line in the Hoosier State. Later this 11-mile Anderson-to-Alexandria road, which opened in 1898, became a component of the 400-mile Union Traction Company of Indiana.[10]

Debate developed about whether *all* traction roads that operated between municipalities should be called interurbans. As electricity made animal, cable, and steam street railways obsolete, streetcar owners,

This versatile freight motor once served the Cedar Rapids & Iowa City Railway, a durable midwestern electric road. During the twilight years of the Interurban Era the secondhand market for modern rolling stock resulted in freight and passenger equipment moving from road to road. Originally No. 58 served the Washington & Old Dominion Railway, and later it became the property of the Kansas City Kaw Valley Railroad.

Krambles-Peterson Archive.

especially in New England but elsewhere as well, started to construct "rural trolleys." These operations linked multiple communities, and usually their lightly built track structure, which commonly featured little grading and sharp curves, appeared on country roads. Equipment was nearly always identical to the rolling stock that transported riders along city streets, being small open cars in the summer and closed ones in the winter. And their standards of operations were essentially those of street railways. But "true" interurbans in the minds of many operated alongside public roads or on private rights-of-way outside corporate limits, installed heavier rail often with stretches of straight ("tangent") track, owned larger pieces of equipment, and functioned more like steam railroads. There were also electric lines, particularly in Pennsylvania, that had characteristics of both rural trolleys and interurbans, explaining the difficulty in making a correct taxonomy. Early in the twentieth century the U.S. Bureau of the Census classified as interurbans electric railways that provided rural or intercity services. This definition, though, was inadequate; after all, rural trolleys were essentially longer street railways. Beginning in 1912 the Bureau believed that it had resolved the issue by permitting each railway to select its own classification. A good definition, however, was offered in 1907 by Edgar Van Deusen, a partner in the New York City investment firm of P. W. Brooks and Company. He considered bona fide interurbans to be "more than fifteen miles in length, which have at least two-thirds of their track outside of municipal limits and operate their cars at a maximum speed of not less than twenty miles per hour."[11]

Some confusion existed about certain electric intercity operations. For one thing, there were "hybrid" companies. The Colorado Springs & Cripple Creek District Railway in Colorado and the Fonda, Johnstown & Gloversville Railroad in New York each had separate steam and electric divisions. There were also carriers that employed "heavy traction." In 1909 the New York, New Haven & Hartford Railroad (New Haven), an established steam road, installed a Westinghouse single-phase 11,000-volt AC catenary system on 33 miles of its main line in Connecticut and later expanded this electrification. In 1915 the Pennsylvania Railroad electrified its 20-mile Main Line suburban service between Philadelphia and Paoli, Pennsylvania, and would place additional trackage under wire. Eventually about 2,800 miles of main-line steam railroads were electrified, including 663 miles of the Pacific Coast Extension of the Milwaukee Road in Montana, Idaho, and Washington State. And a few steam roads had electrically operated tunnel operations, including the Great Northern Railway with its Cascade tunnel and the Michigan Central Railroad with its Detroit River tunnel.[12]

Individuals involved in the interurban industry usually agreed that their electrically powered transport shared several common characteristics. These included a primary emphasis on passenger business and less-than-carload (LCL) freight, use of rolling stock that was heavier and speedier than city streetcars, and operations on often private rights-of-way beyond the limits of a metropolitan area.

WHY WERE INTERURBANS POPULAR?

Just as the steam railroad became popular for multiple reasons – most of all as the replacement technology that was faster and more dependable than any contemporary land, river, lake, or canal transport – much the same can be said for the interurban. Once investors and others grasped the potential of the electric intercity railway, they recognized the advantages of this alternative to steam for passenger travel over short and intermediate distances and for express and small-lot freight shipments.

In general terms the reasons for the growing popularity of the interurban involved the perception that it performed "a service for mankind as notable and perhaps ultimately as great as that rendered by its steam-operated precursor." Observed a writer for the *Chicago Daily Tribune* in 1907, "An entirely new element has entered the social, commercial and even the political life of the country." And there was the common belief that an interurban could solve shortcomings of the existing steam railroad network. "If your town has been left out or stuck on a branch line, you had another chance with the trolley." Little wonder residents of Lee Center, Illinois, a "quiet little rural village off the beaten path for more than 55 years," had long wanted a rail link "to make business prosper." The people of Lee Center believed that a railroad was nothing less than a rite of passage for a community to become a place of importance. In 1910 residents enthusiastically welcomed a locally financed interurban that gave them that connection. For some transportation-starved or badly served residents, an interurban appeared to be their last best hope; they didn't realize, of course, that the automobile would develop rapidly beyond its gestation stage. But early in the century motor cars barely existed; nationally in 1901 only 14,800 automobiles were registered (and no trucks whatsoever).[13]

The public saw interurbans providing a range of benefits. Passenger travel was clean, avoiding the nuisance and discomfort of smoke, soot, sparks, or cinders. Boasted the Kansas City, Clay County & St. Joseph Railway in its initial public timetable: "Dustless – Cinderless – Smokeless." Riders could comfortably ride with open windows in warm weather or take "open cars," popular during the summer months, and still wear their best Sunday clothes. Also farmers did not need to fear hot embers from passing steam locomotives setting their fields, pastures, or wood lots ablaze. There was also the matter of noise. When racing across the countryside, the hissing and smoke-belching iron horse clanked against the rails, but the interurban car, resembling the earlier canal boat and packet, was virtually noiseless, except for the "whiz" of the car and the intermittent singing of air compressors with their characteristic *lung-a-lung-a-lung* sound. And interurban equipment appeared "benign." Commented an interurban traveler in 1903, "There are a good many elderly men and women who are still rather afraid of the locomotive. Compared with an engine and train of coaches, a trolley-car is rather an innocent-looking affair." (The same could also be said about the first railed, mass-transit vehicle, the animal car; horses were so much a part of daily life.) Some contemporaries remarked about their visual experiences in an electric car, being strikingly different from that of a common railway coach. "You can see out of both sides and the back and at times the front as well. You can't do that with a locomotive, tender and baggage and mail cars ahead of you and you probably had other cars behind you." Since interurban companies gladly rented their equipment for group travels, such arrangements became fashionable. Proclaimed an industry source: "The chartered car appeals to the feelings of exclusiveness, sense of ownership and comfort beloved by most human beings." And there were these related thoughts: "Our Special Car Service is what you need when you go anywhere for any purpose in a party," announced a New England traction road in an early advertisement. "Low cost, comfortable, convenient, saves all bother of connection and changing cars." Interurban travel also resembled the informality of steam road local, branch, and shortline trains. "Most of the train crews knew their regular clientele on a first-name basis, and they were not above such homely tasks as running a few errands for a housewife along the line, or seeing to the safe arrival of an unescorted child at his destination." There were even "democratic" dividends. "Everybody in the car is on an equal footing," explained the editor of *Trolley Trips around Scranton, Wilkes-Barre and Hazelton*. "This tends to eliminate the 'bluff,' fostered by the Pullmans in railroad traveling, and leads to an exchange of ideas that to anyone of an observing turn of mind is most interesting."[14]

That friendly relationship between customers and carriers prompted U. S. congressman William B. McKinley, founder of the Illinois Traction System, to comment, "We stand today closer related to the general public than the railroad companies ever did, because our lines come closer to the people and afford much more accommodation, while we can render unsurpassed service between city and city." McKinley knew so well that from the end of the Civil War onward a troubled relationship existed between the public and steam railroads, sparring repeatedly over rates and service, although somewhat mitigated with state and federal regulatory measures that came in the 1870s and 1880s. But the coming of interurbans improved the intercity transportation climate; few electric roads were accused of committing acts of corporate arrogance. "[Steam roads] have enjoyed the right of way so long and given the least possible service for the patronage received for so many years that the new era of electric cars sets hard upon them," observed the *Long Beach* [California] *Tribune* in 1901. "Long Beach has been especially at their mercy."[15]

Relating to service, electric roads dispatched cars more frequently than their steam counterparts. While a steam railroad might provide "double-daily service" on its main or secondary lines, interurbans usually operated throughout the day on perhaps hourly schedules. Their track speeds could be as great as or greater than their steam counterparts', although "limited" trains on steam roads were "ballast scorchers." Although some of the larger interurbans dispatched their versions of "limited" or mostly nonstop cars, all companies provided excellent local service. Patrons liked that cars stopped almost everywhere. By using a hand signal in the day or a lantern, lighted match, or burning newspaper at night, the observant motorman stopped to pick up a rider whether at a trackside shelter or a roadside crossing. "Passengers wishing to stop cars should signal the motorman with arm extended horizontally across the track by day and a light swung across the track by night at a distance of not less than 1,500 feet from approaching cars," the Lake Shore Electric

Longer interurbans were likely to dispatch "limiteds," cars that made fewer stops and were faster than locals between terminals. About 1907 a maker of "real-photo" postcards captured two limiteds that each operated between Cleveland and Toledo, Ohio. The steam one belongs to New York Central affiliate Lake Shore & Michigan Southern Railway, and the electric one is operated by the Lake Shore Electric Railway. Frequently interurbans, because of either tradition or law, needed to build expensive viaducts in order to cross their steam competitors.

Author's collection.

Railway told patrons. "The motorman will answer with two short blasts of the whistle, signifying that he sees and understands you." Furthermore, cars went into the heart of a city or town, eliminating the need to walk or pay for a hack or omnibus from a remote or inconvenient depot. Explained Congressman McKinley, "Frequency of service, convenience to the neighborhood, and a disposition to travel direct from the center of one community to the center of another without having to change are the principal factors in the capture of this local transportation business by the electric interurban lines."[16]

The list of positives continued. When it came to passenger fares, interurbans usually charged less per mile than steam carriers, perhaps two or three cents or even less rather than the four or five cents or more for their competitors. In order to attract commercial travelers or "drummers" and other regular riders, including commuters and school children, electric roads commonly offered coupon ticket books, making trips even cheaper. "One of the most important effects of the introduction of electric interurban lines has been the cheapening of travel," observed the *Journal of Political Economy* in 1906. "The average passenger fare per mile on the chief interurban lines [in Ohio] is a little less than one and one-half cents. Broadly speaking, the steam-railway fares average about double those of the electric lines." Said the *New York Times*, "It [interurban] can hold its own with the steam railroads in any contest of rate cutting which the latter may initiate and earn a profit." Indeed, a spokesman for the Brotherhood of Locomotive Firemen, a union that showed no love of interurbans, argued, "If steam railways had charged less fare for passengers many electric railways would never have been built." And in an age of railroad carnage, interurbans proved safer, having fewer deaths and injuries per passenger mile than their steam counterparts. All of these factors had great appeal and fostered modern urban-rural interdependence. Remarked a Seville, Ohio, resident, who knew well the Cleveland, Southwestern & Columbus Railway (Southwestern), "Shoppers can take advantage of Cleveland sales, and everybody can enjoy an outing to a motion-picture show. City folk can come out to buy cheaper butter, eggs and produce and also to live in cheaper housing."[17]

Within a decade of the appearance of electric intercity interurbans there was excitement about the improving quality of equipment. In one example, the rolling stock of the Illinois Traction System impressed a rider who traveled over much of its 400-mile system. "They are running luxurious buffet chair cars, limited trains rush from city to city, express matter and freight are carried in special cars, and last of all, the trolley line sleeper, as I can attest, is an absolute success."[18]

An attraction that enthusiasts may have overlooked was the possibility of funeral cars. Although some city lines provided this equipment, a range of intercity electric roads offered this service. Usually it was the larger, metropolitan-based interurban that maintained a funeral car. One such carrier was the Southwestern. In 1911 this Cleveland-based company rebuilt an older passenger car for funeral assignments, naming it the *Dolores*. The car's livery was appropriate, being painted dark blue with gold lettering, striping, and numerals. A student of the road provided this description: "Behind the motorman's vestibule was a plush lined compartment, with the doors opening outward. Rollers mounted in the floor made it easy to roll the casket in, then strapped into place. Fold down racks provided a place for floral offerings. The former smoking section was reserved for the immediate family, with wicker chairs plus additional fold up chairs." Other members of the funeral party could travel in what was once the general seating area. Poor roads and bad weather would not prevent the casket, flower arrangements, and mourners from arriving at either an on-line or nearby cemetery, and there was the advantage of keeping the funeral-goers together.[19]

Even if an interurban lacked a specially equipped funeral car, it could still provide this service. "The first funeral train ever sent out by the Holland Interurban road [Grand Rapids, Holland & Lake Michigan Rapid Railway] was that which yesterday carried the remains of Mrs. David Bertsch, who died Thursday at the U.B.A. [Union Benevolent Association] hospital [in Grand Rapids], to Holland for burial." This November 1902 account continued, "The leading car was decorated in front with a large bunch of white chrysanthemums and carried the casket in the baggage compartment. Another of the big coaches was occupied by the funeral party."[20]

Well known to all was that interurban express service could surpass what steam roads provided. For individuals who demanded faster delivery times for package and LCL shipments, electric cars made a real difference. An interurban, with its "merchandise dispatch" that used either a passenger or box-motor car, might deliver a shipment in a few hours that otherwise would take much longer for a steam carrier. Customers commonly received same-day or overnight service, whether for a piece of furniture or an order of dry goods, drugs, or hardware. Passenger cars, perhaps with attached trailers, met the daily time-sensitive needs of city bakers and newspaper publishers. Farmers, who shipped perishable products to urban markets, could expect rapid delivery of their milk, cottage cheese, eggs, and produce, and refrigeration would not be required. They did not need to haul their products to a distant railroad station but instead went to a much closer shelter or siding.[21]

Other benefits became clear. It had long been realized that the technology and economics of the steam locomotive made it impractical to space stops closer than three or four miles. "A steam railroad could not afford to give frequent service with such short stops as would be necessary." But traction equipment could make more stops and could accelerate quickly, and that permitted better, faster service. "It is, therefore, possible for interurban cars to make comparatively frequent stops while maintaining a high average speed," concluded a government report. An electric car was far from being a poky local or branch-line steam train.[22]

The ability to stop and start "on a dime" was but one attraction. The physical layout of an interurban might make it much more attractive than building a steam-powered main line, branch line, or shortline. "A trolley car, weighted down as it is with a heavy motor, will stay on the track in going around a much sharper curve than could possibly be negotiated by any train on a steam railroad," boasted an interurban executive. "Furthermore, the trolley car will climb a heavier grade than is possible on steam lines, even with a doubling up of locomotives. For this reason the interurban projectors find it possible to twist their roads around obstructions and to reach one small town after another which it would not be profitable for the steam road to deviate for." On some lines this twisting prompted wags to suggest that an electric road had "more jogs in it than the road to success."[23]

The operational costs contributed to the popularity of interurban projects. Even though the price tag for equipping an electric road exceeded that of a steam shortline of comparable size, once installations occurred, savings multiplied. There was no need for coaling towers and water tanks, and routine maintenance on an electric car was considerably cheaper than for the iron horse. Labor costs were also less. Two-man crews were typical and not the five or more required on a steam passenger or freight train. Then there was the relative absence of restrictive work rules, keeping costs per train mile far below those of steam roads. As early as 1900 the Interstate Commerce Commission (ICC) found that the average operating expenses of steam roads were 64.6 percent of gross earnings while those of interurbans were just 54 percent. The ICC offered this comparative example: "The operating expenses of the Missouri Pacific last year were 69.9 percent of gross earnings, while those of the Southwest Missouri Electric Railway, which parallels it for the whole length of the latter, were only 58.2 percent."[24]

Convenience of operations was still another attraction. Promoters liked to point out that "it was just as feasible to run separate express cars as it is to run separate passenger cars, and neither service is at all dependent upon the other." And there was this advantage: "Steam road schedules are as rigid as iron. Provisions can be made for large crowds by sending out squads [of cars] instead of singly." Not to be ignored was that when crewmen had completed a day's work, they could just walk away, allowing the equipment to spend the night unattended anywhere on the line. The next morning, after several minutes to pump up the air, the car or box motor was ready to leave. Before steam locomotives could whistle off, there were tenders to be filled with water and fuel, fires to be nursed, and other time-consuming chores to be completed.[25]

Then there was the nightmare of public roads. Generations of travelers had cursed road conditions, especially in those places plagued by a vicious and viscous brand of mud, that ubiquitous "gumbo." A traveler in 1907 had this to say about road conditions in northwestern Ohio: "A heavy rain had fallen over night, and the soft, pasty mud which that powdered dust made was a study in physics and chemistry. It was slippery, slimy, treacherously dangerous ooze." This old saying rang true: "Be sure to choose your rut carefully. You will be in it for a very long time." Admittedly, mud did not bother a horse too much, and this animal could pick its way around chuck holes. Furthermore, a horse could plod through several feet of water, requiring bridges only over deeper streams. Efforts, though, had been made to improve public roadways, including plank, macadamized (layers of crushed stone with an applied bonding agent), gravel, seashell, and brick surfaces. Yet out of the national network of 2.2 million miles of roads prior to World War I, about 2 million miles consisted of dirt construction, and only later did "all-weather" roads become more common. When motorists took to these arteries during dry conditions, they needed to wear goggles and linen dusters for protection from the clouds of choking dust that every automobile raised. Interurban promoters took advantage of the harsh seasonal restrictions and the drawbacks

This photograph of a team of mules pulling an automobile out of the mud dates from about 1915, but the location is unknown. In this case "good roaders" have yet to work their magic.

Author's collection.

of travel by cart, wagon, buggy, or after 1900 the "horseless carriage." In 1903 an observer said this about the motor car: "Automobiling is a brave pastime for the rich who do not mind getting down on their backs in the road and hammering straight up at bolts and things, with grease dripping down in their faces." It wasn't hard to laud intercity traction. "This week a farmer WALKED 4 miles to town with a basket of produce," commented an Iowa editor in 1909. "This week a farmer's wife drove to town with her butter, and most everybody in town heard of it because it was about the only country butter received here the past week." The explanation was clear: "Verily, the bad roads have well nigh cut off the country from the town, and the town from the country." Growing automobile usage led to increased local and state spending, and in 1916 the federal government started to finance the "good roads" cause, but only after the Interurban Era was in full swing.[26]

Even in the mid-1920s muddy roads were ubiquitous. This photograph, taken on April 23, 1925, shows a county road that crosses the electric Kewaunee & Galva Railway west of Kewaunee, Illinois.

Kewaunee Historical Society.

If the decided advantages for passenger and package and freight operations were not enough, there was another recognized benefit of having an electric road – rising property values. "Real estate along electric lines in northern Ohio has nearly doubled in value since they were built," observed an Oberlin, Ohio, businessman, "and the first question a prospective buyer of a farm asks is, 'Haw [sic] far is it from an electric line?'" And there was this observation: "In Ohio you invariably find an increase of from 10 to 50 per cent in value over lands remote from interurban railways, and the same conditions apply to Illinois, Indiana and Iowa." Similar spikes occurred toward the close of the building period. With completion of the Kansas City, Clay County & St. Joseph Railway in 1913, a sociology student from William Jewell College, located in Liberty, Missouri, and served by the new interurban, found that "land near the line has increased 50%. Farms worth $30,000 previous to the construction are now held at $60,000." He added, "Not only has there been a great increase in farm land but also in city property." And interurban companies might work closely with real estate developers, operating special cars to take potential buyers to the suburbs or beyond. The 1908 prospectus for a proposed electric

Early on investors in the Cleveland, Southwestern & Columbus Railway believed in the future of this Ohio interurban. The vignette on this stock certificate reveals an active scene where one of the Southwestern's big wooden cars has stopped to serve patrons. Perhaps a steam-powered passenger train was included to show how it belched out annoying coal smoke.

Author's collection.

road in Iowa stated simply: "The construction and operation of the IOWA RAILROAD will enhance the value of farm and other lands adjacent to its line."[27]

Urban real estate, too, felt the positive impact of the interurban. When the Indianapolis Traction Terminal, the largest and most impressive interurban edifice to be built, opened in 1904, this $1.5 million structure affected property values. "The erection of the Terminal Building and Station in Indianapolis has increased property valuation in its vicinity millions of dollars, and has correspondingly added to the growth and improvement of the city." This phenomenon also occurred in such places as Detroit, Michigan; Louisville, Kentucky; and Los Angeles, California. Earlier much the same had taken place with street railways. Almost immediately after the electrified Akron [Ohio] Street Railway opened in late 1888, "property along the lines of the road has increased fifteen to twenty-five per cent in value."[28]

Interurbans offered additional financial advantages. Throughout the years of optimism and expansion, a growing number of investors believed that this transportation form provided excellent opportunities for stock values to advance as companies developed. An example comes from the Pacific Northwest. In 1907 the Spokane & Inland Empire Railroad Company, which began as a line between Spokane, Washington, and Coeur d'Alene, Idaho, acting through its agent the Union Trust Company of Spokane, touted its preferred cumulative shares: "AN ATTRACTIVE

INVESTMENT – SAFE AND PROFITABLE – NOW PAYING 5½ PER CENT." Bonds looked to be another good investment option. During the first decade of the twentieth century some financial advisors considered securities of larger interurbans to be appropriate instruments for protecting assets of "widows and orphans." If an interurban, whether large or small, had become involved in electric power generation and distribution, prospects looked bright for stock appreciation and uninterrupted bond-interest payments. When compared to the infant motorcar industry with its scores of struggling firms, an electric railroad was seen as a safer investment than any automobile company. As time went by, interurban investors, though, had mistaken a short-run boom for a new era.[29]

Not to be overlooked was the potential employment that interurbans could provide. Although less labor intensive than steam carriers, electric roads hired train crews – motormen and conductors – linemen, electricians, track and maintenance workers, and agents and other white-collar workers. In November 1907 Hugh J. McGowan, president of the Terre Haute, Indianapolis & Eastern Traction Company, told delegates to the annual meeting of the National Business League of America that they should appreciate what the industry had done for the working man: "Employment has been created for thousands." This was no exaggeration. Another interurban executive noted that this meant "hundreds of thousands of dollars paid in wages."[30]

Civic boosters – and citizens generally – considered electric intercity railways as guaranteeing the economic stability of a community. They also had the same thoughts about steam railroads, especially with the placement of major repair facilities. Observed A. B. Stickney, founder and president of the 1,500-mile Chicago Great Western Railway, when he announced in 1894 the selection of Oelwein, Iowa, as the place for its relocated shops complex: "As an element of permanent prosperity to a village or city, railway shops are superior in value to any other manufacturing establishment, inasmuch as they continue to run as long as the railway runs, which is perpetual, for although men die, the railway, like the babbling brook, 'runs on forever.'" It is hardly surprising that the editor of the *Pittsburg* [Kansas] *Headlight* in 1911 considered the hometown Joplin & Pittsburg Electric Railway as ensuring local prosperity. He praised the company for its part in the building up of the community, for its electric distribution system, and for its value of convenience and employment, and concluded with this optimistic statement: "The city will always remain the center of the electrical railway system that will grow as the time passes."[31]

Those businessmen and their employees who had been involved in the building of streetcars or their components or could enter these fields likewise welcomed the interurban. An expanding traction industry increased

Excitement is in the air as work begins on the 11-mile Albia Interurban Railway, later Albia Light & Railway. The year is 1907 and the place is the west side of the public square in Albia, Iowa. Workers are in the process of placing ties in the brick street, and soon they will install rail and overhead wire for the first of two lines, one south to Hocking and the other northwest to Hiteman.

Author's collection.

demands for passenger and freight equipment but also for a plethora of manufactured parts, including insulators, trolley wheels, catchers and retrievers, harps and pole bases, lamps, package racks, and seats. By the early twentieth century communities of varying sizes, but concentrated in the Midwest, benefited from prospering interurban-oriented manufacturers, which had a profound effect on local economies. Other suppliers profited; lumber dealers, for instance, sold cross ties, bridge timbers, and right-of-way poles.[32]

Not to be ignored was how an interurban corridor blended into the natural scene. "The lighter trolley line, which can follow the natural lay of the land, is less disfiguring to the landscape than the heavily graded steam road," opined a contemporary. "From a purely aesthetic standpoint a ride by trolley offers many more attractions than travel on the steam cars between the same points." Another said, "Interurban travel meant that there was a greater association with the land that you were going through." There existed that "hill and dale" dimension of many lines.[33]

As another burst of interurban construction was about to continue following the Panic of 1907, traction executive and promoter Hugh McGowan explained some of the reasons for this ongoing excitement. "There is an awakening and thrill of life in every town and village through which an interurban line runs, never felt before. Commercial opportunities which laid [sic] dormant are made possible and become profitable realities. New markets are opened. The reciprocal relations which develop between the city and town and between the village and farm are beneficial to all." He added, "Summing up interurban development throughout the United States we find that this new means of transportation has won favor with rich and poor alike. Hundreds of thousands of dollars have been saved to the people in reduced fares, which the enhancement in the value of lands contiguous to interurban lines has reached millions of dollars. Investments in interurban lines which have been properly located, financed, constructed and operated have yielded substantial profits, and their securities are sought by conservative investors."[34]

Hugh McGowan was hardly alone with his thoughts. His contemporaries believed that *if* an interurban was properly placed, the future looked bright, likely financially guaranteed. "One thing is certain," opined an observer in 1907, "an interurban trolley line connecting two cities, with good agricultural country as the meat in the sandwich, will pay almost from the start from its passenger traffic, the express and freight business being the nature of a by-product and pure 'velvet.'"[35]

It is no wonder that *virtually every* interurban opening or extension triggered some type of celebration. Completion in 1902 of the Pacific Electric Railway line to Alhambra and San Gabriel, California, led a journalist to write: "An electric shock struck Alhambra yesterday. It set the people agog. It almost completely depopulated the town." His piece continued: "After many months of anxious anticipation the new electric cars of the Huntington syndicate opened for business at 6 o'clock. The suburbanites had been up before sunrise, and the first car carried a goodly load. The town turned out *en masse* to experience the novel sensation of riding to the city [Los Angeles] by electricity."[36]

UNBUILT SCHEMES

Resembling their steam road counterparts, interurban advocates developed plans that remained nothing more than well-intentioned ideas. Although electric intercity mileage peaked at 15,580 miles in 1916, the same year that the steam network reached its maximum coverage, thousands of additional miles of electric lines were contemplated between 1895 and 1925. In Ohio, the state with the greatest interurban footprint, a plethora of unbuilt schemes were part of its traction history. Industry historians George Hilton and John Due pointed out this example: "At least eleven interurban companies proposed to build into Tiffin, although only one, the Tiffin, Fostoria and Eastern, ever did so." They further noted, "No fewer than three companies, none of which ever built track, were reported in 1901 to be grading rights-of-way from Tiffin to Port Clinton, and another was said to be grading from Tiffin to Sandusky." In 1910 *World's Work* estimated that nine out of ten projected interurbans were stillborn, and *Brill Magazine* editorialized that the failure of paper roads was "something frightful." Many of these unfulfilled plans came during the two great waves of building, the first between 1901 and 1904 and the second between 1905 and 1908.[37]

Texas stands out as the leading example of these dashed dreams. The state ultimately claimed almost 500 miles of functioning interurbans, the greatest mileage in any state west of the Mississippi River except California. Yet by the early 1920s interurban advocates in the Lone Star State had projected an astonishing total of more than 22,500 miles![38]

All sections of Texas experienced traction fever. "Interurbans are the wave of the future," proclaimed a Galveston enthusiast, and many agreed. Understandably the commonly discussed routes were in the most populous regions, and in some cases they covered substantial distances. More than a dozen attempts were made to link Dallas and Houston, Dallas and Austin, and Houston and Austin. A line between Austin and San Antonio was another popular objective. Even in sparsely populated West Texas, promoters sought interurbans. In December 1910 Farwell businessmen received a charter for the Rock Island, Texico, Farwell & Southern Railway. The plan was to construct a 75-mile electric road between Farwell and neighboring Texico, New Mexico, and southward from Farwell to the Cochran-Yoakum county line.[39]

Like the Farwell project, nearly all of the paper interurbans in Texas (and elsewhere) sought to connect communities in a linear fashion. The common format was to have a line from A (often a place with a substantial population) through smaller towns and villages B, C, and D to E (likewise a city or town with considerable population or growth potential). A few had destinations that were never precisely designated: "ports on the Gulf of Mexico," "up the Pecos Valley," or "West Texas oil fields."[40]

Not surprisingly, variations in routing strategies existed with these unbuilt Texas interurbans. One involved the "hub" concept. An example occurred in 1914 when the Brenham business community, spearheaded by the Young Men's Business Association, sought to make their town the premier retail center between Austin and Houston. The plan was to build a half-dozen electric lines that would radiate out of Brenham and connect with such communities as Independence, William Penn, Washington, Chappell Hill, Phillipsburg, Millersville, and Gay Hill. "All [electric] roads will lead to Brenham" became the cry. Another illustration came two years earlier. Shreveport, Louisiana, promoters received a charter for construction of their Texas-Louisiana Traction Company.

> **PUBLIC MEETING!**
>
> A Meeting will be held at AMMON'S HALL in
>
> # GEORGETOWN
>
> THURSDAY,
>
> ## JULY 21, 1910
>
> (AT 8 O'CLOCK P. M.)
>
> For the purpose of discussing the practicability of building an
>
> # ELECTRIC ROAD
>
> With Terminals at
>
> # UNION AND VERSAILLES
>
> Connecting Phillipsburg, Georgetown, and other intervening Towns. All persons interested in the proposed improvement are requested to be present.
>
> ## COMMITTEE

In July 1910 residents of the hamlet of Georgetown, Ohio, had the opportunity to voice their opinions about building a 25-mile interurban between Union, located in Montgomery County, northwest of Dayton, to Versailles in Darke County. Alas, only talk prevailed, and this proposed project failed to move to the incorporation or "paper" stage.

Author's collection.

This interurban sought to build three lines that radiated out of this Pelican State trade center: Longview, Texas, via Marshall and Jefferson, Texas, and Mansfield, Louisiana.[41]

Another, albeit rare, plan was the "triangle." In winter 1911 out-of-state promoters announced their intention to create an extensive three-sided system. Their interurban would extend from Dallas–Fort Worth to San Antonio, then to Houston, and return to Dallas–Fort Worth.[42]

Whether the proposed Texas interurbans were linear, spoked, or triangular, they varied greatly in length. Lines ranged from the tiny Burkeville Railway, designed to span the 3 miles between the Newton County towns of Burkeville and Wiergate, to the monster north–south trans-Texas Minneapolis, Kansas City & Gulf [Galveston] Electric Railway (MKC&G). While the Burkeville and MKC&G projects represented extremes, the average length of the more than three hundred roads proposed was about 65 miles, being somewhat longer than typical midwestern interurbans.[43]

Intercity electric promotion in the Lone Star State followed nationwide trends. Enthusiasts tended to be either local businessmen and professionals or civic organizations or out-of-state capitalists and syndicates. Occasionally these types joined forces. Among individuals who sought to establish traction lines was Haskell real-estate promoter M. R. Hemphill, who in 1911 attempted to tie Haskell with Rule, a dozen miles to the west, being an extension of his localized Haskell Traction Company. That same year members of the Commercial Club of McKinney pushed for a 36-mile road between their hometown and Bonham. At the turn of the century "outsiders" from Akron, Ohio, announced their intention to build an interurban in El Paso and Hudspeth counties. The emerging "Rubber King," Frank A. Seiberling, cofounder of the Goodyear Tire and Rubber Company, and a business associate, Frederick E. Smith, president of the Second National Bank of Akron, ultimately acquired only a street railway franchise in El Paso. Stone and Webster, a major utility holding company headquartered in Boston, became heavily involved in Texas traction promotion. The firm successfully linked Dallas and Fort Worth, Fort Worth and Cleburne, Galveston and Houston, and Beaumont and Port Arthur, but several other of its publicized projects failed to materialize. When the Quanah & Medicine Mound Traction Company won incorporation in 1909 to build the 18 miles between the towns of its corporate name, Missouri capitalists joined members of the Quanah Chamber of Commerce to try to turn this dream into reality.[44]

Although an exact profile of promoters who sought to construct interurbans in Texas would be difficult to compile, the majority of local sponsors probably lacked previous railroad experience. This may be an explanation for these widespread failures. Backers came from the ranks of agriculturalists, bankers, merchants, oil men, professionals, and real-estate brokers. A few had been involved in street railways and sought to expand their intracity properties into full-fledged interurbans, or they had participated in steam road construction. Wichita Falls businessmen Joseph Kemp and Frank Kell, for example, had established a positive reputation for their steam properties, the foremost being the Wichita Falls & Northwestern Railway. Kemp and Kell also embraced electricity, becoming principals in the Wichita Falls Traction Company. Toward the end of the interurban building cycle these men sought to construct a 135-mile high-speed electric railway between Wichita Falls and Dallas. In this instance the previously successful formula of "Think like Kemp and work like Kell" fell short.[45]

It is hardly shocking that Texas, with a burgeoning population and growing wealth, became the place where promoters sought to construct thousands of miles of interurbans. But even in sparsely populated Nevada dreams of having electric intercity traction flourished.

At first glance Nevada seemed an unlikely environment for interurbans. Its population was tiny, just 42,335 in 1900, and the only state in the Twelfth Census to lose residents, declining 10.6 percent from its 1890 total. Could such a sparsely settled place support an interurban? Moreover, the steam road mileage of 1,750 miles appeared adequate; Nevada, in fact, claimed the distinction of having more railroad mileage in proportion to population than any other state. Unquestionably the physical terrain posed challenges for any interurban. The need to conquer deserts and mountain ranges would escalate construction and maintenance costs.[46]

Interurban promoters, nevertheless, saw opportunities in Nevada; a new day for this remote state had presumably dawned. About 1902 a second mining boom helped to rouse Nevada from more than two decades of economic stagnation. Not only did thousands of gold and silver miners flock to the Bullfrog, Goldfield, and Tonopah districts, but copper production surged when mines in White Pine County entered full-scale production after 1908, causing population to spike. Irrigation efforts also portended well for the state. Most of all, the Truckee-Carson water project, begun in 1903, offered the possibility for agricultural development of huge tracts of vacant land, attracting potentially tens of thousands of plowmen. In 1911 a journalist beamed about this agricultural spurt: "Never in the history of Nevada had there been such an influx of colonists and homeseekers as at present. Hardly a week passes but what some of the state papers chronicle the coming of new settlers from various parts of the union to acquire land in Nevada."[47]

Between 1906 and 1919 interurban enthusiasts in Nevada sought to tap potential patrons, namely miners and farmers, by proposing more than 400 miles of electric lines in nearly a dozen and a half projects. A South Bullfrog capitalist, for one, revealed his plans in 1906 for a 20-mile electric road between his hometown and the boom camp of Rhyolite. And the state's last proposal, the Tonopah, Divide & Goldfield Electric Railroad, likewise appeared in that gold mining district, seeking to build the 6 miles between the first two places of its corporate title.[48]

Although efforts to bring electric intercity traction to the Sagebrush State lagged behind similar ones in the interurban heartland of the Midwest, average lengths were typical, about 30 miles. The shortest were the two paper roads that actually opened, the Nevada Interurban Railway and the Reno Traction Company. Best classified as rural trolleys, the former covered the 3.5 miles between Reno and the Moana Hot Springs and the latter connected Reno with Sparks, a distance of about 5 miles. The longest line proposal came in 1908, when Boise, Idaho, businessmen announced their intention to link Twin Falls, Idaho, with Wells, Nevada. Their projected 114-mile Idaho & Nevada Southern Railway would traverse about 70 miles of Elko County in Nevada.[49]

The same year as the proposed interurban to Wells, Nevadans learned of another sizable project: electrification of the Virginia & Truckee Railroad. Owners of this steam shortline considered installing an overhead trolley in Reno and a third-rail system on the remainder of its 31-mile main line to Carson City and on the 15-mile Minden branch. The plan was not unique. Elsewhere in the country some steam shortlines either considered or became electric roads. These new interurbans included such widely scattered former steam roads as the Bamberger Electric in Utah; Cincinnati, Georgetown & Portsmouth (a former narrow-gauge road) in Ohio; Jamestown, Westfield & Northwestern in New York; Pacific Coast (also a former narrow-gauge road) in California; Roby & Northern in Texas; and the Washington & Old Dominion in Virginia.[50]

The Fallon Electric Railway Company is a classic illustration of the unbuilt interurban in Nevada. Officially launched on May 27, 1913, by Churchill County investors and led by Dr. C. A. Hascall, a local physician, the plan called for building initially from Fallon "in a generally southerly direction to Harrigan, Churchill County, Nevada, also to run from a point at or near the City of Fallon in a general easterly direction to Stillwater, Churchill County, Nevada." Later these promoters considered a route that would extend from Stillwater northeast for approximately 30 miles into the Dixie Valley, on the east slope of the Stillwater Mountains. The road's backers entertained more serious thoughts of having their line turning east from Harrigan, 7 miles south of Fallon, and crossing the Springs Salt Flat and Sand Springs mining districts, terminating about 40 miles southeast of the Churchill County seat.[51]

The reasons for promoting the Fallon Electric road paralleled those that motivated so many interurban enthusiasts. Residents of the rail-starved areas to the east and southeast of Fallon sought improved transportation. Only a short Southern Pacific Railroad branch from Hazen to Fallon served the immediate region. Freight service was poor, and passenger accommodations were no better. Travel over public roads was even worse. Local sugar growers cried out for a better way to move beets to processing plants, and some interests wanted an electric rail artery to spur production of borax and other minerals.[52]

Determined to improve transportation and to build Fallon into more than a town of 1,625 residents and, of course, to profit personally, proponents eagerly peddled company securities. Although the road issued $500,000 of capital stock (divided into 10,000 shares at a par value of $50 each), the cash amount investors bought was modest. By summer 1913 only $18,000 was on hand, and Dr. Hascall had contributed most of that, investing almost $16,000.[53]

Multiple factors explain the weak security sales. By 1914 the national fervor for traction schemes had cooled; the great bursts of construction

Although hardly a Texas "paper" railroad, the tiny Roby & Northern Railway (R&N) possessed an unusual history. The 5-mile road opened in 1915 as a steam shortline, designed to connect the inland town of Roby with a branch of the Missouri–Kansas–Texas (Katy) Railway at North Roby junction. In 1923 the nearly insolvent R&N fell into the hands of the West Texas Utilities Company, a unit of the giant Insull traction and electric power combine, and the new owners electrified the property. Even though the R&N generated only modest revenues, it lasted until the eve of World War II. For years the company claimed to be "The Best Short Line Railway in America," and perhaps it was.

Author's collection.

WEST TEXAS

A HALF decade ago, West Texas was the Southwest's last frontier. Today, West Texas is beginning to come into her own. Rich in present and prospective possibilities, rich in soil, rich in climate, and above and beyond all else, rich in the sturdy Anglo-Saxonism of her people, West Texas is fast developing into one of America's finest empires.

West Texas points to her ranges, from which come the world's standards for cattle. She points to the long tiers of her counties which produce a substantial portion of the world's cotton supply in freedom from the boll weevil menace. She points to her great farms, her magnificent wheat fields, her record as a kaffir and milo producer. She points to the huge bank deposits of her citizens.

West Texas points to her steadily multiplying new industries and to that trinity which attracts them—desirable land at reasonable purchase, abundant power at reasonable cost and superior labor at reasonable price.

West Texas points to her reputation for hospitality, for proving herself and for carrying on, and with a proud flourish, West Texas points to the fact that she has made "Going West" worth while.

By way of example, West Texas calls your attention to Fisher County. Thirty miles square, half of her land is already in cultivation, and three-fifths of the remainder is tillable. The 1921 cotton crop was 31,000 bales.

Join the procession that is moving toward West Texas. Settle, preferably, in Fisher County, near her capital city, Roby—but settle in West Texas, anyway!

WEST TEXAS UTILITIES COMPANY

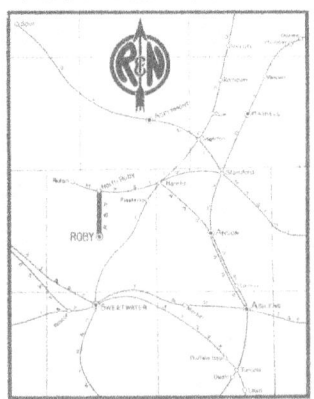

ROBY & NORTHERN RAILWAY COMPANY

OFFICERS

G. W. Fox, *President*

Paul Crowley, *Operating Vice-President*

Arthur Kenderine, *Traffic Manager*

P. P. Sheridan, *Superintendent*

Geo. Mains, *General Freight and Passenger Agent*

NOTES

Satisfactory service—both passenger and freight—awaits in all relations with patrons of the Roby and Northern Railroad Company. Complaints, suggestions and compliments should be mailed direct to the chief operating official at Roby, Texas.

No responsibility is assumed for errors in time tables, inconvenience or distance resulting from delayed trains or failure to make connections. Schedules herein are correct, in change without notice.

Central time is used throughout the R.&N. lines.

SCHEDULE OF TRAIN SERVICE

READ DOWN					READ UP		
No. 6 Daily	No. 4 Daily	No. 2 Daily			No. 1 Daily	No. 3 Daily	No. 5 Daily
1 00 PM	5 45 PM	8 30 AM	0	Lv. ROBY Ar.	9 45 AM	6 35 PM	3 00 PM
1 10 "	*	*	2	Alkih	*	*	2 50 "
1 15 "	*	*	4	Rainbolt	*	*	2 45 "
1 30 PM	6 00 "	8 55 AM	5	Ar. North Roby Lv.	9 30 "	6 20 PM	2 30 PM
				(M.-K.-T. Ry.)			
			5	Lv. North Roby Ar.	9 10 "		
	6 15 "			Stamford			
	8 30 "		41		7 05 "		
	11 45 AM		13	Cisco	3 40 "		
	2 20 AM		162	Dublin	12 42 AM		
	6 47 AM		269	Ar. WACO Lv.	8 10 PM		

*Stop on signal

MISSOURI-KANSAS-TEXAS LINES
CONNECTIONS AT WACO, TEXAS

SOUTH	No. 9 Daily	No. 7 Daily	No. 5 Flyer Daily	No. 25 Limited Daily	No. 2 Daily	No. 1 Texas Special Daily
Lv Waco	6:00₁	1:45₁	11:40₁	11:50₁	12:25₁	12:35₁	4:40₁
Ar Temple	7:15₁	2:45₁	12:43₁	1:05₁	1:30₁	1:45₁	5:42₁
Ar Granger	10:10₁		1:35₁	8:15₁	2:25₁	7:46₁	
Ar Austin	12:01₁	5:00₁		4:05₁		4:25₁	7:50₁
Ar San Antonio	4:00₁	7:30₁		7:15₁		7:15₁	10:25₁
Ar Houston		7:35₁		6:30₁			
Ar Galveston		9:30₁					

NORTH	No. 2 Texas Special Daily	No. 4 Limited Daily	No. 24 Daily	No. 6 Flyer Daily	No. 26 Daily	No. 8 Daily	No. 18 Daily
Lv Waco	1:15₁	4:30₁	4:25₁	4:15₁	4:20₁	4:55₁	5:00₁
Ar Hillsboro		5:30₁	5:30₁	5:10₁	5:25₁		
Ar Waxahachie		6:30₁		6:15₁			
Ar Ft. Worth			7:30₁		7:25₁		
Ar Dallas	4:05₁	7:30₁		7:25₁		7:30₁	7:30₁
Ar Denison	7:05₁	11:05₁	11:10₁	11:50₁	11:25₁		
Ar Kansas City	7:45₁	12:30₁		12:25₁			
Ar St. Louis	11:25₁	7:10₁		7:51₁			

"KATY" SERVICE

The Missouri-Kansas-Texas Lines operate, north and south from Waco, three exceptionally fine trains, the "Texas Special," the "Katy Limited" and the "Katy Flyer." Each train carries drawing room sleeping cars, offers superior dining-car facilities and is made up of thoroughly modern equipment.

Reservations for these "Katy" trains may be made from Waco either north or south by telegraph from the Western Union office at the Roby station of the Roby and Northern Railroad Company.

Electrically Operated Passenger, Freight, Mail and Express Service

had already taken place. Admittedly, parts of the West experienced a delayed development, but for out-of-state investors risks seemed high in such a remote place as Churchill County. Moreover, the county's sparse population (2,811 in 1910) limited opportunities for local stock subscriptions. Two additional events had a negative impact: the outbreak of World War in 1914, which shook investor confidence, and in 1916 the appearance near Fallon of the Nevada Cooperative Colony, a utopian settlement of socialists. "What sensible investor sinks money into an electric railway project so near a band of socialists?" asked the *Electric Railway Journal*. "These are people who plan to capture Nevada for the likes of [Eugene] Debs."[54]

Because of limited funds, proponents of the Fallon Electric Railway formulated a creative way to construct their interurban on a shoestring. The strategy was to spend their nest egg on surveying and bridge and culvert work. With this accomplished, volunteer labor, coming from "online" agriculturists, would grade the roadbed. (These graders would likely receive company stock for their efforts.) The next stage would be to float bonds based on the physical improvements (bridges, culverts, and roadbed). These funds would be spent for the rail, ties, poles, wire, rolling stock, and other necessities. Bond sales would also pay for part of the actual installations and would finance power generation and needed support facilities. Self-help would continue to come into play. Track and pole gangs would consist of volunteers or those willing to accept a combination of cash and stock for their labor.[55]

The Fallon interurban project resembled the "farmers' railroad" movement that earlier had sprouted on the Great Plains. These consumer-launched ventures, consisting of farmers and local businessmen, sought to reduce freight rates and the power of "railroad monopolists." Specifically, backers would sponsor organizational meetings, incorporate, survey routes, and direct construction. Since capital would be scarce, everyone along the projected line would be asked to donate right-of-way and to contribute, if possible, their labor. (Company stock would be their immediate reward.) Available animal teams with plows and scrapers would shape the roadbed, and cross ties would be harvested locally or from more distant stands of timber. With grading completed and ties furnished, the emerging railroad would be bonded to raise funds to purchase rail and rolling stock. The ultimate fate of the finished property would remain flexible. The railroad might be sold or leased to a trunk road with the understanding that customers would receive the best possible rates and service, but more likely, it would be operated indefinitely as a cooperative enterprise. With several exceptions, though, these farmers' railroads remained only on paper.[56]

Even adopting a farmers' railroad approach, the Fallon interurban was not to be. The project stalled. Dr. Hascall tried to reenergize the scheme by persuading a mining promoter from Portland, Oregon, to examine the projected route. Although "strongly impressed with the possibilities of the road," this potential investor failed to make a financial commitment. Then the fatal blow came in the summer of 1916. The local press reported that Dr. Hascall, "everybody's friend and Fallon's consistent and persistent booster," had left the community for Montana. Feeble attempts for a resurrection followed, but they were just that – feeble. With America's entry into war in 1917 and the likelihood of the transcontinental Lincoln Highway being built through the region, interurban fever vanished.[57]

The unbuilt during the Interurban Era also involved urban terminals. The D. H. Burnham and Company–designed Indianapolis Traction Terminal, which opened in 1904 and featured nine stories of offices, businesses, and travelers' facilities, indicated the value of such a complex. The success of this "Temple of Electric Transportation" prompted traction executives in other cities to consider similar structures. Some were built, but others were not.[58]

Residents of Kansas City wanted a central interurban terminal, being inspired by the Indianapolis monument to the Interurban Era. Already this growing Missouri metropolis had become a showcase for the nationwide "City Beautiful Movement." Its signature structure, Union Station, received its first trains in 1914 and gave the city "a station unexcelled." After completion of the Kansas City, Clay County & St. Joseph Railway in 1913, a group of downtown merchants and other boosters created the Interurban Central Station Company. The goal was to build a facility, estimated to cost about $1.75 million, that would serve the four (later five) interurbans that radiated out of the central business district. Not only would the central station provide greater convenience for commercial travelers, shoppers, and other patrons of these electric lines, but it would reduce street congestion. Yet bickering over location and other disputes led to inaction. Time passed, but in 1918 a practical site seemingly had been found. Still nothing happened. Another push for the terminal came in 1923 when the location was slightly altered and a second firm, Kansas City Interurban Terminal Company, announced plans for a more expensive structure, costing nearly $3 million and occupying the city block from Ninth to Tenth Streets on McGee Street. But enthusiasm for the project waned as interurban usage declined. The automobile was rapidly taking passengers away from the electric roads, and transit buses were gaining popularity. Yet a transit hub, which served both traction and bus riders, seemed sensible. As the Interurban Era was in eclipse, a developer outlined plans for a combination office building, hotel, parking garage,

Early in the twentieth century residents of Coggan, Iowa, could send a picture postcard that showed that their Linn County community had both streetcar (*left*) and interurban (*right*) service. They did not. The town, though, was on the Cedar Rapids branch of the Illinois Central and also received trains of the Chicago, Anamosa & Northern Railroad, a twilight-era shortline.

Author's collection.

and bus terminal. Success followed in 1930 when this $5 million structure opened. Kansas Citians now had access to the upscale 300-room Pickwick Hotel and a modern bus facility, but there would not be a place for interurbans.[59]

Even if an interurban project remained a paper proposition, it did not prevent those individuals who longed for electric cars to fantasize about having them. In some communities, which never saw intercity traction, boosters produced picture postcards that showed such service. This was the golden age of the picture postcard, and fakery occurred with some frequency. Coshocton, Ohio, the largest community in the state that lacked an interurban (1910 population of 9,603), did see cards circulate that depicted interurban cars on its main streets. Perhaps these bogus cards made residents, especially its "go-getters" and "live-wires," feel somewhat better about their disappointments. Citizens had had their hopes dashed and civic pride damaged when at least four firms failed to build from Coshocton to Newark or Zanesville.[60]

THE PARTIALLY BUILT

While hundreds of interurban schemes nationwide never left the drawing board, in scattered instances electric railways were neither paper entities nor operating concerns. The precise number is unknown, but partially built interurbans dotted the landscape. There were also those electric roads that opened but failed to complete their intended objectives, falling in some cases far short of their announced endpoints.

The Gainesville, Whitesboro & Sherman Electric Railway (GW&SERy) is but one interurban where construction workers shaped a portion of the line. This Texas company, incorporated in 1906, sought to connect the 39 miles between the towns of its corporate name. Dirt flew, and by summer 1908 the roadbed had been completed a dozen miles east of Gainesville. When financial problems stalled construction, the GW&SERy entered receivership. Yet court protection and new leadership failed to bring about a revitalization. In 1914 the *Electric Railway Journal* reported that the moribund firm still sought to become a going concern. "The company is desirous of [interesting] outside parties in the railway with a view to its construction and operation." There were no immediate takers. After World War I George Easley, a Dallas businessman, acquired the rights and reorganized the partially built property as the Gainesville & Sherman Traction Company. He, too, was stymied.[61]

A much grander project than the Gainesville, Whitesboro & Sherman, but dating from approximately the same time, was the Twin City & Lake Superior Railway. In a plan resembling several long-distance interurban schemes, backers of the "Arrow Line" promoted a double-track speedway with third-rail power between Minneapolis and Duluth. The route would be mostly straight, being more than 30 miles shorter than its steam road competitors and bypassing intermediate towns. By 1910 approximately 50 miles of the Arrow Line had been graded. Soon mounting financial woes and the Soo Line's upgraded passenger service between the two Minnesota cities caused this partially built interurban to collapse.[62]

The complexities of a failed interurban, which included construction, can be found in an Iowa experience: efforts to open an electric line between Red Oak, seat of Montgomery County, and Des Moines, the state capital, a distance of approximately 100 miles. Tracks would run through Winterset and Greenfield, county seat towns, and several smaller communities, most of which either lacked steam car service or were relegated to a branch line.

Before the Panic of 1907 there had been discussions of building interurbans in the territory to be served by the Red Oak to Des Moines route, but nothing tangible had happened. With the return to more prosperous times, talk turned to action. In April 1908 traction advocates, championed by B. B. Clark, a Red Oak canning executive, and Horace Deemer, a Red Oak lawyer and jurist, organized the Red Oak & North Eastern Interurban Promotion Company (RO&NEIPCo). Even though Red Oak residents appreciated that the Chicago, Burlington & Quincy Railroad (Burlington) operated its Chicago to Denver main line through their town and had branches that extended north and south, they considered the Burlington to be an uncaring monopoly. They also wanted a *direct* connection to Des Moines, the state's largest city and its major wholesale distribution center.[63]

Immediately the RO&NEIPCo began to create awareness for its objectives and to raise funds for preliminary work. In the booster spirit of the day, the goal was to make Red Oak "The City of Progress and Enterprise" and "The Hub and Metropolis of S.-W. Iowa." A common promotional pitch went as follows: "Red Oak need waste no effort in trying to get factories. Get a new road first and the factories will come of their own accord." Promoters invited citizens to learn more, suggesting that they visit its office, located on the south side of the public square: "Come in without knocking. The latch string is always out."[64]

Although the exact route between Red Oak and Des Moines fluctuated, the RO&NEIPCo found backing in the rural and urban locales between its announced endpoints. Then with what leaders considered to be ample enthusiasm and adequate start-up money, they forged ahead. In June 1908 they signed a contract with Roberts and Abbott, a Cleveland, Ohio, engineering firm. As interurbans proliferated, support companies emerged, and serious promoters could find engineering, construction, and financial assistance from a single firm. RO&NEIPCo instructed Roberts and Abbott to determine building costs and potential earnings for "an electric passenger railway and also as an electric freight railway." Preliminary work commenced. "The road from Red Oak to Des Moines is going through," crowed the *Red Oak Express*, "and it is going just as fast as money and energy can push it."[65]

Potential patrons learned in detail about the unfolding developments. The *Express*, for one, updated readers with its weekly "Some Interurban News." The survey was ongoing, and that pleased backers. By September 1908 the field party had finished its work between Des Moines and Mount Etna, an "inland" village more than halfway to Red Oak, and it had turned to the remaining section between Mount Etna and Red Oak.[66]

With survey profiles and data in hand, the RO&NEIPCo increased its efforts to raise capital. Winterset, the Madison County seat, which suffered from poor service at the end of a Rock Island branch, and Greenfield, seat of Adair County, which was also plagued by limited service on a Burlington appendage, became key communities that endorsed what Red Oak citizens had started. "Everyone along the route wants a railroad," observed the *Greenfield Transcript*. "This is [an] altogether different proposition from anything ever offered our people before and it is earnestly desired by the Transcript that the people have a thorough understanding of the matter. When it is seen in the proper light the men in charge will have no trouble in disposing of the stock."[67]

Proponents of the Red Oak & North Eastern Interurban Promotion Company considered McKeen gasoline cars to be ideal for their proposed "wireless interurban." These cars even sported that interurban look, although their knife-nosed fronts made them distinctive. There were other choices, including products of the Kobush-Wagenhals Steam Motor Car, equipment that also resembled interurban cars.

Author's collection.

But soon a change in plans occurred. The Red Oak & North Eastern Interurban Promotion Company decided that the cost of a conventional interurban would be too expensive; after all, a power source, substations, poles, and overhead wires would be required. The front page of the November 19, 1909, issue of the *Express* featured a photograph and story about "The New Interurban Cars." Instead of electric rolling stock, promoters opted for the recently introduced internal-combustion McKeen cars, built by the McKeen Motor Car Company of Omaha, Nebraska. The brainchild of W. R. McKeen Jr., superintendent of motive power for the

Union Pacific, these self-propelled rail cars were designed to be cheaper than bona fide interurban equipment and more flexible and economical than steam-powered trains. The McKeen firm made these claims: "Highly economical motor, self-starting, instantly reversible, exceedingly easy to control and above all dependable." Officials of the Red Oak company believed that "passengers on the R.O. & N. E. railway [popular name for the RO&NEIPCo] will ride in the latest and most approved gasoline motor cars such as are already in use on the following roads: Union Pacific road in Nebraska, Kansas and Colorado, Illinois Central in Illinois [and] Chicago & Northwestern [sic] in Wisconsin."[68]

The Red Oak newspaper suggested that McKeen cars were just as good as, if not better than, standard interurban equipment, and they would have the same impact on service. "The cars of this kind are most comfortable at any time of year or in any kind of weather. No cinders or smoke to bother. Easy-riding and speedy." The endorsement continued: "Farmers living along the Red Oak & Northeastern would have no need of automobiles. There will be cars every hour on the new road. When a farmer wants to come to town, what will he do? Simply go to the nearest place where the interurban crosses a road, hail a car and get on." Even though McKeen cars had the habit of inconveniently breaking down between stations, backers believed that their redefined (and less expensive) interurban offered the best in intercity transportation.[69]

The choice of McKeen cars was rationalized in the *Express* by a subsequent piece on "Handling Interurban Freight." Although the described schedule reflected what some electrics provided their freight customers, the plan for this traffic sector suggests that of a traditional steam shortline. "There will be two regular freight trains a day, one each way. A freight will run from Greenfield to Red Oak and from Red Oak to Greenfield. [This] will constitute one division of the road. The other division will be from Greenfield to Des Moines." Presumably the motive power for freight trains would be steam and not internal combustion. Yet the writer indicated that the company, typical of electric interurbans, planned to install frequent sidings, allowing farmers the convenience of shipping and receiving freight, particularly livestock. With McKeen cars moving up and down the line, readers were reminded that "with a passenger car with capacity for light freight, milk cans, etc., passing every hour, and a freight train twice a day, could the farmers wish or ask for anything better in the way of shipping facilities?"[70]

The decision to use McKeen or other types of internal-combustion cars was hardly unique during the Interurban Era. Take, for example, how the Topeka, Eskridge & Council Grove Railroad planned to operate its proposed 45-mile line. In 1906 management announced that it would "acquire gasoline-electric cars for interurban passenger and milk-hauling

Remnants of the partially built Des Moines & Red Oak Railway, previously Red Oak & North Eastern Interurban Promotion Company, remain visible more than a century after the project petered out. This March 2015 photograph shows the remains of the deep cut graders had carved through Jenks Hill in Mills County, Iowa, southwest of Red Oak.

Roxanne McFarland photograph.

service" and use steam locomotives for freight operations. This never occurred; the company folded in 1910 after completing about 4 miles of roadbed in greater Topeka.[71]

With the crucial decision made to reject electricity, perhaps prospects were brighter for the Red Oak to Des Moines road. About this time the Red Oak & North Eastern Interurban Promotion Company had become the Des Moines & Red Oak Railway Company (DM&RO). Supporters believed that finally the project had moved beyond the "promotion company stage." With Des Moines in the corporate name the expectation was that it would be easier to gain financial support, especially in the capital city.[72]

Yet the DM&RO faltered. An altered name did not enhance resources; financial problems plagued the gestating road. Promoters concluded that construction costs, especially on the southern section, in the short term would far exceed their means.[73]

Even with money concerns, the DM&RO did not quit, becoming just another failed paper road. In 1912 the company committed its resources to building *southwest* from Red Oak rather than *northeast* toward Greenfield, Winterset, and Des Moines. It commenced construction on a 14-mile line that began at a connection with the Omaha line of the Wabash Railroad near Imogene, in Fremont County. Workers hurriedly grubbed out trees and underbrush on the hastily surveyed line. With newly acquired grading machinery, which the company planned to use later on the Des

Moines core, graders fashioned the roadbed from the Wabash interchange to near the outskirts of Red Oak. As work progressed the company purchased cross ties, bridge timbers, and culvert pipes that were distributed along the route. Then activities abruptly stopped. The costs of the survey, labor, equipment, and other supplies left little money to acquire rails, track materials, and rolling stock.[74]

Still, backers of the DM&RO did not surrender. They hoped that by winning a tax levy from Red Oak they could finish the Imogene section and jumpstart the original project. In a spirited election held in August 1912, where supporters sponsored rallies and placed placards that proclaimed WE ARE FOR THE RAILROAD AND RED OAK in the windows of sympathetic store owners, voters overwhelmingly approved the subsidy. When the tally was announced, celebrations followed. "The serenaders or 'shot gun' parade was some noisy and were indiscriminate in their favors, and their performance was looked upon with all due forbearance. Some of the younger boosters became almost over-enthusiastic, but no harm was done."[75]

Red Oak taxpayers could not save the Des Moines & Red Oak. The payment of tax dollars would not be immediate but made over an extended time period. Other political units, including Des Moines, either avoided votes on tax subsidies or defeated them. Stock sales, surely influenced by citizen inaction or voter rejection, sputtered at best. As a result it did not take long before the company collapsed. Farmers and others then hauled off the scattered ties and bridge timbers (probably under the cover of darkness), and nature began to reclaim the naked roadbed. Partially built meant only disappointment and financial loss for those who were convinced that an electric interurban, even "wireless traction," would be in the best interests of on-route communities large and small.[76]

While they hardly fell to that category of partially built interurbans that never operated, there were related instances where functioning, even profitable and enduring, electric roads were unable to complete their incorporated or publicized plans. Three good illustrations come from Ohio, the state with the greatest interurban mileage. The Northern Ohio Traction & Light Company (NOT&L), one of the oldest, largest, and most important electric roads in the Buckeye State, had its eyes on linking Cleveland with Wheeling, West Virginia. Although the NOT&L served Cleveland, Akron, and Canton and extended as far south as New Philadelphia and Uhrichsville, the remaining 46 miles to the Ohio River were never constructed. Another Ohio company, Scioto Valley Traction Company, the state's most heavily built interurban and only third-rail operation, spanned the distance between Columbus, Circleville, Chillicothe, and Lancaster, but it failed to extend the Chillicothe line to Portsmouth and the Lancaster branch to Athens. The Toledo & Western Railway

(T&W), probably the first electric road intended to transport both passengers and carload freight, successfully opened a line between Toledo and Adrian, Michigan, and Toledo and Pioneer, Ohio. Although the T&W started to grade west from Pioneer, it floundered in its efforts to connect with interurbans in neighboring Indiana. If these three projects had been completed as planned, they would later have been blighted by the automobile and truck.[77]

In some cases an interurban later reached its announced endpoints by providing connecting bus service. Such was the case with the Milwaukee Electric Railway & Light Company. Its planned line to Madison got no further west of Milwaukee than Watertown, Wisconsin, because of the financial problems caused by the Panic of 1907. Yet coordinated bus service allowed it to accommodate passengers between the state's two largest cities.[78]

BIG SCHEMES

Before the Railway Age itself took hold, transportation dreamers proposed some exceedingly long lines. As early as 1829 William Redfield, an amateur scientist caught up in the enthusiasm for the emerging "Age of Steam," wrote a widely disseminated tract (revised a year later) that advocated a bold scheme for a railroad to connect the Atlantic Ocean with the Mississippi River. A few years later Horatio Allen, chief engineer of the South Carolina Canal & Rail Road Company, told delegates at a railroad convention in Estellville, Virginia, that he believed that a railroad could and should be built between Charleston and the Ohio River. Even more ambitious proposals occurred during the "Demonstration Period" of the 1830s and 1840s. The most widely discussed (and debated) plan for a long-distance railroad began in the mid-1840s. Asa Whitney, a New York merchant involved in the China trade, became an untiring advocate for a railroad to the Pacific Ocean and was convinced that there were "those persons now living who will see a rail-road connecting New York with the Pacific." Others agreed and took up Whitney's cause.[79]

Resembling their steam-road counterparts, there were electric railway enthusiasts at the dawn of the "Interurban Era" who thought big. In 1892 visionaries suggested an electric railway that would run 252 miles "as the crows flies" between Chicago and St. Louis. They bragged that the frequently dispatched cars of their Chicago & St. Louis Electric Railway (C&StLERy) would offer exceptional – arguably fantastic – service. A *St. Louis Republic* headline proclaimed: THE DISTANCE OF TWO HUNDRED AND FIFTY MILES TO BE COVERED IN TWO AND ONE-HALF HOURS. The fastest contemporary steam-powered passenger train between the Windy City and St. Louis, which traveled over the Chicago & Alton Railroad

(Alton), took eight and a half hours to make this 283-mile trip. Unlike the Alton and other steam roads, passenger service on the C&StLERy would not operate at night, "the tracks being reserved for high-class freight, mail and express service."[80]

Although the Chicago & St. Louis Railway represented lunatic-fringe thinking, considering the state of interurban technology, additional long-distance electric projects appeared during the first decade of the twentieth century, those halcyon years of promotion and construction. Writers for newspapers, popular periodicals, and trade publications reported an array of amazing schemes, including ones that would connect Omaha with Denver, Chicago with Boston, and the most ambitious of all, the Transcontinental Electric Railroad that would span the continent. "The day is seemingly not far distant when the electric railway system of the country will reach transcontinental proportions, when it will be possible to board a well-appointed, comfortable and speedy electric train at Boston and alight at San Francisco," prophesied a writer for the *Philadelphia Ledger* in 1907. "The conception is by no means visionary." And there were those major proposals that were less grand, including the 300-mile Missouri Central Railway that in 1904 planned to connect the city centers of St. Louis and Kansas City via Columbia.[81]

The Minneapolis, Kansas City & Gulf Electric Railway represents these grandiose, albeit totally failed plans. Its promoters, which included the former president of the Chicago City Railway, put on an advertising blitz in 1907 to attract support for a projected line between the Twin Cities and Galveston, Texas, an interurban that would serve Des Moines, Kansas City, Wichita, Oklahoma City, Dallas, Houston, and scores of intermediate places (roughly the route of today's Interstate 35). Backers believed that they had compelling arguments. "Startling is the fact that there is not one through trunk line from the lakes to the Gulf, the Garden Spot of the World. There must be a through Trunk Line North and South. This railway will intercept all the great avenues of transportation running East and West, and from these sources we will receive an interchange of passenger and freight business that is almost beyond comprehension." There was more. "A savings in time and money in transportation of passengers and freight will always be rewarded by large profits." The construction strategy seemed sensible. The company would build in pieces. "As each section is completed it will be immediately placed in operation, thus producing revenues. The first section will be from Minneapolis to Des Moines. The country traversed assures this section a success." The plan, however, called for some metropolitan centers to be skirted but reached by electrified feeders. The promotional copy was emphatic: NEVER WILL WE BE CONFRONTED WITH THE PROBLEM OF MUNICIPAL OWNERSHIP,

RENEWAL OF CITY FRANCHISES, AND OTHER NUMEROUS EXPENSIVE DEMANDS.[82]

Notwithstanding the alleged merits for potential investors and patrons, enthusiasm for the MKC&G failed to take hold, at least in terms of financial support. The impact of the Panic of 1907 hardly helped. This expansive interurban became another paper folly. Yet it revealed that there were enthusiasts who "dared to plan," exploiting the perceived advantages of intercity traction.

The big interurban scheme that came the closest to becoming reality was the Chicago–New York Electric Air Line Railroad, commonly called the Air Line. As its name implied, this interurban would link America's two greatest cities, New York and Chicago, and in a direct "air-line" fashion. Unlike the case of the Minneapolis, Kansas City & Gulf, investors came forward, and the Air Line actually turned a wheel, although only in Indiana and only for a short distance.[83]

Why did the Air Line trigger widespread excitement? Although the plan was hardly that dissimilar from others – namely connecting two large, distant metropolises – it was well advertised, and its backers were unrelenting in their optimism and promotion for what they envisioned: a high-speed "people's" electric air line between the Windy City and Gotham. In the words of one excited official, "This is the dawn of a new era in the field of transportation."[84]

The idea for the Air Line originated in the fertile mind of Alexander C. Miller (1852–1918). When a teenager, this Ohio farm boy "went railroadin'," braking for the Lake Shore & Michigan Southern. Later he worked as a telegrapher, station agent, and dispatcher for the Chicago, Burlington & Quincy. In 1902 Miller resigned his chief dispatcher's job on the Burlington to organize the Aurora Trust and Savings Bank in his hometown of Aurora, Illinois, and served as its president. Before he left banking after four years, he became involved with the not-so-successful Miller Train Control Corporation, a firm that developed its own version of the electric block signal. A tall, "heavily built" man, Miller was "partial to Stetson hats and big black cigars, exuding quiet ability."[85]

Alexander Miller conceived the Air Line while conducting business for his signal company. He frequently traveled between Chicago and New York City and realized that the crack passenger trains of the New York Central (NYC) and the Pennsylvania (PRR) railroads took eighteen hours or longer to make the trip. With the NYC the first leg from New York City was *north* 150 miles to Albany before tracks turned *west*, and Chicago-bound passengers were further from their destination than when they started. Reasoned Miller, why not a *straight* path between the two terminals? "To a thinking man," wrote Miller, "a direct, high speed railroad, electric of course in the Twentieth Century, to connect the greatest commercial centers on the continent is absolutely inevitable."[86]

Miller was not about to let his idea die. He found supportive railroaders and businessmen in the Chicago area who agreed to assist him in building his dream interurban. Although the company was organized in October 1905 under the laws of Maine, it would not be until July 1906, which coincided with the height of the second rash of interurban construction, that the public learned about the grand plan.[87]

Advertisements in an assortment of daily newspapers, including a full-page splash in the July 8, 1906, issue of the *Chicago Sunday Tribune*, offered details. The bold-faced banner read: "Chicago to New York in 10 Hours – Fare $10. New Direct Line Electric Road Startles the Transportation World. Route 160 Miles Shorter Then the Shortest – Time 10 Hours Quicker Than the Quickest – Fare $10 Cheaper Than the Cheapest." The bluster continued. The Air Line would run 743 miles in mostly a straight line between terminals, cutting off 237 miles from the NYC and 168 miles from the PRR, and would take ten years to complete. The anticipated trip would consume about ten hours and would cost passengers $10 (what detractors mockingly called the "10 hour/10 dollar scheme" or the "Hot Air Line"). The interurban would have four parallel tracks (later reduced to two) placed on a 100-foot-wide right-of-way with third-rail power, and electric generating stations or substations positioned every 50 miles or so. Rather than single cars, a steeple-cab "Lectromotive" – a piece of rolling stock that was yet to be built – would pull trains "for high speed passenger, mail and express service." There would not be any highway or railroad crossings at grade, and gradients and curves west of the Allegheny Mountains would be minimal. The company would deal with the rugged terrain in the Pennsylvania region by having the line span valleys on high fills, cross streams on steel viaducts, and penetrate hills and mountains through deep cuts and tunnels. This would be no side-of-the-road interurban! The pricey construction strategy would pay dividends by substantially reducing operating costs, and income would be further enhanced by the millions of people who lived along the Air Line corridor, estimated at one-eighth of the country's population. To tap cities near the interurban, including Toledo, Cleveland, and Pittsburgh, management planned feeders served by shuttle trains, an approach that the Minneapolis, Kansas City & Gulf also proposed. Further resembling that paper road, the Air Line would be constructed in sections. The First Division, which would stretch 100 miles between Chicago and Goshen, Indiana, was expected to generate enough income to finance construction of subsequent divisions as the road marched eastward. Bonds would not be sold, but rather 20,000 shares of stock (later increased) priced each at $100 (later reduced to $25) would be issued,

Somewhat surprising is the style of the stock certificates issued by the Chicago–New York Electric Air Line Railroad. Unlike so many other interurbans–built or unbuilt–the certificate did not contain either a fancy logo or vignette. Yet this particular certificate reveals two important aspects about this monster interurban scheme: it is for only five shares–sales were aimed at small investors–and the certificate number, 12927, indicates that early on the "10-hour/$10" line attracted investor support.

Author's collection.

making the interurban a truly cooperative or people's undertaking. Interestingly, stockholders would receive preference in the hiring of company officials and employees.[88]

Miller and his associates relied on more than newspaper advertisements. The company produced eye-catching investment brochures and launched a slick monthly magazine, *Air Line News: Published in the Interests of the Chicago–New York Electric Air Line Railroad*. The inaugural issue appeared on October 1, 1906, and Charles Burton, a veteran journalist and former Illinois state printer, took on the editorship.[89]

The 10-hour/$10 interurban got off to an auspicious start. "The first day of September, 1906, was a historic day, because it witnessed the beginning of the construction work on the Chicago–New York Electric Air Line Railroad," beamed the *Air Line News*. "The first dirt was thrown about two and one-half miles south of Laporte [sic], Indiana, and in consequence Laporte [sic] is now known the country over. In honor of the event a great picnic was planned in a neighboring grove, to which Laporte [sic] citizens turned out en masse and many from neighboring towns and from Chicago. The orator of the day was Hon. George E. Clarke of South Bend, Indiana [a prominent attorney], whose eloquent address in full has been printed in pamphlet form."[90]

The fact that the Air Line actually began construction energized the project, even though management admitted that it had run surveys only as far as western Ohio. As the months passed, *Air Line News* reported in excruciating detail each step of the building process, and lavish photographs of the unmistakable progress adorned every issue.[91]

Since the Miller administration rejected debt, equity would finance the First Division. Investors, though, were not buying shares of the interurban itself, but rather they were acquiring a stake in its affiliated Co-Operative Construction Company, also incorporated in Maine. To comply with Indiana law, the Air Line organized its First Division as a separate entity, the Goshen, South Bend & Chicago Railway, and it would be built officially by the Co-Operative Construction Company.[92]

Why stocks and not bonds? After all, virtually every interurban used debt financing together with stock sales and stock trades for land and other considerations. Experienced (and conservative) investors often preferred the steady payments that bonds provided, not wanting to worry about the uncertainties of common stock prices and dividends. Air Line management, however, viewed bonds as potentially a millstone; fixed debts had to be serviced regardless of economic conditions. Miller and his associates also seemed suspicious of "big money," blasting "financial jugglery." A no-debt philosophy surely appealed to small, unsophisticated investors who were likely caught up in the anti–big business or antitrust sentiments of the Progressive Era or who simply wanted to cash in on the interurban craze. The company focused on these individuals. "The opportunity to become a part owner in this modern system of Electric railroads and to share in the profits of construction and operation is one that should have your most serious consideration, even though you have but a small sum to invest." The company went so far as to claim: "Success and Big Profits Are Assured. Profits almost beyond Calculation. Here Is Your Opportunity! The Chance of a Lifetime! The Nation's Need Is Your Opportunity."[93]

Just as the Miller group had hoped, its promotional efforts of "The Opportunity of a Century" attracted investors. Money poured into Air Line coffers. "The winter of 1906–'07 found the company with 15,000 get-rich-quick subscribers on the books and more than two millions of cold cash in a Chicago bank," recalled Blake Mapledoram, the company's chief engineer. "When the stock was offered to the public at $25 a share, a mob of buyers swarmed into the building [Chicago's Majestic Building on Monroe Street] to an extent that regular tenants could hardly get near their own offices."[94]

It would be the modest investor, independent of Wall Street "stock jobbers" and "monopolists," who made possible the start of construction and promised hope for completion. Proclaimed the Air Line prospectus: "This is an organization **OF THE PEOPLE, BY THE PEOPLE, FOR THE**

PEOPLE." Supporters of the larger interurban projects expected "capitalists" to provide much of the financing. Still there were traction firms, also with big ambitions, that courted persons with thin pocketbooks.[95]

The Minneapolis, St. Paul, Rochester & Dubuque Electric Traction Company illustrates a people's interurban. Rather than using its hard-to-remember corporate name, the project became known as the Dan Patch Electric Railroad or simply the Dan Patch Line, honoring Dan Patch, the famous harness race horse owned by the road's Minneapolis promoter Marion Willis (Will) Savage. In a letter to a potential investor from Lisbon, Ohio, Savage explained why his road was different. "The Dan Patch Electric Railroad is truly a People's Railroad, built by the people and for the people. It was conceived in an earnest desire to offer a better investment to the common people – the small investors – than had even been offered to them before." He continued: "It is being honestly constructed according to the most approved methods of modern Railroad construction. It will be efficiently managed in the interests of all the people who hold its stock. Its only purpose is to make money for the stockholders. The stockholders of this Company will receive the same returns on their capital as I will receive on mine. I guarantee that the interests of every stockholder, whether large or small, are equally protected with my own." Concluded Savage, "I have invested my money in the enterprise, obtaining my stock at the same price as the other stockholders. We insure equal rights to all, special privileges to none."[96]

The Dan Patch Line became more than a paper proposition. On July 4, 1910, the first train ran from 54th and Nicollet Streets in Minneapolis to Antler's Park on Lake Marion in Lakeville, Minnesota, and at the end of the following year the line reached Northfield, creating a 42-mile road. Some additional grading occurred before construction stopped. In the process Savage rejected electric traction, selecting cutting-edge internal combustion freight and passenger equipment. While this decision did not in itself prove disastrous, Savage's death and financial problems led to a reorganization in 1918, and ultimately the property, renamed the Minneapolis, Northfield & Southern Railway, developed into a thriving switching road.[97]

Just as Will Savage cultivated the small investor, the Air Line relied on grassroots support – the people – who at times became exuberant, even giddy, shareholders. In 1908 *Air Line News* reported the launching of the "Air Line Stockholders' Association of the World," an organization arguably unique among interurban projects. Activist stockholders in Kankakee, Illinois, decided to form an organization that would promote the Air Line. They claimed formation of "Camp No. 1" and made known their objectives:

FIRST: – Mutual benefit to all "Air Line" stockholders throughout the world.

SECOND: – to secure as many new stockholders for the Chicago–New York Electric Air Line as lies in our power.

THIRD: – to use our influence to prevent malicious and unfair criticism of the Chicago–New York Electric Air Line Railroad Company.

FOURTH: – to encourage and help the "Air Line" management in every honorable way to construct the road from Chicago to New York.[98]

But Camp No. 1 would not be the sole unit for a handful of Air Line stockholders. Other camps, perhaps as many as fifty, appeared, sprouting up elsewhere in Illinois and the Midwest and also in California, New York, and several other locations. "Not only has this action [Camp No. 1] resulted in a greatly increased volume of business from Kankakee and vicinity and has been a splendid tonic of encouragement to the management and to the stockholders generally," reported *Air Line News*, "but the example is being followed in other localities." Miller considered this enthusiasm "a most astonishing thing."[99]

These camps also served as support groups, reinforcing the feeling among investors that they had made wise financial decisions. In an age when fraternal organizations, well known for their social functions, reached their greatest popularity, these Air Line camps arranged outings to increase bonds of commitment, thereby strengthening a determination to see through the completion of this long-distance interurban. In July 1910 stockholders from a New York City camp paid fifty cents each to participate in a cruise on the Hudson River, and during their trip they surely discussed the Air Line. Even if a camp did not sponsor a special event, management encouraged camp representatives (and others, too) to visit construction sites as "their interurban" took shape.[100]

Whether coming from a camp member or not, the Miller organization encouraged comments (positive, of course) that would be printed in the *Air Line News*. This letter, published in the September 1909 issue, was representative: "When the 'Air Line' enterprise was first announced, it appealed to me instantly as one of two things; either it was an exceptionally great opportunity, or it was a colossal swindle. I made up my mind long ago which it was." The Niagara Falls, New York, resident saw the Air Line as the former. "This man," noted the *Air Line News*, "is one of the most enthusiastic stockholders who has been out to see the railroad."[101]

The initial thrust revealed a project that might be capable of realizing its ambitions. "By the fall of 1907 our equipment consisted of 60 mule teams purchased in St. Louis for $22,000, 42 wheelers, three locomotives with flatcars and self-dumping dirt cars, a Vulcan 2½-yard shovel, a steam grader, a warehouse with $10,000 worth of supplies, a powerhouse, a three-car barn complete, and two $11,000 electric passenger cars, built at Niles, Ohio, to carry stockholders over the line free," recalled chief engineer Mapledoram.[102]

While the Air Line seemingly had the resources to build the First Division, the construction process proceeded at a snail's pace, largely because of the extraordinarily high standards management demanded. After all, this interurban was to have that straight-as-an-arrow level main line and no public road or railroad crossings at grade.

The Air Line, nevertheless, exploited its limited operation. "The visiting prospective stockholders were greatly impressed," remembered Mapledoram. "After a breath-taking ride over the initial stretch of Air Line speedway, they were practically speechless and were ready to buy all the stock they could immediately afford and to subscribe for a few additional shares on the installment plan. Air Line prosperity was on the ascension." He further recalled, "One of the motormen, C. P. Lyon, fell heir to more than $1,000,000 from an English estate, invested some of it in Air Line stock, and stayed on the job, not wishing to give up the pleasure of running the fast cars."[103]

Enthusiasm from stockholders – who usually took only one or a few shares – failed to realize Miller's grandiose dream. The interurban, which ultimately appeared, resembled other struggling midwestern traction roads. Although the Panic of 1907 dampened stock sales and caused installment payments to be missed, the company, which lacked a bonded debt and had cash reserves, continued to build. The first portion had been the short feeder stem between La Porte and South LaPorte that opened in June 1907, and by early 1908 the designated main line stretched westward from South LaPorte to Westville. The electrified line inched along, and by early 1911 it reached Goodrum station, south of Chesterton, a place that honored a large Air Line stockholder. In completing this 25-mile core work gangs had placed steel bridges over the lines of the Monon and Pere Marquette railroads and a temporary wooden structure over the Wabash Railroad. They also had constructed a million-cubic-yard cut to fill the expansive valley or "bottom" carved out by Coffee Creek. Laborers then laid heavy steel rails (85 pounds to the yard) on durable white oak ties and installed the DC power supply. The company, however, selected orthodox overhead wires rather than a third rail, expecting later to use what was known as the Farnham Third Rail System. Critics considered the Air Line to be the "No-place to No-place Route," and for the main line that seemed an apt description.[104]

Yet Air Line management did its best to have an electric road that served more than scattered villagers and farmers. Management organized and promoted a separate company that slowly built a modest line from the county seat and college town of Valparaiso northward to a connection with the main line at Goodrum and then onward for the few miles to Chesterton. Unlike the Air Line corporation, this dozen-mile Valparaiso & Northern Railway sold bonds to finance construction and broke with the policy of straight and level feeders. This "cross line" officially opened on February 17, 1912.[105]

It would be from the northern part of the Valparaiso & Northern that the Miller "system" sought to exploit traffic generated by the "magic city" of Gary, located on the shores of Lake Michigan. In 1906 the United States Steel Corporation (USS) created Gary and nurtured its development. This heretofore largely empty expanse of sand dunes became the site of a complex of mills and finishing plants owned by Indiana Steel Company, a USS subsidiary, and where the Gary Land Company, another USS affiliate, oversaw this planned metropolis. By 1908 population surpassed 10,000, and two years later it reached 16,000. Prognosticators expected that more than a quarter million people would eventually call Gary their home.[106]

To serve this "City of the Century" and to gain access to Chicago, the Air Line organization replicated the structure, financing, and building concept it employed with the Valparaiso & Northern. It would be through affiliates Gary & Interurban Railway and Gary Connecting Railways that in January 1913 interurban cars linked the main stem from near Goodrum to Gary and beyond the short distance to Hammond, Indiana, and connections to the Windy City.[107]

Although the Miller organization had cobbled together an interurban network that served two cities – Gary and Hammond – other communities were much smaller. Construction costs had been exceedingly high, and the family of lines had racked up huge debts. Income was inadequate to sustain operations and made worse when the Gary mills experienced a steep downturn in the latter part of 1914. Their workforce plummeted from 14,000 to less than 5,000, and the city "was so hard hit by the business depression." Moreover, upstart automobile "jitneys" cut into fare-box revenues.[108]

In 1915 the Air Line combine, which in September 1914 stockholders had restructured as the Gary & Interurban Railway, entered bankruptcy. "[The Air Line] was utterly uneconomic," is the concise conclusion reached by George Hilton and John Due. Fortunately for patrons some trackage survived, being fused shortly into the more durable suburban lines of the Gary Street Railway. But those Air Line enthusiasts, who lost every penny they had optimistically invested, must have been shocked by the unfolding of events. Perhaps some shed a tear in 1917 when the core line between South LaPorte and Goodrum, with its tangent track, steel bridges, and colossal Coffee Creek fill, was abandoned. Yet the Valparaiso line, as part of Gary Street Railway, lasted until 1938. About the time of the Valparaiso closure, Blake Mapledoram, the former chief engineer, noted that "passing through La Porte, I dropped off a New York Central train and walked over the Air Line's former right-of-way. Nothing was visible except the million-yard cut and the embankments. Trees six or eight inches in diameter were growing where once had been a high-class roadbed."[109]

Some observers of "America's Greatest Railroad" considered this ill-fated venture to have been a swindle. Apparently, though, this attempt to construct a super interurban had not been a stock-selling scheme; it was a sincere but misguided effort to maximize the perceived advantages of intercity traction. In fact, there were only rare instances of outright fraud with interurban projects, markedly different from what happened with the promotion and construction of steam railroads. With interurbans it appears that limited business acumen rather than dishonesty came into play. An observer thought these words by Irish writer Oscar Wilde appropriate: "The value of an idea has nothing whatever to do with the sincerity of the man who expresses it."[110]

The ultimate outcome of the Chicago to New York project was hardly what backers had expected (or hoped). "The men who are building the 'Air Line' have a firm grasp on the greatest idea in the world," its advocates had argued, "and they are achieving marvels in the task of converting that idea into the greatest electric railroad in the world." Alas, this monster proposal of the Interurban Era, which attracted national attention and widespread investor enthusiasm, ended with a whimper and not with a bang.[111]

SUCCESSFUL SCHEMES

When an interurban began operations, financial backers and residents along the route expressed gratification and possibly relief. Opening day celebrations became commonplace, being a time of great joy in community after community. The arrival in October 1896 of electric cars of the Frederick & Middletown Railway to the transportation-starved community of Middletown, Maryland, prompted a resident to pen this joyful piece:

> At last! At Last! The dreams of years
> That racked our anxious brain
> Through night and day, through toil and rest,
> Has not been dreamed in vain.
> We stand in wonderment and awe,
> And gaze upon the sight;

> While in our hearts there rolls a wave
> Of rapturous delight.
> Long years we toiled with might and main
> While hope turned to despair
> To bring the "iron horse" across
> Our Valley dear and fair
> And while we labored on and on
> Our idol to obtain,
> Behold! There sweeps across the land
> The magic trolley train.
> The iron horse is soon forgot,
> And on the trolley comes;
> Then soon it rolls along OUR way,
> And to the Valley hums.
> It climbs Catoctin's lovely slope,
> Sweeps down our Valley side,
> And o'er the hills, and on to town
> The wonderous trolley glide.[112]

The number of these gala inaugural events cannot be accurately determined, but they tallied in the hundreds. There could even be more than one observance for an electric line. After all, "system building" occurred as the industry matured by the second decade of the twentieth century, paralleling what earlier had happened with numerous steam shortlines. A larger corporate structure might well absorb small electrics that may have opened during the first wave of building. The Detroit United Railway, which at its height operated more than 400 route miles, consisted of a dozen predecessor companies. The 617-mile Ohio Electric Railway, the largest interurban in Ohio, claimed a corporate genealogy of even more components. With the debut of an expanded or consolidated interurban, celebrations, including speeches and special runs, became the order of the day.[113]

Although the interurban industry began to fall apart by the time of World War I, a process that accelerated rapidly in the 1920s and early 1930s, there were longer lasting and undeniably "successful" companies. Such interurbans as the Samuel Insull family of electric properties in greater Chicago – Chicago, Aurora & Elgin; Chicago, North Shore & Milwaukee; and Chicago, South Shore & South Bend – and others, including the Illinois Terminal (previously Illinois Traction), Pacific Electric, and Piedmont & Northern, endured for decades either as freight and passenger carriers or as solely freight haulers. Portions of some lines remain active in the twenty-first century, with the South Shore line being America's last true interurban, trackage that retained both freight and passenger service.[114]

Yet "successful" is tricky to define, and these early casualties of auto and truck competition may well have been successful, perhaps not financially but with the people that they served. Consider the Columbus,

The recently formed Iowa Southern Utilities Company, previously Centerville, Albia & Southern Railway, issued a "system" map that it used on its stationery. The company is guilty of a degree of map fakery: it shows its two lines and those of principal connecting roads to be largely arrow straight.

Author's collection.

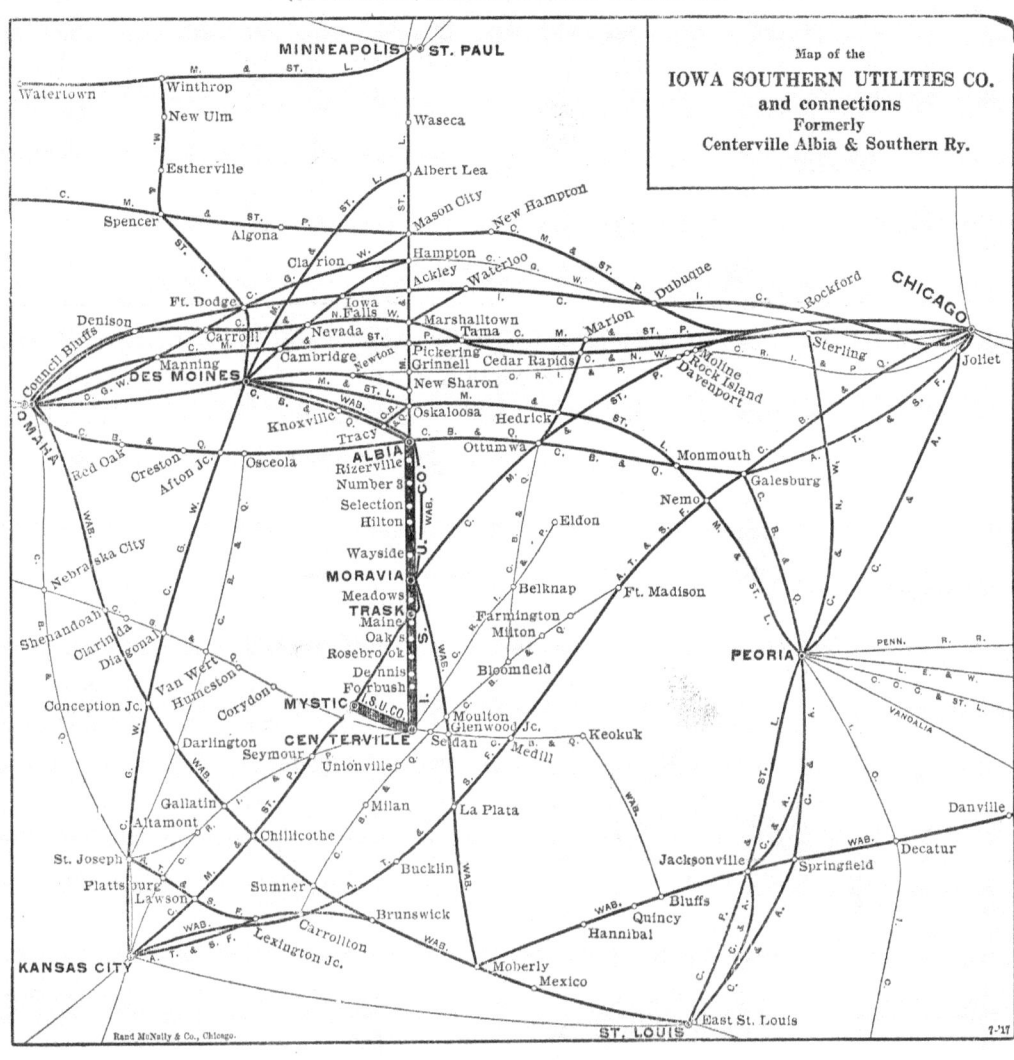

Magnetic Springs & Northern Railway, an 18-mile electric road that linked the central Ohio towns of Delaware and Richwood and reached the small resort community of Magnetic Springs, 11 miles west of Delaware. Although the "Magnetic Springs Route" had a short life – fifteen years – it provided residents and other users with good, reliable service

ENTHUSIASM 51

before the appearance of more dependable automobiles and better public roads, and it made easier "taking the waters" and enjoying other pleasures at "the Springs."[115]

An example of the long-lasting service provided by an interurban is the 30-mile Iowa Southern Utilities Railroad (ISU), née Centerville, Albia & Southern Railway (CA&S) and Centerville Light & Traction Company (CL&T). Unlike most electric roads, the ISU had a pre-electrified component. What became its longest line extended the 25 miles from Centerville, the Appanoose County capital, northward to Albia, seat of Monroe County. A steam shortline between these two towns, originally the Centerville, Moravia & Albia (CM&A) and then the Albia & Centerville (A&C), dated from the 1880s. At the close of that decade the CM&A was leased to the Iowa Central Railway, and in 1890 it was reorganized as the A&C. The Iowa Central continued to operate the railroad until 1910, when New York City and Centerville interests acquired ownership. These investors named their enterprise the Southern Iowa Traction Company (SIT), viewing the property as a future interurban. The line could conveniently link the Burlington and Rock Island passenger stations in Centerville with those of the Iowa Central, Wabash, and Burlington in Albia. The latter was made possible by running over the Albia Interurban Railway that connected Union Station (Iowa Central, Wabash, and the former Albia & Centerville) with the Burlington depot, about a mile away. The SIT would also serve Moravia, a thriving farming community about midway between the two terminals, where passengers could transfer to trains of the Wabash and the Milwaukee Road. The interurban, with its frequent service, would tap several coal camps, allowing miners and their families the convenience of shopping in Albia and Centerville and also Moravia. The saying went that "miners spend; farmers save" – a possibly true statement. The interurban would surely derive additional profits from LCL and carload freight; after all, the Albia & Centerville and lessee Iowa Central had been predominately freight haulers.[116]

Although the Southern Iowa Traction continued to be run by steam, a change soon came. In 1914 two Centerville men, banker D. C. Bradley and attorney Frank Payne, who were both involved with local street traction, took charge and christened the road the Albia, Centerville & Southern Railway. Bradley and Payne speedily directed conversion from steam to electricity, and by summer that transformation was complete. With the AC&S becoming a true interurban it was time to "celebrate in a big way." That September nearly one hundred Centerville residents, representing the professions and leading businesses, took the electric cars to Albia to "participate in the jubilee." They met their hosts at the Albia Commercial Club and then the two hundred or so attendees, accompanied by the municipal band, walked to the nearby Methodist Episcopal Church for an

The newly acquired car No. 26 of the Centerville, Albia & Southern Railway waits at the crossroads community of Hilton, Iowa, with its uniformed conductor, J. L. Johnson, standing near the center-entrance door. On August 18, 1915, an amateur photographer captured one of the two new Centerville, Albia & Southern cars at the Chicago, Burlington & Quincy Railroad depot in Albia. Baggage and express have just been unloaded, and the car is about to return to Centerville, via the trackage of Albia Interurban Railway, to the joint Minneapolis & St. Louis and Wabash "union" station about a mile distant. It will then proceed on its own private right-of-way.

Author's collection.

evening banquet "where numerous talks were made, appropriate for the occasion, interspersed with much music and other features."[117]

Five years before the Southern Iowa Traction electrification, the Centerville Light & Traction street railway decided to expand, having its eyes set on Mystic. This booming coal-mining community had a population of nearly 3,000 and was only 7 miles to the northwest of the Appanoose County capital, but it lacked a direct steam railroad connection. Centervillians liked the idea, and it did not take long before 165 "go-getters" in the area, spearheaded by "the Committee of 15," subscribed the $75,000 needed to defray construction costs. Work progressed rapidly. Then opening day for the interurban came on April 22, 1910, and cheer and optimism were in plentiful supply. "A new era opens for Centerville. The day of a new prosperity is at hand," editorialized the *Centerville Iowegian*. "With this new line proving a paying investment, as it is confidently predicted it will, other interurbans will fast follow." Continued the editor, "When President F. S. Payne identified himself with the Light & Traction interests here, it was because he saw a future. He saw Centerville as a babe that was to grow to the stature of the metropolis of southern Iowa, attracting trade from a large area. So the building of the road has done more than open up new commercial possibilities – it has helped Centerville find itself – helped it to measure its resources and find out it could do big things."[118]

A union between the two interurbans did not take long in coming. In 1916 the CL&T became the Iowa Southern Utilities Company (ISU), and later that year the CA&S entered the fold. The consolidated properties met local expectations. Seven round-trip passenger runs between Centerville and Albia and a few more on the Mystic line handled a healthy ridership. Freight service, provided by two box motors, was less frequent but adequate for the needs of the several on-line coal mines and other customers. Patrons praised the two center-entrance passenger cars acquired from the American Car Company of St. Louis for $7,000 each. This rolling stock featured spacious smoking and "ladies'" compartments. Miners, as expected, flocked to the electric road. Since some of these men were described as "unkempt" and even worse "coarse and rowdy," women and children might have concerns. But these separate passenger compartments "provided privacy for female passengers as the road hauled many miners who sometimes became quite boisterous, particularly on pay-days."[119]

Although the ISU earned greater revenues from its expanding electricity sales than from its rail operations, the latter did a good freight business, dominated by coal from local mines that fueled the power plant near downtown Centerville. And the Great Depression did not crush the interurban. As the industry faltered nationally, ISU remained active; a more powerful 50-ton Westinghouse-built steeple-cab locomotive regularly pulled strings of mostly coal hoppers. But reflecting larger trends, passenger operations became financially burdensome. In the post-World War I era "automobility" cast a shadow over interurban travel. By the late 1920s the number of round-trip runs between Centerville and Albia had dropped to three, and Mystic service likewise had been cut. Then as hard times deepened, the company won regulatory approval to exit the passenger business, and on July 1, 1933, the last cars rolled over the two lines.[120]

The electric road continued to experience change. Another corporate reorganization took place. Largely for legal and tax reasons, the

ISU electric road in 1941 became the Southern Iowa Railway (SIR), but it remained a freight hauler. Although the interurban abandoned part of its Mystic trackage in 1944 and all of the Moravia to Albia section four years later, it continued to haul coal to the generating facility and handled bricks, fertilizer, lumber and other traffic. In 1959 revenues increased when a Haydite aggregate plant, a unit of the Carter-Waters Company, opened on the stubbed Mystic line. While no money maker, the SIR also for nearly a decade, beginning in 1954, hosted "Electric Railway Excursions" in conjunction with the Iowa Chapter of the National Railway Historical Society, making the line a must destination for "juice" enthusiasts.[121]

The end came for the traction road in the mid-1960s. The utility sold what in reality had become a belt railway for Centerville to the Southern Iowa Industrial Railroad, an undercapitalized and mismanaged concern. This company operated not with electricity but with internal combustion, in this case with two diesel-powered ex-Burlington motor cars. This reflected a pattern that occurred when some former interurbans morphed into gasoline or diesel shortlines. By 1968, though, the little Iowa carrier had folded, and salvageable materials, including rail and overhead wire, had been removed and sold. Yet some pieces of rolling stock were saved, going to museums in the Midwest. This historic equipment became reminders of an interurban that served the public well and lasted far longer than most.[122]

INTERURBANS IN DAILY LIFE

2

FARMERS

It would be farmers who became avid supporters of interurbans. When lines were available, these people of the soil relied on this transport form until the maturing Automobile Age and "Good Roads" crusade pulled them away. Agrarians considered the interurban to be a practical way to enhance their incomes and quality of life, mitigating the drudgery and long hours of farm work and ending their rural "imprisonment." When it came to the passenger business, interurban companies depended heavily on two classes of riders: farmers, villagers, and their families riding to a town or city, and commercial travelers going from one city or town to another. Most traction roads also handled agricultural traffic. Farmers regularly used less-than-carload (LCL) services provided by conventional passenger equipment and box motors to market their dairy products, eggs, fruit, and truck produce and, at times, to ship carloads of livestock, grain, and other bulk commodities. And they relied on interurbans for delivery of a plethora of LCL shipments and, where possible, carload freight. Concluded a North Carolina State College sociologist, "In fact these [interurban] cars are used for practically every conceivable transportation function which rural communities need."[1]

As the Interurban Era evolved, America remained largely an agricultural nation. Although the superintendent of the census reported in 1893, based on data collected three years earlier, that the "frontier" had closed, frontier-like conditions remained in scattered areas, including the Great Plains, intermountain West, and Florida. The urban population did not eclipse the rural population until after World War I. Moreover, the farming sector began to thrive following the drought and depression of the late nineteenth century. While farm incomes fluctuated before the agricultural recession of the 1920s, the period from 1909 to 1914 became the benchmark "parity years" when farmers enjoyed real prosperity. Good prices for wheat, cattle, hogs, dairy, and other products made this happen.

The value of farm lands and structures reflected these halcyon days, rising from $16.6 billion in 1900 to nearly $40 billion in 1910, and this upward trend continued through World War I. Farmers, especially those who resided in the Corn Belt and close to metropolitan centers, commonly lived in comfortable homes near established communities with churches, schools, stores, and other facilities. "There has never been a time when the American farmer was as well off as he is today," declared President Theodore Roosevelt's Country Life Commission in 1909, "when we consider not only his earning power, but the comforts and advantages he may secure."[2]

It did not take long before farmers grasped the potential of the interurban. Progressive agrarians realized that "poor country roads meant poor country schools, poor churches, poor community relationships, as well as financial losses." The trip by cart, wagon, or buggy over roads made impassable by mires of mud or blocked by snow might have been a long safari, but electric cars made it at most a day's journey, and that previous day journey became a jaunt of several hours or less. During the rise of interurbans in Midwest the *Cincinnati Post* observed, "In the old days you could find hundreds of country dwellers who never left the confines of their home township from January to December." A writer for *New England Magazine* agreed, commenting, "A family in 1895 saw town so infrequently that their visit was always more or less of an occasion, involving a long drive or an expensive ride by train. Urban entertainments and other attractions, except for the circus, were very much out of their lives." And in the case of one Iowa farm family, they went to church in a neighboring village only occasionally because the task of pulling a wagon on bad roads was too much for their horses, who needed to be rested on Sundays. "It was five miles from us, and five miles in days of bad roads was a real barrier." Intercity traction changed everything. "To-day, on account of the trolley connection, the members of the country family are not more remote as regards time, and not much worse off in the item of expense of travelling to and from the theatre, or concert or religious meeting in the city, than are the suburbanites of towns within the metropolitan district of Boston." Somewhat earlier an Anderson, Indiana, resident had witnessed the impact an interurban had on rural life. He told a friend who planned to build an electric road between Newcastle and Knightstown: "Nearly all the farmers in this County that live near the electric line do all their traveling on the electric line; you do not see the number of teams and horses in Anderson now that we did before this line was completed." For those farm families who lacked access to an interurban, life remained largely self-contained on their home place and in their immediate neighborhood, even into the era of World War I. "The automobile had not yet extended the radius of the farmer's life from four or five miles to forty or fifty," recalled Carl Van Doren about rural Hope, Illinois, during the early twentieth century. "Except to go to school or church and to visit a few relatives, my brothers and I left the farm hardly a dozen times a year."[3]

Farmers commonly backed interurban projects in several ways. Promoters, whether they were local individuals or representatives of traction "syndicates," knocked on farmhouse doors to sell their securities, and they were usually not disappointed. If the preferred route came through property owned by the agrarian, they likely showed their survey maps and suggested (even requested) a donation of a right-of-way strip. Their efforts were frequently rewarded. "Farmers were so anxious to be on the line of an electric railway that they gladly donated land for the right of way," wrote a contemporary. At times the farmer might receive stock, an annual pass, or some other consideration in exchange for the land deed or an easement agreement.[4]

Some farmers became so excited about having an interurban in their neighborhood that confidence men found them easy prey. In one case a Warren County, Ohio, agrarian in 1903 purchased $2,000 of stock in a mythical electric road, thinking that it was the Rapid Railway, a Cincinnati-based traction company that was then constructing a 33-mile line between the Queen City and Lebanon. When the swindled man talked with the Rapid Railway president, he learned that his certificates were bogus. "The farmer refused to give his name and could give no description of the man who had sold him the worthless paper, but vouchsafed the information that he was not the only one who had been duped out of his money." In another instance, some Nebraska farmers who individually had purchased as much as $3,000 worth of stock in what was apparently the fraudulent Omaha & Nebraska Central Railway (O&NC), took action in 1909 against the company. In their suit they charged that salesmen misrepresented the proposed interurban when they claimed that a new railroad grade near South Omaha was that of the gestating O&NC.[5]

Some farmers, though, did not want an interurban line to slice through their fields or pastures, being "in earnest opposition to interurban development." In April 1896, not long after the first intercity electric road made its debut in the Midwest, a Michigan farmer, Henry Lippincott, who knew little about intercity traction but was certain that he did not like it, made clear his feelings in this thought-to-be amusing poem that appeared in the *Coopersville [Michigan] Observer*:

> They tell me thet they're going ter run a sort o' 'lectric train
> From Grand Rapids to Grand Haven, and oll cut across my lane.
> I want yer all to hear me now, and harken t'all I say;
> Fer if they try ter run that hi-fa-lu-tin thing my way,
> I'll dynamite 'em certain, or in somehow do 'em harm,
> I won't have that 'ere lightnin' flashin' on my old chicken farm.

> Yer know that feller Dawkins that is farming by the mill?
> Jist ask him 'bout the lightnin', fer it struck his brother Bill,
> And knocked the life right out o' him – laid him deader than a nail,
> And then they think o' buyin it fer running on a rail.
> I kant see what's got in em, cause fer me ther ain't no charm,
> I won't have that ere lightnin' flashin' on my old chicken farm.
> I know it's scientific, an' some people think it smart
> Ter have the thing ter pull 'em, stead o' riden on a cart.
> They say "we mus' be stirrin," – an – "the scheme oll make a hit."
> "We farmers is too old" – an – "the young mus' manage it."
> I'm waitin' fer the'r hittin', and I'll raise a big alarm
> Ef enny of em try ter run across my chicken farm.
> Why, the people oll be stricken, all the hosses run away,
> The milk all gittin' sour, lightnin' makes it spile that way.
> The hands instead o' plowing, oll be ridin' on the thing,
> An' any amount o' trouble yer the pesky thin oll bring.
> I tell you what, I'm kickin', and oll raise my mighty arm,
> If any of em try ter run acrost my chicken farm.[6]

But once farmers recognized the advantages of intercity traction, they nearly always altered their tune. "Five years have sufficed to change entirely the sentiment of farmers," proclaimed the *Columbus* [Ohio] *Dispatch* in 1906, "and now many who were successful in forcing interurban roads to take routes that left their land at a distance regret their action." A Columbus-based interurban, the Columbus, Delaware & Marion Electric Railroad, stated bluntly: "The novelty and luxury of riding on the traction cars has now become a necessity with rural populations." This enthusiasm replicated agrarians' excitement about the coming of the iron horse. Said the *American Railroad Journal* in 1850, "In the West, the feeling in their [railroads'] favor amounts almost to mania, and every farmer there is contriving how he shall secure one within convenient distance."[7]

During the interurban building process, agrarians could reap financial rewards. They might receive cash payments or company stock for their labor, teams, and equipment, or they provided provisions for the work gangs. When the Puget Sound Electric Railway was being built in 1902, the son of a farmer recalled, "During the construction days on the line, my father sold milk to the crews when they worked on the portion of the line nearby." Enterprising agrarians perhaps sold other "liquids" as well.[8]

It became widely understood that easy access to a functioning "juice" line gave the farmers and their families ample opportunities to enhance their quality of life. Most apparent was the farmer's ability to get perishable products quickly to urban customers, be it milk, cream, butter, eggs, fruit, or produce. In some markets milk sales proved to be highly lucrative, almost depression-proof. It became commonplace to see rows of raw milk in their uninsulated, unrefrigerated 10-gallon metal cans (sometimes covered with wet blankets to retard heat) resting on a wooden freight

It is evident from this ca. 1920 photograph of car No. 78 of the Fort Dodge Line that milk is part of the daily business that these crew members handled.

Byron Olsen collection.

platform. The pickup might occur almost literally at the farmer's property. This ability to exploit a profitable commercial marketplace became "a most indispensable convenience." Some interurbans concentrated on daily milk shipments; Michigan United Railway was one such road, being nicknamed the "Milk Can Route." And interurbans considered other needs. The Los Angeles Pacific Railroad, a future component of Pacific Electric, had no difficulty winning away from local teamsters the shipping business of lemon growers along its Hollywood, Redondo, Santa Monica, and Venice lines. Previously the fruit suffered from the roughness of the trip, but the interurban solved that problem. "[The farmers] stated their grievance, and the result is the 'Lemon Growers' Express,' which carries the delicate spheroids to market as gently as in a baby's cradle." A Princeton University professor offered these thoughts: "The ease and promptness of this [interurban freight] service have called into being a great deal of business which was not previously carried on at all."[9]

Then the farmer might be able to ship carload lots of grain, livestock, and the like and to receive fertilizer, lumber, machinery, or some other bulky order at a siding located at a nearby station or siding. Farmers who lived along the lines of the Illinois Traction System, for example, took advantage of attractively priced coal. "The McKinley Lines [Illinois Traction] loads coal at the [on-line] mines and dumps it anywhere along the right-of-way, the farmers combining to buy their fuel in carload lots." The accessibility to an interurban for LCL or carload shipments allowed the farmer to take advantage of upticks in the market. Some lines, particularly those that served Indianapolis and Louisville, made it possible for livestock producers to transport cattle and hogs to buyers much faster than by steam roads. "Stock cars are always ready to catch a sudden turn in the market," and that meant more income.[10]

For the farmer an interurban provided a host of additional attractions, some major, some less so, but collectively explaining his exuberance for intercity traction. The agrarian relished the possibility of bringing electricity to his farming operations. "Cheap and convenient power" had real appeal. "The time will come," prophesied an interurban executive in 1907, "when on farms near electric railroads, fields will be plowed and harvested, machinery operated, even cows milked by the same power which takes the farmer's family to town and his products to market." Although field work became the bailiwick of gasoline tractors and other pieces of internal-combustion machinery, electricity lighted farmsteads, operated milking machines, and provided power for other chores. Said a traction advocate in 1908, "The farmers may have an economical and very satisfactory electric light service in their houses and barns thus reducing work of care for lamps as well as danger from fire or explosions from lanterns and lamps in barns, sheds, etc." Yet at the height of the Interurban Era, most farms lacked access to commercial power. Electricity for much of agricultural America did not come until the late 1930s and 1940s, facilitated by the New Deal–created Rural Electrification Administration.[11]

Interurban service increased farming efficiencies. One involved labor. Intercity traction created a more mobile labor force, whether that of the surplus farmhand during the "dull season" finding work in town or that of the "city-dweller who is brought to the farm when he is most needed, and when wages are the highest." Then there was the more efficient use of a farmer's time. "The savings in time to farmers who now are compelled to give from one-half to a whole day in making trips or in the carrying of stock and grain to the nearest station will be something remarkable." If a machine part required replacement, a telephone call to the implement or hardware dealer meant that the needed item would arrive in less than a day – perhaps in a few hours – by passenger car or express motor, and not a day or longer as if sent by a conventional train. Or the farmer could take the interurban and fetch the part himself. Such a trip became a simple and routine matter. If another chore necessitated a trip to town or city, there was this advantage: "Farmers lacking interurban access are now compelled to take their teams off important work in order to send some members of the family or helpers to town."[12]

A farmer, however, still might need a horse to reach an interurban stop, even though he might be able to walk or "borrow a ride." But traction executives thought of a way to make connecting horse travel more attractive. About 1910 the Iowa & Illinois Railway, which linked the Hawkeye State cities of Clinton and Davenport, offered a version of the later "park and ride" and "park and fly" automobile lots. At stations and major road crossings the company erected wooden sheds where rural patrons could tie up their horses without charge before boarding a car. However, there was this caveat: "Bring your padlocks to protect against horse thieves."[13]

Even during the high-flying parity years farmers were often frugal, knowing that an agricultural depression might be lurking down the road. An interurban offered this savings: "Farmers now required to keep teams for use of helpers need no longer do so as the frequent service [of the interurban] will enable farm hands and servants to go to and from evening entertainments and other occasions without requiring the use of the team." Maintaining work animals was labor intensive and expensive, demanding large quantities of oats and hay. Electric cars conceivably allowed farmers to reduce their numbers and hence the acreage needed for their feed. Corn, wheat, or some other cash crop could replace oats plantings.[14]

There were additional benefits for the farmer gaining access to an interurban line. There were matters of business to transact in town or city – perhaps with a banker, lawyer, or grain dealer. There were also social and educational activities. They might include a meeting of a fraternal lodge like the Knights of Pythias, the Masons, or the Modern Woodmen of the World, the Patrons of Husbandry (Grange), or a political organization. It might also be an agricultural demonstration or "institute" hosted by a land-grant college or county extension agent. In fact, interurbans were considered an important factor in arranging for these farmer meetings. In 1913 Michigan Agricultural College selected four cities with good interurban service – Grand Rapids, Kalamazoo, Pontiac, and Saginaw – as sites for its annual Round-Up Institutes. "In this way nearly every farmer in the southern half of the state could attend an institute by going not to exceed thirty miles from home. With interurban connections it was possible for them to attend the sessions and return home each night." There were other functions that might be kept quiet. "One elderly farmer from northern Scott County [Iowa] relied on the CD&M [Clinton, Davenport & Muscatine] in a special way. A regular weekend tippler at Davenport nightspots, he sometimes drank too much and needed to be dutifully assisted off that last evening run by accommodating CD&M motormen."[15]

The farm wife likewise grasped the advantages of an interurban. She may have been the one who managed the farm accounts, realizing that electric traction reduced operating costs and bolstered income. Since so many farm women relied on eggs for their "pin money," the transportation of these perishables (including dressed poultry) made these sales practical and profitable. In addition to "cash money," farm wives commonly traded their produce, especially butter, for essential items from the grocer or other merchants. If the house became electrified, the farm wife would not need to maintain the kerosene lamps, and she might acquire an

It is understandable that the Toledo & Chicago Interurban Railway selected a photograph of a rural shelter for the cover of its January 21, 1912, public timetable.

Author's collection.

About 1925 a woman, presumably a farm wife, waits at Norman's flag stop in Virginia for an interurban car of the Washington & Old Dominion Railway.

W&OD files, Herbert H. Harwood collection.

assortment of electric appliances, ranging from an iron to a hotplate. Like her husband, she could receive goods quickly from favored merchants, whether dry goods or a parlor chair. As the medical comforter, the farm wife could conveniently take a sick child to the town or city physician or specialist and need not rely wholly on the beloved country doctor.[16]

It was easy to show graphically this positive change in farm life. An essay in a 1904 issue of the *Yale Review* described a recently published four-part drawing. "Nos. 1 and 2 revealed the old and familiar style of marketing. In No. 1 is represented the farmer and his wife in the early morning hours before daybreak, harnessing the horses by lantern light, and putting butter, vegetables, potatoes, and eggs in the wagon preparatory to the journey into the city. In No. 2 we see the pair returning at sunset, tired and dusty, their wagon now laden with sugar, flour, clothing, etc." The other two panels depicted the impact of intercity traction. "Nos. 3 and 4 represented the new and improved style of marketing. The farm produce is seen, in No. 3, standing on a platform in the yard by the side of the track of the electric line. The farmer is at the telephone giving his order to the city merchant. No. 4 showed the return of the electric car. The goods required from the city were being unloaded." What was the past exceptional trip had become the ordinary.[17]

INTERURBANS IN DAILY LIFE

Then there were the social and cultural advantages. If so inclined, the woman of the farm could easily pay social visits to family and friends in town or city, participate in a sewing or quilting circle, or attend club and church functions. While the family might continue to worship in its country or village church, a new denomination in an urban center might make for a more satisfying spiritual life, whether it be Christian Science or a Pentecostal faith. In an era of popular women's organizations, ranging from the Women's Christian Temperance Union and the Daughters of the American Revolution to the International Order of King's Daughters and the P.E.O. Sisterhood, access to their meetings and "doings" became practical by taking the cars. A farm wife might encourage (even dragoon) her husband and children to attend a concert, play, or related event. The Cleveland & Eastern Traction Company was one interurban that tapped this desire. The road, untouched by direct steam railroad competition, regularly operated theater car specials on Saturday evenings to the Public Square area of Cleveland. "It was a great thrill for the farm folk of far out Garrettsville and Fullterton and Webster Crossing to reach the big city and its glare of electric lights." A garden, library, or museum might be the personal or family destination for these agricultural residents. It could also be a meal in a downtown restaurant; these establishments, with the advent of an interurban, noticed new patronage from farm families. Such an experience surely pleased the wife, relieving her of preparing dinner over that hot kitchen stove. With cars running frequently and into the nighttime hours, taking advantage of such diversions was equally doable. A government report put it this way: "The contact with town and city life which is thus made possible contributes greatly to the breadth of view, culture, and happiness of the farm family."[18]

Mental health benefits conceivably came with interurbans. "It is fair to presume that the loneliness of the farmer's wife is at an end," speculated the *Chicago Tribune* in 1907, "and if that be so the unfortunate percentage of suicides in the agricultural districts will surely decrease when a farmer can take his wife and children and in a few minutes be dropped at the nearest cross roads, or even at the village, [for the city] which was visited only once in a season when the roads were good, and when the general farm team was not otherwise occupied." In the 1890s a magazine writer observed that monotony and loneliness on a farmstead for women could be devastating and asked, "Why do the insane asylums hold such an enormous proportion of farmers' wives?" Isolation was the contributing factor. "Every day of her life she goes through the dreary, monotonous round of work."[19]

Interurban travel affected farm children. Boys and girls could attend school in a town or city and not have to trudge a mile or more to that little red schoolhouse with its lone teacher who managed grades one through eight. And they did not need to stay in town in order to attend an academy or high school. Commuting daily became practical and not that expensive. Just as the quality of everyday life improved for the child's father and mother, the same held true for these children of agriculture. Examples abound. "A boy can remain at home, do his work on the farm during the day, and yet take his girl to the theater, or to a lecture, or a dance that night, and get home in time to do the chores in the morning at least," observed a journalist. "The farmers are coming oftener to the city. They find they can get city types of clothes as cheaply as they formerly could the antiquated garments which once distinguished the agriculturalist. The gawky country boy and girl is disappearing so rapidly that there will soon be little material in that line left for the comic weeklies, because the type is being wiped out by the interurban railroad." Offspring who had completed their education might take jobs in the town or city but still be attached to the farm or village. "Often a son or daughter who has obtained employment in a store or factory and who would formerly have been obliged to board in the city, visiting the home folks once or twice a month over Sunday, is now able to live at home under its wholesome restraints." In 1914 the president of the Bangor Railway & Electric Company concluded that "social conditions on the farm have been greatly improved as a result of the electric railway" since the advantages of the city were easily available. This Maine interurban executive believed that the problem of keeping the younger generation on the land had been solved – less flight to the bright lights of a "wicked" city.[20]

Just as agriculturists by the turn of the twentieth century welcomed the telephone and rural free delivery of U.S. mail, electric intercity railways also had a profound impact on rural America. "There is no public utility that helps the farmer as much as the interurban railways," opined one writer. "The interurban has been found to completely transform and change the habits of the resident rural community." That dependable farm-to-urban conduit with its frequent, inexpensive, and dependable service was commonly viewed by agrarians as the *chief* function of this transportation form. A contemporary observer went so far as to say in a hyperbolic way: "[An interurban] helps to break down any distinction between city and country life. Most important of all, an antagonism is disappearing that is almost as old as human society – the opposition between urban and rustic." Another said, "It knits city and country." Still, Liberty Hyde Bailey, who chaired the Country Life Commission, believed that "the fundamental weakness in our civilization is the fact that the city and the country represent antagonistic forces." This may or may not have been true. Economists George Hilton and John Due explained the likely impact of the interurban on rural America. They toned down that assessment of eroding urban-farm tensions by contending that the interurban's "principal influence was, clearly, in conditioning the rural population to a greatly increased mobility that was fully realized only with the general acceptance of the automobile." Automobile and "Good Roads" advocates generally agreed, seeing the "Age of Gasoline" has having this impact on the farmer: "Less danger; greater comfort and pleasure in travel; better attendance at church and school; better education; better market; better prices; more sociability." The opinion of some farmers that the motor car was a "devil wagon" had long since past.[21]

VILLAGERS

As the Interurban Age evolved, thousands of villages dotted the American landscape, ones that the contemporary humorist George Ade said "prop two cornfields apart." Many of these settlements claimed only several hundred or fewer residents. Likely the village scene featured a general store (with post office), blacksmith shop, mill, and perhaps several other businesses. Then there was usually a school and a church or two, a score or so of houses, and maybe a depot, although some villages lacked a railroad. In larger communities there was usually a hotel, boarding house, saloon (depending on prohibition laws), pool hall, livery stable, mercantile houses, barber and butcher shops, newspaper office, professional offices, bank, drugstore, fraternal lodges, grain elevator, lumber and coal yards, and mill. And in the Southlands a village probably had a gin, compress, and cotton warehouse, or maybe a textile factory. Additional residential structures and churches could be found in these more populous places.[22]

Villagers, however, expressed more misgivings about interurbans than did neighboring farmers. The major concerns came from retail business owners. Would not electric cars draw away customers to larger towns and cities? Would not their livelihood be damaged or ruined?

Some villagers became so alarmed at the possibility of an interurban wreaking havoc that they took action. The small college town of Oberlin, Ohio, was one such place. Local merchants were content to rely upon the modest service provided by Lake Shore & Michigan Southern Railway, the only line through Oberlin, and they did not fancy an interurban to Cleveland. "RUIN!" proclaimed a handbill that they distributed in 1897. "Follows in the Wake of the Electric Railroad! *Elyria* has Three Steam Railways and Two Electric Roads. Result, Six Big Business Failures recently and Five of them within Three Days. *Oberlin* has one Steam Railway and No Electric Railroad. Result, One Small Failure in Twenty-five years."[23]

Oberlin storekeepers were not alone in their thinking. By polling a range of merchants in communities with populations of less than 5,000 early in the century, the U.S. Department of Commerce and Labor sought an answer to whether an interurban caused economic hardship. In the process it received these negative comments: "Trade about 6 per cent less in 1903 than in 1902." "Bleeding us and feeding cities." "Better class of trade goes exclusively to large town." "Reduced fare to city injurious."[24]

There was the real possibility that village merchants might feel the sting of wandering customers. Yes, there was the convenience of the general store and the likely friendliness of its proprietor, who customarily extended credit. But urban centers had businesses that provided strong financial incentives to take the electric cars. It was not unusual for a city merchant to refund all or part of an interurban fare if the customer spent a specified amount, perhaps $10 or more. (For some time this had been a customary practice for patrons who traveled by conventional steam trains.) These aggressive sellers might advertise in newspapers (efficiently distributed by interurbans) and occasionally regional guides and timetables to lure potential village and small-town shoppers to their stores.[25]

One creative twist to entice villagers for shopping excursions appeared in Lima, Ohio. Known as the "Lima Trading Ticket," it was the brainchild of the Lima Merchants' Trading Association and designed for those rural, village, and small-town residents who lived along the Western Ohio Railway, a 115-mile interurban that served greater Lima. The ticket worked this way:

> Individuals wishing to go there to shop purchase these tickets from the Western Ohio station agent for the same price as the regular ticket. When such person makes a purchase in any of the Lima stores whose names appear on the ticket, the clerk of that store, upon request, stamps the amount of the purchase on the ticket, and, if, the purchases at all the stores amount to from five to twenty dollars (depending on the distance from Lima), upon presentation of this ticket to the station agent of the Western Ohio, the full amount of the fare paid for the ticket is refunded.[26]

Interurbans themselves might offer travel incentives to lure outlying residents into town or city for their buying needs. One road that did this was the Grand River Valley Railroad (previously Grand Junction & Grand River Valley Railway), better known as the "Fruit Belt Route." When merchants in Grand Junction, Colorado, a regional trade center, ran newspaper specials for groceries, mercantile items, and the like, the traction road sold $6.00 coupon books for $5.00 and sometimes for $4.50. When shoppers took advantage of these reduced fares, businesses in the village of Fruita suffered.[27]

There might be a combination of merchants and interurbans promoting these shopping outings. The Southern New York Railway is one such company. This interurban (formerly Oneonta, Cooperstown & Richfield Springs Railway), which operated between Oneonta, Cooperstown, Mohawk, and Herkimer, commonly dispatched "Trade Day Specials," designed to bring villagers and others to Oneonta stores. The local chamber of commerce might pay the transportation charges, or the company might offer reduced excursion rates.[28]

Even if villagers failed to receive a financial incentive to travel to a town or city on a buying trip, they might be recipients of special considerations from merchants. It was not uncommon to read advertisements in newspapers and elsewhere that stores welcomed shoppers to make their place of business the center for their buying activities. In the advertising space sold by the Fox & Illinois Union Railroad for its January 1, 1915, public timetable, Campbell and Phelan, the "Clothes Shop" in Morris, Illinois, told those who came to town from farm or village: "Check Your Parcels at Our Store." Perhaps Campbell and Phelan and other merchants offered toilet facilities and other amenities.[29]

There were commentators who thought that interurbans allowed villagers to travel too often. Surely this was the result of being bombarded by "big city specials." Said one, "The electric roads have seemed to the shopper to constitute a bargain in transportation, so that people traveled frequently and perhaps needlessly, through a feeling that they were saving money." The villager seemed drawn to urban shopping emporiums as the moth to the lamp.[30]

Interurbans also facilitated the use of mail-order houses, a retail industry dominated by two post–Civil War corporate giants, Montgomery Ward and Sears, Roebuck. These mercantile houses, which bypassed the middlemen, selected goods with rural and village customers in mind. Through volume buying they could sell at attractive prices. Their popular illustrated catalogs – "wish books" – permitted potential customers to examine at leisure their buying choices. An interurban, which frequently handled "pouched" mail and occasionally had a Railway Post Office compartment in its cars, allowed for the convenience with which goods could be ordered and then delivered by express or mail. Even if an interurban lacked a U.S. mail contract, nearly every major traction road established a relationship with a privately owned express company, whether Adams, American, National, United States, or Wells Fargo. Not until after 1913 did the U.S. Post Office handle parcel post shipments.[31]

Villagers might also use the mail – postal card or letter – to buy items directly from an area store. In November 1908 the Auburn, New York, firm of Foster, Ross and Company, "Auburn's Greatest Department Store," which carried a line of "dry goods, upholstery, rugs, crockery, house furnishing, etc., etc.," advertised in the regional *Trolley Talk* timetable: "When you are in the city come and see what we can do for you. If you cannot come to town, write. Our Mail Order Department will shop for you." There was this incentive: "We prepay transportation on all Cash orders amounting to $5.00 and over." Any purchase would then be shipped

In a classic village interurban scene, express shipments, including a crated bicycle for a young girl, are being unloaded in Bluemont, Virginia, from a car of the Washington & Old Dominion Railway.

E. Everett Edwards photograph, Herbert H. Harwood collection.

over the Auburn & Syracuse Electric Railroad. A postal communique or telephone call to a business might involve what so many Americans considered a necessity of life, especially during the summer months – block ice. "The interurban trolley seems to furnish a solution of the problem of how to furnish ice for country towns and farmhouses."[32]

Just as the Department of Commerce and Labor received negative responses to its merchant questionnaire, it learned that some village and small-town businessmen considered the interurban a good thing. "Sales have increased over 50 per cent in five years." "Can get goods more promptly." "Sales rapidly increasing; country prospering; aid in getting of goods." "Easier to get goods; carry less stock." These retailers could partake of what later would be called "just in time" deliveries, materially speeding the flow of goods through distribution channels. This better way of receiving inventory is seen with this example: "The rapid service of the traction 'express' allowed the [merchant] to sell chairs with the same certainty of delivery as though he had them in his own stock room." There was this observation: "With the arrival of interurban electric cars and rural free-deliveries and telephones and many other improvements in rural districts, a pace of progression has set in, even in the most out-of-the-way village, that is rapidly changing the ideas and methods of the country merchant." Another writer said much the same. "The village merchant at

Car No. 78 of the Indiana Railroad, previously Union Traction Company of Indiana, stops in the commercial center of the somnolent village of Chesterfield, Indiana, located 14 miles southwest of Muncie. Although this photograph dates from June 25, 1940, it could have been taken decades earlier.

J. F. Cook photograph, Krambles-Peterson Archive.

first was startled at the possible competition of the great city stores. Then he found he could solve the problem by the use of the means of transportation which has brought the city competition to him. All he had to do was to increase his stock, add to its variety, discard unsalable types, and study modern styles. Dealing in goods by wholesale, the freight charges alone would insure him a good profit, which the individual customer would go to the city only so long as the city furnished better styles or smaller prices."[33]

The coming of an interurban might produce this positive effect: population growth. The village could attract permanent residents from outlying farmsteads, "who, because of the improved methods of transportation, can reach their farm easily." A retired farm couple might take advantage of the amenities of the larger towns and cities while remaining in their familiar neighborhood and no longer needing to maintain a horse and buggy. Retail trade and local economic interests would surely benefit from this growth. It would be the automobile, better roads, and changes in commercial agriculture that by midcentury made so many villages and small towns "broken" communities.[34]

The debate between village opponents and proponents of interurbans continued, although it largely subsided by the end of the initial wave of construction. The electric intercity railways had become a reality. Those villagers who benefited from this convenient and reasonably priced way to shop applauded its presence and felt that they enjoyed a better lifestyle. Interurban companies were quick to emphasize their positive impact on smaller communities. When the Columbus, Delaware & Marion Electric Railroad described Green Camp, Ohio, located southwest of Marion, it stated: "Green Camp opens up another rural district, giving it an outlet for

farm and dairy products and allowing a population of 500 people to enjoy the pleasures and benefits of Interurban Communication."[35]

It is easy to understand why commercial travelers took advantage of interurban lines. A car could take them directly into the commercial heart of a town or city. On October 9, 1938, car No. 32 of the Clinton, Davenport & Muscatine Railway is turning from Third Street onto Perry Street in downtown Davenport, Iowa.

John H. Humiston photograph, author's collection.

COMMERCIAL TRAVELERS

Men who traveled from place to place selling their wares or services have long been part of the nation's commercial scene. During the colonial era and early national period itinerant peddlers walked, pushed a cart, rode horseback, or used an animal conveyance to offer a variety of oddments. Then with the developing Railway Age these men of commerce – "drummers," "commercial travelers," or "knights of the grip" – began to patronize steam cars "to make their towns." They customarily worked for wholesale houses and manufacturers and paid periodic calls on active and potential clients. The commercial man might represent a whiskey distiller, a woman's garment house, or a maker of hand tools. By the post–Civil War era the growing number of these peripatetic individuals covered hundreds of miles each month, frequently over the rapidly expanding web of iron and steel rails.[36]

Even with development of the sprawling railroad network, steam-car travel could make for long, arduous trips, especially if commercial travelers needed to take a route that offered minimal passenger service.

INTERURBANS IN DAILY LIFE 73

The Lake Shore Electric Railway brought commercial travelers into the heart of Huron, Ohio. A car has just arrived, and a "knight of the grip" is presumably walking to his local destination.

Author's collection.

Gilman City, Missouri, is an example. Early in the twentieth century this northwest Missouri community, with a population of about 600, had only a single passenger train that operated each way over the Quincy, Omaha & Kansas City Railroad. The eastbound train arrived about noon, and if salesmen wished to travel later toward Kirksville, Missouri, or Quincy, Illinois, they needed to wait nearly twenty-four hours before continuing their journey. Yet in a leisurely way that is what they did. "Commercial men, toting their heavy sample cases, could call on customers that afternoon, complete their business the next morning, and take the train to the next town."[37]

No matter the frequency of steam-road service, making the train might become a challenge for a salesman with sample cases and trunks. If he missed the local, there would likely be an inconvenient, even excruciatingly long, wait before he could leave that village or town. "I made the train by the small margin of a hair; it was pulling in at the depot when I arrived," boasted a veteran commercial traveler. "There was no time to check baggage. Quickly I ordered the drayman to back right up to the baggage car and dump my trunks in without being checked. The station agent was one of the sort that every travelling salesman carries around a club for. He started right in to veto proceedings, but he was a minute late. The conductor shouted, 'All aboard!' I threw a half-dollar to the driver, telling him to hurry and drive off. The train pulled out, and I swung onto the rear platform."[38]

Although less numerous than farmers and villagers, the ranks of commercial travelers grew steadily. By the start of the twentieth century there were an estimated 500,000 traveling salesmen in America, and about a tenth of them lived in or near Chicago, an expanding traction hub. It did not take long for them to appreciate the interurban. Its value increased as these roads connected with one another to form networks or "systems." Even disconnected lines enhanced a salesman's travel experiences, allowing him to combine electricity with steam.[39]

Convenience and time were essential in making the most of a commercial traveler's occupation. He usually wanted to be in the heart of a community or the central business district and to make as many calls as possible. It was common for him to utilize "sample rooms" – temporary showrooms – that hotels provided at little or no cost, a venue where he could display his wares and meet customers. The interurban was ideal. Cars traveled to commercial centers, either on their own tracks or over city streetcar lines. Steam roads, perhaps built *after* a town or city was established, might have their stations in inconvenient locations. The saying went: "The trolley cars pierce these places, the steam roads skirt them." The commercial traveler might alight from a car in front of his destination, and his sample cases could be delivered promptly. If he traveled on a steam road, he would need to find and pay a drayman to provide this service. Frequent electric cars offered another advantage; he might not even think about consulting a timetable or need to juggle his travel times based on limited steam-car service. "[Commercial travelers] soon learn that the frequent schedules suit their convenience and that they are not compelled to arrange their plans to suit the convenience of the train schedules," opined a Galveston, Texas, source. Said another: "Commercial travelers can come or go at any hour of the day, where previously they had to spend half their time waiting for trains." Still another recalled, "The good thing about the trolleys was that you could go to all kinds of little towns and, later in the day, when you'd made your sales call and were ready to leave, there was certain to be another car along soon." A contributor to *McClure's Magazine* offered these comments: "Go, for instance, to Indianapolis, and take a spin of fifty-three miles to Muncie over the lines of the Union Traction Company. You do not have to calculate your train time by a nautical almanac. You can go at any hour of the day."

In 1902 the developing Pacific Electric slammed steam competitor San Pedro, Los Angeles & Salt Lake in this newspaper advertisement: "Ride in comfort on trains that make fast time over a smooth track. The Salt Lake Route sells ten ride tickets with limit 30 days. Remember the electric cars carry you when you are ready to go and bring you back when you are ready to return. Tickets unlimited. Good for anyone at any time. Why waste time waiting for steam trains when you can take a car at any cross street every fifteen minutes?" As the Northern Texas Traction Company/Tarrant County Traction Company put it: "Always a Car When You Want it." In the interurban world "double-daily except Sunday" trains did not exist, and even in major urban areas "frequently the daytime [steam] trains are extremely few in number." The commercial traveler appreciated that an interurban might allow him to make his calls in a day or two and not need to be on the road riding steam trains for an extended period. "I envy the fellow who retires at night to his own fireside," wrote a seasoned traveling man. "Strange beds and hotel food wear on one after a while." With the speed and convenience of "the cars" the traveling man potentially could visit more customers, which perhaps would make it easier for him to meet any company-set sales quotas. And he would always look sharp for meeting his business contacts, not having to have his clothing marred by sooty locomotive smoke. The repeated mantra of the industry was this: "The attraction of interurban patronage depends upon speed, frequency, convenience, cost and comfort of the service rendered in comparison with similar facilities offered by competing [steam] lines."[40]

Interurban officials realized the importance of having salesmen board their cars. "It must be recognized that commercial travelers with trunks and sample cases afford a steady source of revenue to any transportation line prepared to handle them," editorialized the *Street Railway Journal* in 1905. "Such regular commercial travel is the backbone of the transportation business as it is steady, month in and month out, and is practically independent of the weather and other local conditions. That this class of traffic should be catered to goes without saying."[41]

Traction roads did just that. In 1906 the Ohio Interurban Railway Association and a similar organization in Indiana merged to form the Central Electric Railway Association (CERA), which included thirty-eight interurban companies. Somewhat later CERA expanded its membership to traction lines in several adjoining states. This organization labored hard to attract and retain the commercial traveler. Not only were those sample cases and trunks usually carried at no extra charge, but the CERA developed a discount coupon book. Salesmen appreciated the opportunity to buy $12 worth of travel for $10, permitting them to make their trips in multiple directions from their home community even less expensive than the already competitive (with steam road) fares. These coupon books had the added value of lacking time restrictions. And the CERA adjusted rates, often downward, as business conditions changed. The organization issued maps showing how its lines could be optimized and published consolidated timetables. Some members bought space in regional railroad guides and the *Official Guide of the Railways*. CERA also worked closely with the Order of United Commercial Travelers and the Travelers' Protective Association of America, the largest national salesmen organizations, a relationship that was in everyone's best interest.[42]

While interurbans customarily charged less for travel than steam carriers, even higher traction fares apparently did not deter the commercial traveler. Take the Rochester & Sodus Bay Railway (electric) that competed for about 45 miles with the Rome, Watertown & Ogdensburg Railroad (steam). "The steam road runs from half to three quarters of a mile from the center of the towns along the route; the electric road uses the highway for the greater part of the distance, and runs down the main streets. The cars have a baggage compartment, and make a special feature of delivering the trunks of commercial travelers at the doors of the local hotels, saving the cost of transfer, and although the electric road charges slightly higher fares than the steam road, it gets probably ninety per cent of the business." That type of competition for the much sought after commercial traveler is one reason why the New York Central Railroad, parent company of the Rome, Watertown & Ogdensburg, gobbled up the Rochester & Sodus Bay and several other interurbans and placed them in its New York State Railways subsidiary.[43]

Equipment also reflected this industry desire to please the commercial traveler. Interurban cars often contained smoking sections or attached parlor cars, ideal venues for business conversations and social intercourse. Some offered food services. The Waterloo, Cedar Falls & Northern placed in its parlor-observation units Tom Thumb kitchenettes where attendants prepared sandwiches and light refreshments. More elaborate meals could be enjoyed on the Chicago, North Shore & Milwaukee Railroad (North Shore Line). Noted a public timetable from the mid-1920s, "Trains with Dining Cars attached are run from both Chicago and Milwaukee at hours to suit the convenience and save the time of the passenger. The man of business may eat his breakfast while traveling to Chicago or Milwaukee and have luncheon or dinner on the return trip, in this way conserving time." A handful of companies offered sleeping cars, designed largely for their business clientele. The Illinois Traction System, Interstate Public Service Company, and Oregon Electric Railway are representative roads that provided overnight accommodations.

Early in the twentieth century the Holland Palace Car Company of Indianapolis built two sleepers that for a brief period operated between Indianapolis and Columbus via Dayton and Lima. Advocates of traction sleeping cars made a cogent case for such equipment over relatively short distances (when compared with Pullmans on steam trains). "They will secure traffic by offering passengers a full night's sleep between these points [Indianapolis and Columbus], and relative freedom from noise and

The Willdred Flats, located in Sandusky, Ohio, and convenient to the cars of the Lake Shore Electric, represents what preservationists have dubbed "interurban architecture."

National Register of Historic Places.

dirt. It has solved the problem of how to travel comfortably between cities too far apart to permit a business man to take time for the journey by day, and yet so near together that the passenger traveling in the sleeping-car on a steam railroad must either go to bed very late or get up very early. The electric cars will take all night for the trip, and there will be no cinders to drift in at open windows in the summer time." These cars were also designed "to render a double service, being used in the daytime as a parlor car, and at night as a sleeping car," a dual purpose also designed to please traveling men.[44]

Just as hotels courted commercial travelers – often boasting private baths, good and reasonably priced meals, and fireproof construction – entrepreneurs built housing that catered to these "men of the grip" and their families. Early in the twentieth century so-called interurban architecture appeared. A fine illustration is the Willdred Flats, located in Sandusky, Ohio, about midway between Cleveland and Toledo, and served by the heavily patronized Lake Shore Electric Railway. This interurban tied together these two Buckeye State metropolises and also linked Sandusky with Norwalk, Ohio. Constructed in 1906–1907, at the height of interurban fever, this three-story brick structure of classical revival styling, with

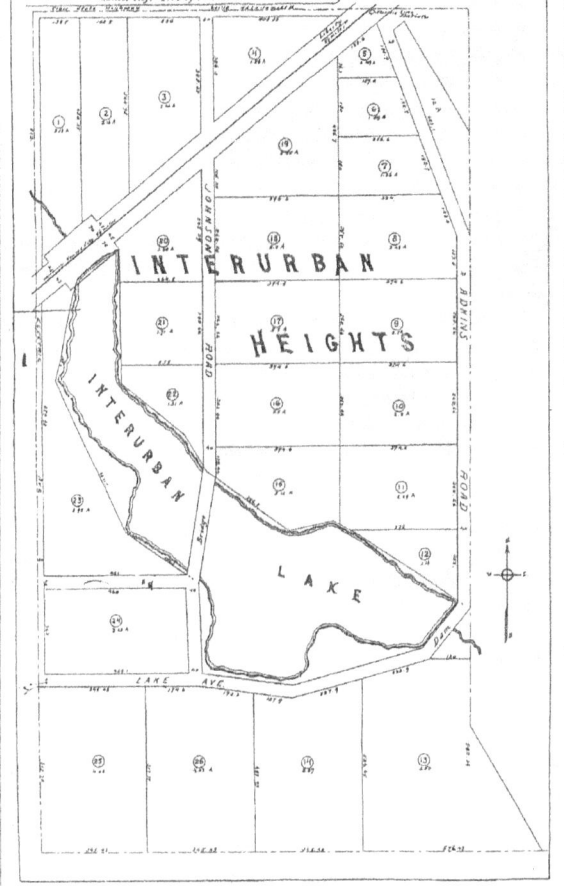

Shortly before World War I, the recently completed Kansas City, Clay County & St. Joseph Railway, with two lines radiating out of Kansas City, Missouri, allowed rural and suburban residents to commute conveniently to several locations. The Kirkland Realty Company took advantage of this "juice" road with its promotion of Interurban Heights near Liberty, Missouri.

Author's collection.

its portico of Ionic columns and balconies, situated at 1116 Columbus Avenue, was erected by a local businessman who occupied one apartment and rented the other three to traveling men. Three years later a salesman who liked the convenience of the Lake Shore Electric purchased the property. It would not be until 1916 that he would add a detached garage, responding to the growing popularity of the automobile.[45]

By the time the automobile culture became established, commercial travelers largely abandoned the interurban for the "tin lizzie." They could now follow their own schedules and travel literally from door to door. Argued the Kansas City Car Dealers Association in 1918, "The

The dapper man (left) is unquestionably a commercial traveler. He seemingly has his eyes on the group of young ladies, likely students from Millikin University, who on July 23, 1912, are about to board Illinois Traction System car No. 235 in Decatur, Illinois.

Kranbles-Peterson Archive.

salesman [with an automobile] has doubled his soliciting capacity and therefore made himself more value to his house. Few men regard their cars as 'pleasure cars.'" This more convenient alternative coincided with occupational changes; commercial travelers were rapidly evolving into modern salesmen. They no longer were old-time "flashily dressed" drummers who relied heavily on personality and "gift of gab" but nattily attired businessmen who depended rather on their corporate sales "organization" and more sophisticated advertising – salesmanship on paper – and other advancements in marketing. "The Salesman of today is a standardized product of modern efficiency," opined journalist Don Marquis in 1927, "and he sells billions of dollars' worth of other standardized products without telling a single funny story or attending a single lodge meeting."[46]

Commercial travelers, whether old-fashioned drummers or modern salesmen, long had the reputation of having an eye for young women. Their presence might frighten or at least irritate female passengers. A woman college student who traveled on the North Shore Line remembered encountering a salesman who became too friendly. She cut off his advances. "I was in no mood to be picked up." Human nature has known no bounds on public transportation, past or present.[47]

COMMUTERS

While those commercial travelers who continually patronized interurbans fall into the broad category of "commuters," there were others who fully met the definition. A Wisconsin traction executive defined this "bread and butter" element of the passenger traffic this way: "A commuter, in the generally accepted sense of the word, is one who is an habitual rider at reduced rates." The principal groups of commuters consisted of men and women who lived in suburban or rural areas and used the electric cars to travel to and from work, and schoolchildren and college students who relied on intercity traction in furthering their educations.[48]

Interurbans themselves did much to generate this journey-to-work traffic. Their promoters and owners often became involved in suburban real-estate development, creating trolley or interurban additions to cities and towns and establishing more remote communities. They considered electric lines as adjuncts to their land speculation and exploited desires of those urbanites who wanted to escape the hustle and bustle of smoky, congested, and crime-ridden cities. "To the city dwellers these interurban roads make possible the dream of years," wrote a business journalist in 1904, "and they flee from the crowded cities to settle on two, three or five-acre tracts along the line of these roads, there to enjoy in the midst of their gardens the pure air, the quiet and the healthful conditions of country life."

By way of an illustration, the Denver & Interurban Railroad (Kite Route), working with the Colman Selling Company, glorified "the Beautiful Lakeview Valley" that was "Only Twenty Minutes from Denver on the New Boulder Electric Line." The promotional copy made this claim: "Lakeview Valley is the most beautiful garden spot in Colorado – away from the noise, dust and infection of the city – surrounded by green fields, lakes, and romantic hills – it has an uninterrupted view of one hundred and fifty miles of snow-capped mountains, that, though a long way off, yet, because of the absolute purity of the atmosphere, seem but a little distance." As another incentive: "Chickens and squabs can be raised and splendid profits made by selling them in Denver. There is plenty of good pasture for cows and the creamery of the town will buy the milk." Not everybody embraced this "back to the land" ideal, yet there was a common desire to live in a pleasant and commutable suburb or exurb. For middle-class families these new homes meant a quiet, safe, and sanitary environment and neighbors who shared similar outlooks on life. William B. Strang Jr., founder of Overland Park, Kansas, and builder of the 20-mile

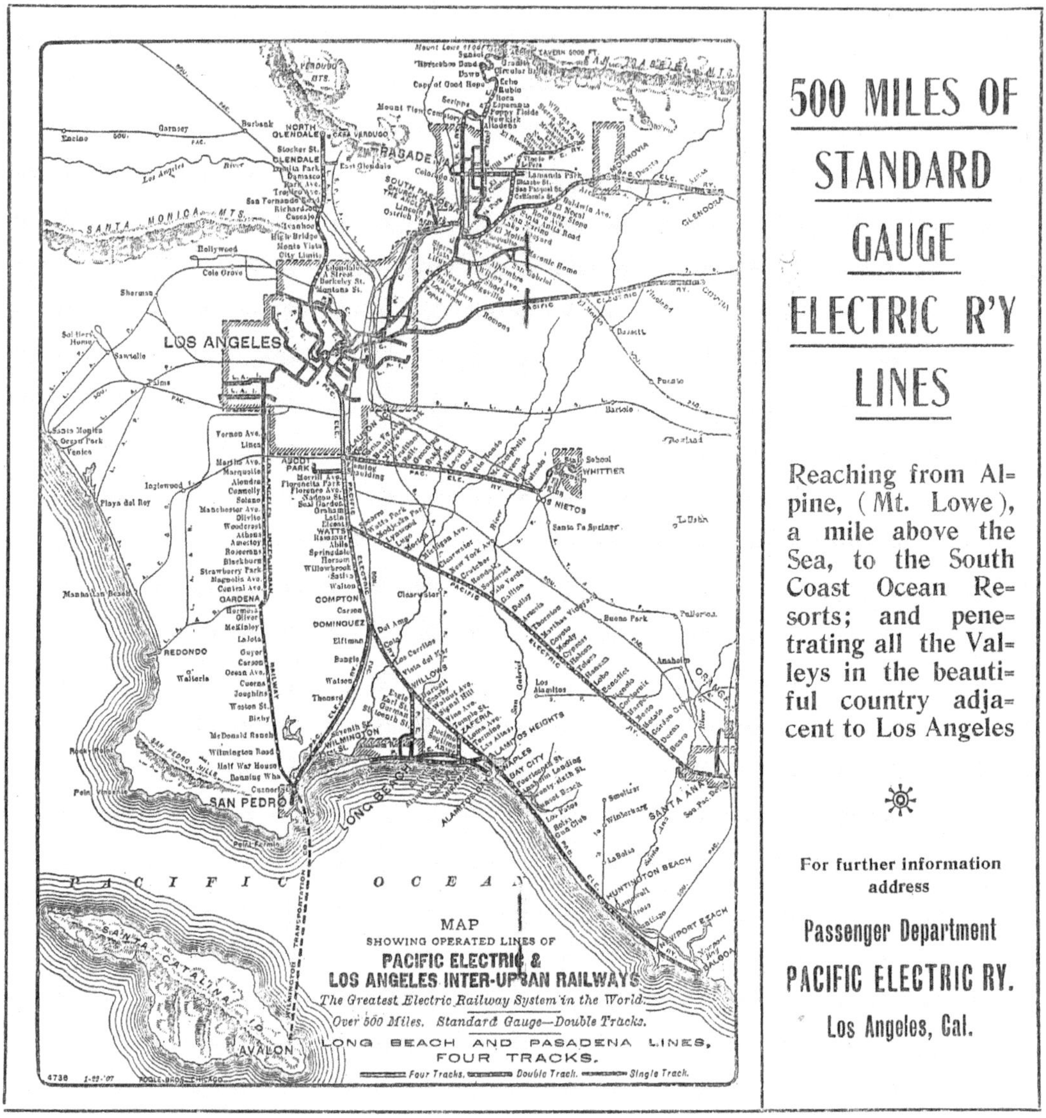

500 MILES OF STANDARD GAUGE ELECTRIC R'Y LINES

Reaching from Alpine, (Mt. Lowe), a mile above the Sea, to the South Coast Ocean Resorts; and penetrating all the Valleys in the beautiful country adjacent to Los Angeles

For further information address

Passenger Department
PACIFIC ELECTRIC RY.
Los Angeles, Cal.

MAP SHOWING OPERATED LINES OF PACIFIC ELECTRIC & LOS ANGELES INTER-URBAN RAILWAYS
The Greatest Electric Railway System in the World.
Over 500 Miles. Standard Gauge—Double Tracks.
LONG BEACH AND PASADENA LINES, FOUR TRACKS.

The map of the sprawling Pacific Electric and Los Angeles Inter-Urban railways, which appeared in a December 15, 1907, public timetable, graphically reveals how "The Greatest Electric Railway System in the World" allowed commuters, shoppers, and others to easily reach Los Angeles.

Author's collection.

Missouri & Kansas Interurban Railway, insisted that his new community of detached single-family frame homes would be a "country retreat" away from "sordid" city life, and his electric road would become a "great way to happiness." About 1915 the Gary & Interurban Railway extolled its Riverside development in Lake County, Indiana: "On the electric line – between the city and the beautiful Inland Lakes on high ground among the oak trees, commanding a superb view of the whole countryside – the hills and valley of Deep River which flows so peacefully along this tract – there is fishing, boating and bathing. Improvements, macadamized streets, cement curbs and walks, electric lights. Opening Price, $165 and up for a big 330 × 210 foot lot spells profit." Before the Great Depression of the 1930s the nearby Chicago, South Shore & South Bend Railroad (South

In 1909 commuters who are using a car of the Washington, Arlington & Falls Church Railway (right) are most likely government employees who work in the nation's capital. The station is at Rosslyn, Virginia, opposite the Georgetown section of the District of Columbia. The city car on the left belongs to the Great Falls & Old Dominion Railway.

Library of Congress.

Shore Line), an Insull property, established "The Own Your Own Home Bureau," which provided "free information to the public on real estate buildings and plans, and attempts to bring the prospective home owners through the maze of technical details leading up to the building and owning of a home." In fact, the Insull lines promoted suburban living in Chicagoland by offering free passage to allow prospective lot buyers to see what parcels were available. In 1911 the Albany Southern Railroad, which operated between the New York cities of Albany and Hudson, made what was a common pitch: "There are many acres of land along the Albany Southern Railroad that are suitable for home building that can be purchased at reasonable prices and the Company is ready at all times to assist you in locating along its lines. Our commutation rates are very low and the service is prompt. We also furnish electricity."[49]

It would be Henry E. Huntington who emerged as the king of American real-estate promoters. Biographer William B. Friedricks called him the "great metropolitan entrepreneur." Huntington's sprawling Pacific Electric Railway, which developed into the largest interurban in the country, with more than 700 miles of routes that radiated out of Los Angeles, became the key to his Southern California development schemes. The Pacific Electric had an enormous impact on the Los Angeles basin. In the late 1920s the effects were described this way: "The interurban system has knit the surrounding cities into a compact community with the larger city [and] made possible the upbuilding of hundreds of square miles of rural territory." The multiple routes of the Pacific Electric enabled "the wage earner to own his own home in one of the many subdivisions which have sprung up along the company's various lines," and in the process generated a mass of weekday commuters. No contemporary denied that these expanded transportation opportunities enhanced real-estate values. Interurbans had that Midas touch, promoting land speculation and development wherever they passed.[50]

"Traction titans" themselves might take advantage of the good life in a rural setting that electric roads made possible. Henry Everett and Edward Moore, who partnered to create one of the nation's foremost streetcar and interurban syndicates, built country estates adjoining the Cleveland, Painesville & Eastern, one of their properties. The former resided on a 400-acre farm, "Leodoro," and the latter on the larger "Mooreland." Both men used the electric line to commute to their offices in downtown Cleveland, as did most of their wealthy neighbors.[51]

There were those interurban companies, albeit a minority, that depended upon the workday commuter for a substantial portion of their passenger revenues. "The 'commuter,' who rides every day, going from his home to his work," said an interurban official, "is a very profitable source of business to an electric railroad." Tens of thousands of daily riders, who represented a wide spectrum of the public, relied on such well-built electrics. These included the Pacific Electric; the Insull-controlled Chicago, Aurora & Elgin; North Shore and South Shore lines that served Chicago; Illinois Traction (later Illinois Terminal) that reached St. Louis from several Illinois suburbs on its own bridge over the Mississippi River; and the New York, Westchester & Boston that connected Port Chester and White Plains, New York, with New York City and was designed to handle high-volume commuter traffic. In terms of annual ridership the Insull group could report these impressive numbers for 1921: the North Shore Line carried almost 12 million, largely commuter passengers, the CA&E about eight million, and the South Shore Line approximately 2.5 million. These roads resembled the best metropolitan rapid transit systems.[52]

Lesser interurbans also served commuters. The Lake Shore Electric Railway, for one, carried scores of business and professional people between the western suburbs of Cleveland, especially Lakewood and Rocky River, and Public Square. Although much smaller than the Lake Shore Electric, the Great Falls & Old Dominion Railway, built to take pleasure seekers to the Great Falls of the Potomac River, "the Niagara of the South," and to spur real-estate projects in an area "almost completely uninhabited and ideal for development," enjoyed a brisk commuter business from communities and housing that sprang up at trackside, most notably McLean, Virginia. These riders were headed to Rosslyn, Virginia, and streetcar connections to destinations in the District of Columbia. Later when the Great Falls & Old Dominion became part of the much larger electrified Washington & Old Dominion Railway, which stretched westward from suburban Washington to Leesburg and Bluemont, Virginia, additional commuters boarded cars to and from the capital city.[53]

Interurbans, large and small, recognized that they must please their regular clientele, becoming paramount as "jitneys" and automobiles began to take away this business. Charles F. Price, traffic manager for the Western Ohio Railway, said it well: "Commuters' rates should be reasonably low and the service such as to encourage the every-day traveler." According to traction historian Herbert H. Harwood Jr. these riders were "the most volatile commodity known to transportation." He backed the Price argument. "Matters of train performance and fares can suddenly become flash points. Since everyone is trying to get to work on time, and get home as soon as possible afterward, lateness can be a major issue, especially if it's chronic. And fare levels are more important to commuters than to occasional riders, since they are part of one's daily living expenses."[54]

Those commuters who daily boarded interurban cars normally settled down to a staid and predictable routine. They might read a newspaper, magazine, or book, play cards with their traveling companions – pinochle and poker were popular – chat with fellow passengers and crew members, or even knit. And in the process these commuters established lasting friendships. As with commuters on steam railroads, conductors came to know their "regulars." On the less heavily patronized commuter-carrying interurbans, there might be that personal touch. "Here's a man that gets on at some stop, the same stop, the same car every morning," related a former Lake Shore Electric conductor. "Well, if one morning he wasn't here, you'd look down the street. If you saw him running, you'd wait for him. If he wasn't in sight, the motorman would start blowing the whistle, banging the bell, to let him know that he was there." Having given that commuter his chance, the car departed, and surely to the delight of passengers anxious to reach their destinations.[55]

For some interurbans another important group of daily commuters were miners. Roads in the anthracite and bituminous coal regions hauled thousands of these diggers of black diamonds, several Upper Great Lakes carriers transported workers to iron ore pits, and a few western ones carried men who worked copper and other nonferrous deposits. One interurban that typified this service was the Monongahela Valley Traction Company (previously the Fairmont & Clarksburg Electric Railroad and later the Monongahela Power & Railway), the leading interurban in West Virginia. Miners who worked for the Fairmont Coal Company, a large local producer, and who did not live in company housing at Monongah, took the cars to work from their homes in Fairmont, Clarksburg, and on-line settlements or from their small farms.[56]

No matter the volume of daily commuters, interurbans had a pronounced impact on where people lived. Edward Mason, a Harvard University economist, was right when he wrote in the early 1930s that electric railroads increased "the radius of feasible daily travel from urban centers and laid the basis for the tremendous growth in population and area which American cities have witnessed during the last forty years."[57]

When rural and suburban students had access to an interurban line, their options for a better education increased, although by the time intercity traction appeared, some school districts already had begun establishing consolidated facilities. School authorities either provided horse-drawn vehicles (later motor buses) to transport students, or they encouraged parents to provide transportation in a cart, buggy, or sled. Students also traveled alone, riding a horse or pony, peddling a bicycle, or walking.

The interurban, where available, enhanced educational opportunities for thousands of youth and made their school travels and lives easier and richer. This pattern largely continued until daily road travel became practical after World War I. Even at the dawn of the Interurban Era students flocked to these upstart traction lines. In 1897 the *York* [Maine] *Current* noted that cars of the Portsmouth, Kittery &York Electric Railroad were well patronized, and "quite a number of our young people are attending the high school at York Corner, going and returning on the electric cars." Early on rural students who wished to attend Elyria High School in Ohio found that the interurban made that a realistic possibility. Of the 363 students who attended this secondary school in 1906, 125 lived in the surrounding countryside and used the electric cars, and of these, "at least two-thirds would be unable to attend but for the interurban road."[58]

Then there is this example from Iowa. With electrification of the Webster City–based Crooked Creek Railroad, its new owner, the electric Fort Dodge, Des Moines & Southern Railway (Fort Dodge Line), made it possible for students who lived near the line to experience a dramatically improved change in their pattern of education. "High school students could flag a car at any road crossing and commute daily to their schools at Fort Dodge or Webster City," remembered a veteran Fort Dodge Line conductor, "where formerly they would have to board and room in town and get home only weekly, if the roads permitted." A similar situation might work for rural schoolteachers. "[They] could board a morning car at Fort Dodge and, in a matter of minutes, get off the car at a road crossing near their school where, before they had this service, they would have to board and room at some farm home near their school."[59]

If elementary and high school students had the convenience of these electric cars, not only could they live at home, but they could participate

The Oklahoma Railway, the largest interurban system in the state, regularly transported students between the University of Oklahoma campus in Norman and Oklahoma City. But in 1947 this convenient service ended.

Author's collection.

in after-school activities. It might be the debate club, school chorus, or sports team. Developing intercity contests in high school basketball (both boys and girls) and football allowed teams and their fans to attend these much-anticipated games. Some rivalries evolved because schools had convenient interurban connections. Throughout the country the relationship between school and interurban became strong. It came as no surprise to residents of Terre Haute, Indiana, that the Terre Haute, Indianapolis & Eastern Traction Company named one of its big interurban cars "Wiley High School" and adorned its sides with the school's pennants. There were even "school trains" or "school trippers." Several interurbans contracted with boards of education to provide cars exclusively for their students. The Sacramento Northern, for one, operated morning and afternoon school trains between Oakland and Concord, California, and for years these movements customarily required five cars. And for much of its history the North Shore Line maintained dedicated cars for hauling students to and from New Trier High School in Winnetka, Illinois.[60]

Whether with a regularly scheduled car or a special one assigned to students, interurbans tended to have a good on-time record. Recalled a regular rider who in the 1930s took the New York, Westchester & Boston (NYW&B) to school in the Bronx, New York, "In my lifetime I've traveled on many railroads. You could always depend on the accuracy of its [NYW&B] timetables. The trains ALWAYS arrived on schedule." A woman who after World War II attended a Roman Catholic grade school

INTERURBANS IN DAILY LIFE   87

in Waukegan, Illinois, but lived in nearby Zion, had a similar experience. "The [North Shore Line] local was nearly always on time, and usually so in bad winter weather."[61]

College students also became part of the passenger mix. Thousands commuted almost daily to nearby colleges and universities. Understandably these institutions of higher education, ranging from the large University of Michigan in Ann Arbor to little Wofford College in Spartanburg, South Carolina, valued an interurban line. Students could conveniently attend classes outside their home communities while living inexpensively at home. In 1903 the Columbus, Delaware & Marion Electric Railroad promoted the School of Business at Ohio Wesleyan University in Delaware. "Buy a 500 mileage book – use the C.D. & M., take a Business Course and board at home." The University of Iowa in Iowa City drew hundreds of students daily from Cedar Rapids, 27 miles to the north, and surrounding areas, who patronized the Cedar Rapids & Iowa City Railway (CRANDIC). A former female student recalled vividly riding the interurban: "When I was in my first year at the University in 1940 I rode the CRANDIC every day from Cedar Rapids to Iowa City. On the way home from Iowa City I often went to the back of the car to take a nap. Usually the operators let me know when I got to my stop, but once they forgot. I rode back and forth between Iowa City and Cedar Rapids until about 11:00 at night!"[62]

Another example involves the scores of students who relied on the North Shore Line to attended classes at Northwestern University in Evanston, Illinois. They came from its terminal cities and from intermediate towns and villages. During the twilight years of the road, a former student applauded the punctual service and found no stigma for being an interurban commuter, although many Northwestern students lived on campus and drove fancy cars. "There were many other students who rode the North Shore, North Western and the L to school." She recalled that the university provided a comfortable waiting lounge on an upper floor of Scott Hall, the student center, for members of "Men and Women Off Campus."[63]

Some of these regular collegians commuted only during the opening and closing of the academic semester and during holiday vacations. "There were the cheerful and happy, young college students leaving for Ames or Des Moines or Iowa City or Grinnell or Pella or some other college town, their faces aglow with health and a sparkle in their eyes which mirrored their ambitions to become doctors or lawyers or engineers or teachers," happily recalled a Fort Dodge Line conductor. "What a wonderful bunch they were, so honest and upright, so frank in discussing their plans, their hopes and dreams of the future."[64]

Colleges themselves might become proactive and encourage, even finance, an interurban connection. The financially struggling Westminster

October 25, 1913, was a memorable day for the Bethel College community in North Newton, Kansas, for it marked the arrival of service by the Arkansas Valley Interurban Railway. Students, college officials, and traction employees pause for a group photograph in front of car No. 10.

Mennonite Library and Archives, Bethel College.

University, a Presbyterian school that was gallantly striving to become the "Princeton of the West," situated on a high point of land northwest of Denver, wanted students to be able to avoid the steep, mile-long walk to campus from the Westminster station of the Denver & Interurban Railroad. In 1908 the school administration asked this newly opened road to build a branch to serve the campus directly. The interurban agreed, and construction crews soon installed the lightly built electrified appendage that had exceptionally steep grades.[65]

Although Westminster University, which failed during World War I, relied on the resources of the Denver & Interurban for an interurban connection, another small, albeit durable, institution, Bethel College, a Mennonite school located about a mile north of Newton, Kansas, helped to finance its own link to intercity traction. This involved the Arkansas Valley Interurban Railway (AVI), a road that operated between Wichita, Newton, and Hutchinson, Kansas. The college was somewhat remote from urban life, although it had an inconvenient connection to an area streetcar line. But according to the *Bethel College Monthly* this was hardly ideal, and at times it became necessary for "students, teachers and visitors to tramp through mud, rain and storm" to reach the campus. Although early on the quietness of the college's surroundings was considered an advantage, that attitude of "splendid isolation" changed. By 1912 the college community concluded that "regular transportation service would be of great benefit both to campus residents and to students from the city desiring to attend Bethel College. With the introduction of a full college course in 1911, there began a noticeable increase in the attendance from Newton." So what to do? Forging a connection with the AVI seemed the practical solution.[66]

Action followed. Friends of Bethel subscribed $20,000 for bonds to pay most of the costs for the short AVI extension, and the college community applauded their support. "The persons, who bought bonds and thus made possible the Interurban service, have manifested an unusual spirit of philanthropy and careful insight into the needs of the college."[67]

Cars soon arrived. That eventful day occurred on October 25, 1913. "So elated were the campus dwellers, that children and grandfathers, cooks and professors, students and visitors turned out to welcome the visitors from Newton," related the *Bethel College Monthly*. "After the band, standing on the college steps, played enthusiastically several numbers, President [J. W.] Kliewer spoke a hearty word of welcome and appreciation to the large crowd congregated in front of the college. He was followed by Mr. [A. V.] Boyle, the General Manager of the A.V.I. R.R." For several hours this celebration continued, and it included the presentation of a "handsome loving cup" to Rudolf Goerz, a college trustee "who worked faithfully and sacrificingly [sic] to sell the bonds."[68]

College students appreciated (perhaps most of all) an easy way to *leave* campus, especially when rigid rules about behavior and decorum were enforced. Those males who attended Denison University, a Baptist school in Granville, Ohio, took advantage of one of the pioneer intercity traction roads, the 7-mile Newark & Granville Street Railway, a later component of the sprawling Ohio Electric Railway. "Those residents in dormitories or village homes were appreciative of the new opportunities for shopping and amusement outside Granville," wrote university historian C. Wallace Chessman. "Patrons of the 'Owl Car' returning from Newark after eleven o'clock on Saturday night would not be noted for sobriety; bars and brothels already gave the country seat [Newark] the air of a sinful Rome over against its collegiate Athens [Granville]."[69]

Another reason to leave campus was to be with members of the opposite sex. A good example took place in Michigan. On weekends the Detroit, Jackson & Chicago Railway did a brisk business when male students at the University of Michigan in Ann Arbor boarded its cars for Eastern Michigan Normal College in Ypsilanti. The "U" had an enrollment of "three thousand boys and not enough girls, Ypsilanti had a thousand girls at the Normal and not enough boys." The interurban helped to restore the equilibrium.[70]

Military personnel frequently became part-time commuters, resembling some college students. There were interurbans that reached directly (or with streetcar connections) various army and navy bases. One such

Even after World War II and the Korean Conflict, sailors from the Great Lakes Naval Training Station took advantage of the Chicago, North Shore & Milwaukee. It's a chilly December day in 1962 and not long before this high-speed interurban shut down that these men in uniform line up on the platform at North Chicago Junction to board a "Swabbie Special" for Milwaukee and a prized weekend leave.

John Gruber collection.

road was the Inter-Urban Railway (later Des Moines & Central Iowa) that during the world wars served a booming Camp Dodge, located northwest of Des Moines. This army-training facility became during World War I "the third largest city in Iowa," having a population of from 40,000 to 50,000. In both conflicts this Hawkeye State interurban handled thousands of personnel to and from the camp. There were instances when at interchange connections the company attached its freight motors to standard steam-road equipment, including Pullman cars. "It was said the road once moved [during World War I] 3,500 men and their baggage from a connecting railroad to camp, twenty-five miles distant, in five hours." This interurban did more than transport troops for training; soldiers who gained weekend leave passes jammed cars to and from the Iowa capital.[71]

Other interurbans transported even greater numbers of service personnel. The Washington, Baltimore & Annapolis Electric Railway (WB&A) and the North Shore Line were two such roads. The WB&A served both the U.S. Naval Academy in Annapolis, Maryland, and Fort George G. Meade (originally Camp Admiral), northwest of Annapolis. During World War I, the electric road handled nearly 14 million passengers, many of whom were servicemen going to and coming from these military installations and often taking cars for their leaves in Baltimore and Washington,

INTERURBANS IN DAILY LIFE   91

D.C. The North Shore Line became exceptionally busy, especially during World War II. Explained the company in 1942: "[The North Shore Line] serves two of the Nation's most important Army and Navy Establishments – Fort Sheridan and Great Lakes Naval Training Station. In effect, this is the same as though several densely populated new cities had suddenly been added to the many important ones the railroad already serves." This soaring wartime traffic prompted the road to ask civilians to board cars when passenger volume would be less. "Schedule your trips so as not to conflict with the heavy Army and Navy furlough traffic out of Chicago and Milwaukee on Saturday and Sunday nights." Other interurbans made similar requests. The Pacific Electric repeatedly used public timetables, station notices, newspaper advertisements, and radio spots to warn non-military riders about the needs and limits of wartime travel, knowing that at certain times of the day or week their cars would be jammed to the gills with those in uniform.[72]

PLEASURE SEEKERS

Students and soldiers considered interurbans a necessity but also a way to find enjoyment. Others from all walks of life shared similar thoughts and in the process sought "to get a glimpse at the outside world beyond." Interurban officials understood the financial implications of such feelings, and they did what they could to exploit them. As early as the late 1890s the Massachusetts Street Railway Association backed publication of *Derrah's Street Railway Guide*, a 178-page booklet that sold for fifteen cents, promoting "the largest connected system of street railways in the world" and giving pleasure seekers "some idea of the diversity of sights and scenes to be reached by the various electric systems."[73]

An interurban trip was usually a pleasant experience. "I loved to ride those cars out of Indianapolis," remembered a former resident. "It was exciting to see the bustle in the streets, to observe the farms and to view the woodlands and streams." Remarked another: "The advantage of the trip, remember, is not alone that you arrive at your destination, but that every moment of the going affords new and ever-changing pleasure in all that pertains to outdoor life." Some passengers really had no destination in mind when they boarded a car; the ride was the objective, especially when the rural trolley or interurban operated seasonal open cars. "If you take a ride on a summer evening you will see the open seats filled with cool, comfortable people, sociably chatting, with their hats in their laps, while the breeze blows through their hair or whiskers, as the case may be," observed a magazine writer. Some commented on the delightful smells of new-mown hay and wild honeysuckle. Then there might be young

A trip along the Niagara Gorge and to Niagara Falls, New York, surely had therapeutic value for sightseers. This scene of a beauty spot along the Niagara Gorge Electric Railway includes an open car running on a double-track right-of-way. This card was produced in about 1900 by the Sterro-Photo Company of Dolgeville, New York, a firm that in the mid-1890s began to offer scenery views, especially of the American West.

Author's collection.

couples in love who took a moonlight ride. They preferred rear seats so they could "fondle and spoon," a venue superior to the courting supervision of parents and family members that took place in home parlors and on front porches. These pleasure riders "were not going anywhere – they were simply enjoying a spin in the people's automobile." Early in the twentieth century novelist William Dean Howells in his essay "Confessions of a Summer Colonist" remarked that the open cars of the Portsmouth, Kittery & York were popular with summer residents. "Some pass a great part of every afternoon on the trolley, and one lady had achieved celebrity by spending four dollars a week in trolley rides." An industry trade journal supported such commentaries. "The popularity of the open car is due largely to the fact that it affords the least possible obstruction to the movement of fresh air through the car. This gives a sense of freedom to the passenger. The sensation in riding is much more like that experienced in an automobile than in traveling in a car which is closed."[74]

Open car or not, a ride on an interurban supposedly had therapeutic value. "Ordinary, every-day trolleying has its advantages, but the 'trolley traveler' who uses this service in an intelligent manner reaps the greatest harvest. Tired Nature demands relaxation from the daily grind, and nothing so fully meets this demand as a change of scene," suggested a public timetable issued jointly by the Pittsburgh, Harmony, Butler & New Castle and Pittsburgh, Mars & Butler railways. "Intelligent trolley riding will furnish more real, genuine pleasure than any similar investment. Coupled with the pleasure, there is health and the added education advantages to be derived from seeing the historic points of interest that surround the vicinity in which ones lives. Then there is the delight, after a hot day's work

In 1907 individuals who sought to tour New England could easily plan their itineraries by purchasing a copy of the *Trolley Wayfinder*, a publication of the New England Street Railway Club. The cover drawing features the popular summer open car.

Author's collection.

in the crowded, busy, bustling city, of a quiet, cool trolley ride through the peaceful, restful suburban country. It's a tonic that fits one better for the battle of life that must be taken up the following day."[75]

That desire to enjoy fresh air, scenery, and the wonders of the natural world was much exploited by the rural trolleys of New England. "When it comes to cheap and satisfactory recreation, with no punctured tires, no lame horses and no time-card handicaps, the trolley is certainly the very best thing," concluded Albert Bigelow Paine, writing in *World's Work* in 1903. As he continued, "Trolley-lines are cast in pleasant places, along sunny highways, and through the choicest of city streets. [And you can] drop anchor by hill or meadow and by running brook. On the whole there is something good and sociable and old-fashioned about trolleying in spite of the fact that it is about the newest form of travel." In 1919 the writer-poet Richard Le Gallienne found a trip over the Berkshire Street Railway, the only interurban to operate in four states simultaneously – Connecticut, Massachusetts, New York, and Vermont – a delightful experience. "[We] proceeded to jog along at forty miles or so an hour right into the heart of the hills, hills coming swiftly into real mountains, hills and streams and lakes, and all thick with memories, in which, with an original combination of the historic and business senses, for which one can scarcely be too grateful."[76]

Outdoor enthusiasts might take a fancy to these interurban jaunts. One such group was the informal Rambling Club, which consisted of business and professional men who lived in Elmira, New York, and who loved to walk. They commonly hiked all or part of the 25 miles between their hometown and Corning. If the weather turned nasty or if they were tired, these "Ramblers" boarded the cars of the Elmira, Corning & Waverly Railway, which ran hourly, for their return home. That same interurban also provided a convenient way for canoeists to enjoy the Chemung River. Those who wished to experience these charming waters could rent boats at Bill Cotton's Canoe Livery in Elmira and have them stacked three deep on flatcars and transported to East Corning by a box motor and then follow in a scheduled car. At their destination the canoes were unloaded, and these pleasure seekers could paddle downstream to Elmira. And for years the interurban division of the Northwestern Pacific Railroad attracted hikers to lovely Marin County, California. The company publicized that in Mill Valley, located on its third-rail electrified line from the San Francisco ferry wharf at Sausalito, these devotees of the outdoors had access to facilities where they could change clothes and take showers.[77]

Choosing less strenuous activities than a hike or canoe trip were those individuals who took cars so that they might pick wildflowers, mushrooms, or other plants of the fields or woods. The Eastern Ohio Traction Company was one interurban that encouraged such jaunts. Yet it strongly objected to those mushroom hunters who during chilly times tore off boards from their waiting shelters and burned them to keep warm while awaiting a car.[78]

Game hunters also might find that interurbans facilitated their outdoor pursuits. During the 1904 hunting season the Dayton, Springfield

& Urbana Electric Railway–Urbana, Bellefontaine & Northern Railway announced in newspaper advertisements: "HUNTERS! There is good shooting along the line of the D.S.& U. and U.B.& N. During the hunting season, commencing November 15, Dogs will be carried on all cars." About the same time a promotional booklet issued by the Cincinnati, Lawrenceburg & Aurora Electric Street Railroad noted that in season "the sound of the hunter's gun could be heard during the day, and the evening 'runs' into the city [Cincinnati] carried many hunters with bags filled with almost every kind of small game."[79]

There might be hunters with another objective – seeking places to find alcoholic beverages. By the time interurbans became a transportation option, scores of states, counties, and municipalities had passed prohibition laws. So those with a "thirst" needed to be resourceful, and electric cars might make their task easier. Imbibers of drink in western Illinois found the Sterling, Dixon & Eastern Traction Company helpful. "The SD&E benefited from the violent local option elections of its early days," recounted a student of the road. "Voters from Sterling and Dixon changed their minds frequently about having a 'dry' or 'wet' town. Whichever town was 'dry' could always count on the railroad to provide good two-way service to the neighboring 'wet.'"[80]

Then there might be a journey over one or more traction lines. Roads in New England encouraged this travel, especially for pleasure seekers. In 1909 the Hartford & Springfield Street Railway issued a large three-color map entitled "New England by Trolley" to attract such riders. The accompanying narrative indicated that it was possible to take electric cars from New York City to Portland, Maine, and listed approximate fares and running times between intermediate points. Five years before this New England road promoted long-distance travel, a New York publisher released a rather unusual book, *A Trolley Honeymoon from Delaware to Maine*. This breezy and well-illustrated account told of newlyweds Clinton and Louisa Lucas, who decided to "trolley" for nearly 500 miles from their home in Wilmington, Delaware, to resorts along the Maine coast. They had happy times, and they had a few misadventures. Throughout the couple's story of "rural trolleying" there are comments about people they met or observed; some who sought pleasure and others who did not:

> Our fellow-passengers on the Dunellen [New Jersey] car were a medley indeed.
> On the rear seats sprawled a group of men in grimy canvas suits, and nestling at their feet was a generous supply of picks and crowbars. Seated among them was a lean, bewhiskered farmer, bereft of collar and tie, who kept cracking hard-shelled jokes with the conductor. Near us in the centre seat sat a Tennysonian young lady, rapt in the *Idylls of the King*, while at her elbow was a fat negress, whose watery eyes and paroxysm of sneezing testified to the ravages of hay fever. All the front seats, however, had been

The Moulton interurban odyssey in 1909 did not involve a largely straight route between New York City and Chicago. The trip between Toledo and South Bend required traveling through Lima, Ohio, and Fort Wayne and Wabash, Indiana. Efforts to construct a more direct Toledo and South Bend line, however, were nearly achieved before World War I.

Author's collection.

pre-empted by a merry trolley party (the first we had met on our trip), a group of women hatless and radiant in white shirtwaists, who chattered vivaciously over a hand-to-hand feast of caramels. They changed with us into the Plainfield car at the station in the outskirts of Dunellen village.[81]

The Wilmington honeymooners also represent those pleasure travelers who wanted to prove a point, namely how the meteoric rise of interurbans facilitated long-distance trips. In August 1909 J. S. Moulton, a lawyer for the Interborough Rapid Transit Company of New York City, wished to show the possibilities for a journey largely by electric cars from New York City to Chicago. In his account, published in the *Electric Railway Journal*, he began with these comments: "As far as I am able to learn from many inquiries this is the first trip made from New York to Chicago over electric lines for so large a part of the way." In the process of riding over a period of four days on nearly twenty interurban roads, he related a variety of positive comments. "It was remarkable to find that the electric lines, with their long runs and many stops in the different cities and villages, made almost exact schedule time." While on a car of the Ohio Electric Railway, he reported: "At Van Wert, Ohio, the Manhattan Limited of the Pennsylvania Railroad, which parallels the electric line at this point, came up, but we passed the steam train and kept ahead of it." His closing statement: "I had a fine and comfortable trip and shall certainly repeat it at the earliest practicable time."[82]

A year after the Moulton trip a more ambitious multiday, multiroad interurban journey took place. On the morning of May 10, 1910, twenty-one businessmen from Utica, New York, joined by a traction official who

About the time of World War I and at an unknown location the Fort Dodge, Des Moines & Southern Railway operated this multicar train presumably for members of the fraternal Masonic Order.

Byron Olsen collection.

conceived of this "grand voyage," boarded a chartered car of the New York State Railways in their home city for what was likely the longest continuous journey in interurban history. For two weeks these goodwill ambassadors, or "Trolley Pilgrims," traveled approximately 2,000 miles on twenty-eight electric roads in six states: New York, Pennsylvania, Ohio, Indiana, Kentucky, and Michigan, where they visited fellow businessmen in such cities as Rochester, Buffalo, Erie, Cleveland, Columbus, Dayton, Indianapolis, Louisville, Fort Wayne, Toledo, and Detroit. This "Utica Electric Railway Tour," sponsored by the Utica Boosters and the chamber of commerce, was designed to demonstrate the advanced state of intercity traction and to advertise the progressive features of this New York textile manufacturing and trading center. Upon return of the special car, with its pleasure-loving passengers, the *Utica* [New York] *Observer* ruminated on the trip: "At some future time, when the electric roads of this country shall have been further extended and connected under a smaller number of managements, someone will write a history of electric traction development in the country. He will then tell of the 'first long trip' in one trolley car – that of the Utica business men who returned last evening – and it will become an historical event."[83]

Pleasure seekers might not need to be part of an organized group to board a special car. Some interurbans offered specially equipped cars for virtually any type of pleasure outing. In 1916 Detroit United Lines promoted rental of its car the *Yolande*. "THE car – your car – for privately entertaining guests over the interurban lines. It is magnificently equipped with kitchenette and movable tables, with a full complement of table linen, china and silverware. Just the car you want, whether you have a bite to eat

Smaller interurbans might have a parlor car to rent for group outings. The Oneonta, Cooperstown & Richfield Springs Railway made available to the public its attractive *Otsego*. In June 1905 it is seen on a Cooperstown, New York, street.

Author's collection.

en route or not. The gastronomic arrangements are of your own making." The company added: "This special car is available any time over any lines subject to traffic conditions."[84]

Some pleasure seekers, who resembled commuters, were individuals and groups that took the cars to attend regular or special events. These ranged from community festivals to political debates. Fraternal organizations were also part of this mix. An Ohio interurban executive expressed his pleasure that "along our line the members of the various I.O.O.F. [Independent Order of Odd Fellows] lodges are now making trips every week or ten days to some other town, carrying on their work and contesting for a prize which will be awarded the latter part of February. They never go in less than carloads and return at night, always before the time arrives for shutting down the power."[85]

No different from streetcar companies interurban roads realized that the greatest generator of weekend passenger business (and hence revenues) came from a variety of popular destinations. These included amusement parks, amphitheaters, dance halls, county and state fairs, baseball diamonds, race and trotting tracks, picnic grounds, bathing beaches, scenic spots, and campsites (or a combination of these attractions). Without a pleasure-drawing venue, Sundays would be slow traffic days; after all, farm families and village shoppers might remain at home, and commercial travelers and commuters would not likely be on the move. In fact, several

Earlier pleasure seekers detrain from a Lake Shore Electric car at Rye Beach Park, west of Huron, another revenue maker for this Cleveland to Toledo interurban.

Frohman collection, R. B. Hayes Presidential Center.

interurbans, including Paul Smith's Electric Railway in New York State and the Toledo, Port Clinton & Lakeside Railway, were heavily dependent on vacation or seasonal traffic.[86]

Virtually *every* interurban claimed some attraction. Such a facility at trackside or nearby was considered a surefire traffic builder. Even before an electric road turned a wheel promoters frequently planned for such places. In 1901 the instigator of an Indiana interurban told a potential investor, "Two or three pleasure parks and a health resort will be on our line," suggesting that they would stimulate ridership and guarantee financial success. Such facilities might intentionally be placed in a site that would be difficult to reach without taking the cars. The pint-size Albia Interurban in Iowa opened in a remote farm pasture its "Interurban Park," which included a covered pavilion for dancing, roller skating, and other activities. Then there was the mighty Lackawanna & Wyoming Valley in Pennsylvania that became involved with several such attractions, the most enduring being Rocky Glen Park near Moosic, 5 miles south of its Scranton terminal. This destination featured a variety of popular rides, highlighted by its "Million Dollar Coaster," along with food concessions,

The Glens, Cuyahoga Falls, Ohio
On Lines of The Northern Ohio Traction & Light Co.

Meyers Lake, Canton, Ohio
On The Northern Ohio Traction & Light Co. Line

Resembling the Lake Shore Electric, the Northern Ohio Traction & Light Company also served more than a single recreational site. This ca. 1910 picture postcard reveals scenes from its leading destination, Meyers Lake, in Canton, and also its less popular The Glens in Cuyahoga Falls near Akron.

Author's collection.

Since virtually every interurban had some pleasure destination on its line, promotional advertisements were ongoing. In a regional traction guide, published in 1915, the Chicago, Ottawa & Peoria Railway ballyhooed Starved Rock State Park as "Nature's Wonderland of the Middle West."

Author collection.

penny arcade, bathing beach, and a picnic grove that provided tables, stoves, swings, and teeters.[87]

While Rocky Glen Park was a sizable operation, there were interurban amusement parks that were grander, including Kennywood outside Pittsburgh (Pittsburgh Railways), Saltair on the Great Salt Lake (Salt Lake, Garfield & Western) and Redondo Beach (Pacific Electric). One of the largest was Cedar Point, two miles north of Sandusky, Ohio. This park, situated on a spit of land that adjoined Lake Erie, became a good money maker for the Lake Shore Electric. In the 1903 season alone, not long

For decades Cambridge Springs, Pennsylvania, attracted pleasure seekers to its spa facilities. Although on the main line of the Erie Railroad, this town received the interurban cars of the Northwestern Pennsylvania Railway, successor to the Erie Traction Company. Before World War I this Keystone State interurban promoted the Sir Knight's [Templar] Excursion with a special seventy-five cents round trip fare between Erie and Cambridge Springs.

Author's collection.

SIR KNIGHT'S EXCURSION
TO
CAMBRIDGE SPRINGS
VIA
Northwestern Penn'a Railway
Scenic Electric Line

THE INLAND LAKE ROUTE
TO
Erie's Popular Summer Resorts

Cambridge Springs

The famous Spa, internationally known for its beneficial spring waters. The best of hotel accommodations.

75c Round Trip Fare 75c
EACH DAY DURING CONCLAVE
HOURLY SERVICE, Clean, Comfortable Cars

Purchase Tickets At
UNION INTERURBAN STATION
12 North Park Row

For Further Information Address
H. C. ALLEN, Traffic Agent,
508 Downing Building,   ERIE, PA.

after the road opened, it deposited nearly 10,000 fun seekers at the foot of Columbus Avenue in Sandusky, where they transferred to lake steamers for the short trip to the Cedar Point dock. Since the road directly served major population centers, it exploited that brisk pre-automobile passenger traffic. Although the Lake Shore Electric had to battle excursion steamers that plied Lake Erie, still on summer weekends thousands of park-goers filled its cars. The much smaller Toledo, Port Clinton & Lakeside Railway also benefited from these pleasure seekers by having a convenient boat connection at Marblehead to the park.[88]

Cedar Point was (and remains) an impressive place. "Crowds thronged the great bathing beach, boardwalk, lagoons, groves, and promenades. The Opera House imported top talent and multitudes swarmed the convention hall. Cedar Point boasted of having the largest bath house on the Great Lakes, and the biggest dance floor on Lake Erie." Ten bowling alleys and three hotels, including the upscale Breakers, added to its popularity. During the Interurban Era it was arguably the "Atlantic City of the Great Lakes."[89]

A number of interurbans promoted "taking the waters" as a way to enhance passenger revenue. In an era of medical quackery such places had strong appeal. The Santa Clara & San Jose Electric Railway was one road that sought out health seekers. It ballyhooed Alum Rock Park and

Ohio's Lake Shore Electric Railway and most of the larger interurbans served multiple recreational venues. Cedar Point Amusement Park on Lake Erie near Sandusky was the leading one for this road. On September 12, 1930, scores of girls, 4-H club members, leave five special cars, including two two-car trains, at the foot of Columbus Avenue in Sandusky. A Cedar Point steamer awaits to transport them to the park grounds for a day of fun.

Frohman collection, R. B. Hayes Presidential Center.

INTERURBANS IN DAILY LIFE 103

Reservation located on the eastern edge of California's Santa Clara Valley. "At the terminus is found a variety of remarkable mineral springs, including hot and cold sulphur, soda, magnesia, arsenic, iron and other combinations unequaled for their beneficial properties. There are private sulphur, turkish, plunge and tub baths, and the largest public mineral swimming bath in America, containing natural sulphur water and covered with an immense glass roof." Supposedly these waters were "very beneficial for rheumatism, Bright's disease, and other stomach and kidney troubles, malarial afflictions, etc."[90]

Throughout this time park developers, whether interurban or private, made an effort to cater to specific public wants. If alcohol was served, the "cold water" brigade would stay away. Alcohol-free parks, therefore, appeared, designed to eliminate the most objectionable features of places that dispensed beer and occasionally distilled spirits. These entertainment centers would, of course, offer "temperance drinks." The goal then was to create "good order and the absence of everything that very often brings such places into disrepute." Ravinia Park was a place that embraced prohibition and attracted the "better clientele." Opened in 1904 on 30 acres on the south side of Highland Park, Illinois, by its developer, the Chicago & Milwaukee Electric Railroad (after 1916 the North Shore Line), the park featured an athletic field, ballroom, theater, and winter toboggan slide. In time its popular evening operas and other musical events drew a cultured audience from Chicago and neighboring communities, making it different from Rock Glen, Cedar Point, and other parks that were magnets for working-class families and company picnics.[91]

Interurbans, if possible, also took advantage of the surging popularity in community and tent Chautauquas. This religious-turned-cultural phenomenon, which emphasized the arts, education, and entertainment, used both permanent and temporary sites. The original and largest Chautauqua, situated on Lake Chautauqua in western New York, and the smaller Lakeside Chautauqua on Lake Erie in Ohio, depended heavily on the Chautauqua Traction Company and the Toledo, Port Clinton & Lakeside to make their summer seasons successful. These Methodist-affiliated institutions generated strong ticket sales for both interurbans.[92]

Visitors who attended a Chautauqua might be lured into taking a traction outing. This is what a Missouri interurban sought to do for those who came to the Carthage Chautauqua Assembly. A broadside read in part: "All Visitors to the Chautauqua Should take an Excursion Over the lines of the Southwest Missouri Electric Railway. Jasper County is the EMPIRE COUNTY of MISSOURI. Do not miss your present opportunity of acquainting yourself with its scenery, towns, people and resources. Travel by trolley is inexpensive and pleasant."[93]

A version of Chautauquas were church camp grounds, many of which predated intercity traction. One such place that came to rely on an interurban was the Winona Lake Assembly and Summer School Assembly in north central Indiana, an operation that became associated with Billy Sunday, Bob Jones, and other fundamentalist preachers. Yet initially the Winona Interurban Railway, which opened in 1906 between Goshen and Warsaw and four years later added a line to Peru, did not operate on Sunday, potentially its busiest day. Two influential backers of the road, H. J. Heinz, the condiment magnate, and J. M. Studebaker, the wagon and automobile manufacturer, were ardent Sabbatarians, and they ordered that cars run only on weekdays. But the interurban became so unprofitable that it failed to earn interest on its debt, in part because it served a lightly populated territory. If Sunday operations occurred, the financial situation would improve. The average summer attendance at the Assembly reportedly reached a quarter of a million. The major creditor, a Chicago contractor who had accepted $425,000 in Winona first-mortgage bonds, filed suit to force the interurban to start Sunday operations. Fearing receivership, Heinz and Studebaker relented, and in March 1909 cars began to run on a daily basis, being especially busy on the Sabbath. The road's general manager, however, remained so opposed to this change that he resigned. The public, including those who wished to attend the programming at the Assembly, found frequent Sunday service a further attraction.[94]

For those who did not seek a cultural or religious experience, there might be that baseball game. Until the maturing of the National Football League in the 1960s, baseball, led by the American and National Leagues, was the indisputable national pastime. Whether Chicago, Cleveland, Detroit, or some other city or town, interurbans benefited from those who believed that this was the sport to watch, and they commonly dispatched cars loaded with game-day fans. In the South, where electric intercity roads were widely scattered, baseball also drew thousands to minor league, industrial league, semiprofessional, and amateur contests. But unlike regular and special runs elsewhere, these cars were racially segregated. The South's largest interurban, the Piedmont & Northern Railway, which operated two unconnected sections between Charlotte and Gastonia, North Carolina, and Spartanburg, Greenville, Anderson, and Greenwood, South Carolina, adhered to the Jim Crow code. In a 1916 advertisement that appeared in the *Anderson Intelligencer*, "The Electric Way" promoted an Easter excursion from Anderson to Greenville: "Account BASEBALL between Dick Thompson's and J. W. Jordon's Anderson and Greenville Teams. This is Strictly a Colored Train, Plenty Coach Space." Thompson team fans would watch fellow African Americans play at P&N Park located near River Junction in Greenville.[95]

It appears that this special multicar train on the Piedmont & Northern Railway likely on its South Carolina division is for children, perhaps a trip to a park or church event. The lead car is appropriately marked with a white flag, denoting an extra movement.

Krambles-Peterson Archive.

Interurbans, large and small, also took advantage of the public obsession with baseball by sponsoring community and company teams. The Cleveland, Southwestern & Columbus Railway, which consisted of two main lines, one west from Cleveland to Norwalk, Ohio, and the other southwest to Bucyrus, Ohio, exemplifies the former. About 1910 it organized the "Interurban Baseball League," which consisted of teams from six on-line communities. The company promoted games, provided free rides to players, and donated a silver cup to the champion team. The Boise Valley Traction Company, which operated an 83-mile loop route west of Boise to Caldwell and Nampa, Idaho, represents the latter. In 1914 it organized a team popularly known as the "Coin Grabbers." These interurban employees played area opponents at Riverside Park in the capital city. This "Loop-play" attracted hundreds of spectators, many of whom took the cars, including special runs, and the team fostered an esprit de corps among the electric railway workers.[96]

Interurban companies exploited seasonal fairs and similar events. Between January 10 and January 20, 1910, the Pacific Electric transported a reported 77,000 riders to and from the Los Angeles International Air Meet held at the Dominguez Air Field in present-day Carson, California, dispatching cars "direct to main entrance aviation camp every two minutes." This first major air show in the United States, what the *Los Angeles Times* called "one of the greatest public events in the history of the West," was organized by the Curtiss Exhibition Company of New York City, headed by pioneer aviator Glenn H. Curtiss. Not surprisingly the Curtiss firm advertised its services in the *Electric Railway Journal*. "Increase Your

Traffic by Promoting Aviation Meets. Others Are Doing It. Why Not You? AVIATION IS THE SPORT – The greatest drawing card of the day." During the early part of the twentieth century Americans considered "aeroplanes" to be mechanical curiosities and aviators to be daredevils or madmen. These fragile, unstable biplanes thrilled the throngs, and in the case of the Los Angeles extravaganza an estimated 240,000 spectators attended over the course of the eleven-day event.[97]

On some occasions, rather than for pleasure seeking, an interurban provided the means to witness a tragic event. Take what happened following gas explosions at Mines No. 6 and No. 8 at Monongah, West Virginia, on December 6, 1907, that killed more than five hundred coal miners. Since the Fairmont & Clarksburg Electric Railroad served the community, for the next several days thousands of the curious boarded its cars to view the disaster scene.[98]

All interurban travelers, pleasure seekers or not, might encounter problems. Their experiences were usually no different from those who took other forms of public transportation. Pickpockets might work their trade in crowded cars, and there were actual robberies, although rare and much fewer than on steam railroads. And they might be exposed to communicable diseases, including the deadly influenza pandemic that spread rapidly throughout the country toward the end of World War I. Then there were delays caused by broken equipment, floods, and ice, wind, and snow storms. Occasionally passengers became rowdy, especially boys and young men, who might pull down the trolley pole, rock a lightweight car off the tracks, or be engaged in some other type of unacceptable behavior.[99]

WORKERS

Initially construction gangs appeared. After a road opened, there were those employees who labored in the maintenance-of-way or track departments, the electrical and car repair units, and office assignments, ranging from accounting to agency service. The operating sector meant thousands of additional jobs. Most interurbans used two-person passenger crews, motormen and conductors, until the sting of modal competition, which accelerated in the 1920s, led to single car operators.

Who were these workers? The men who did construction, grading, track laying, and related tasks were often immigrant laborers, hailing frequently from eastern and southern Europe or, in the Southwest, especially California, from Mexico. As with steam railroads, farm lads, disliking agrarian life, whether field work or "slopping the hogs," took jobs with these new electric roads. Employees also came from urban areas, feeling the excitement of this transportation technology. Some steam-road

In 1906 workers stop briefly from their toil of grading the right-of-way for Indianapolis, Crawfordsville & Western Railway, later Terre Haute, Indianapolis & Eastern Traction Company, west of Linnsburg, Indiana. Already poles for the overhead wire have been installed.

Crawfordsville District Public Library collection.

employees joined the ranks, thinking perhaps that they could advance more rapidly on an interurban. They might also have been blacklisted for their union activities, including former members of the American Railway Union who had participated in the failed Pullman strike of 1894, or they had run afoul of management for rules violations, particularly "Rule G," which forbade use of intoxicants. There were interurbans that wanted only former steam railroaders as trainmen, "believing that better results could be obtained with experienced railroad men than with men recruited from other occupations." Future interurban employees might already have had streetcar experience. Early in 1901 Casper Jackson, a trolley motorman, contacted the head of a gestating interurban in Indiana to say that he would like to join his company. "Would be glad to have a position as Motor-man on your new Electric Ry. from Newcastle to Knightstown. I am 29, married, graduate from common-school this State, weight 140 lbs. height 5 ft. 7 in. Worked last year, 1900, as Motorman, with New Albany St. Ry. Co. this city. Can give reference. Please file this application till you need me and write me." He penned this postscript: "When do you think your road will be complete? Enclosed find envelope for reply." Some also may have trained informally. Perhaps they rode frequently with a

Although the background of these repairmen and maintenance crew employees of the Northern Ohio Traction & Light Company is unknown, they probably were a mix of local urban and former rural dwellers and surely included a few European immigrants. About 1910 they pose with car No. 41 along with a company official at the Silver Lake Junction carbarns.

Author's collection.

family member or friend who operated a trolley or interurban car, or they may have acquired an instructional book or booklet like *How to Become a Motorman*.[100]

Resembling the job of engineer on a steam locomotive, the motorman's position carried a sense of excitement. With his hand on the controller, and with a modern car running on a good track with ample power, there might be that urge to race a nearby steam passenger train or simply to see how fast the car could go. On the Toledo & Western Railway (T&W) there was "this particular spot [that] was a popular area for the motormen to see how fast they could get the cars moving. Counting the seconds to travel between the mile markers, speeds of 75 to 100 miles per hour were reached routinely." Such lightning speeds may or may not have been achieved. Yet when one T&W motorman bragged that he had managed to obtain the rate of 88 miles per hour, word of this excessive speed reached management, and he was promptly fired. Because of lax discipline on the Washington & Old Dominion, a company official in 1914 complained to the general manager that "a great many employees of this road, who are not competent to operate cars and have never been instructed in this matter are frequently seen running cars, apparently for the fun of it. If it is desired to bring a sense of responsibility among the regular motormen, it will be necessary to stop this playing with equipment by irresponsible

INTERURBANS IN DAILY LIFE   109

The Rochester & Syracuse Railroad employed a large workforce to maintain its double-track, high-speed line between the two largest cities of central Upstate New York. Keeping the property shipshape meant cutting grass at stations and shelters.

Author's collection.

men who are not amendable to discipline and are not criticized for failure to conform to the rules of operation."[101]

Conductors, too, swaggered at times. They were figures of authority and may have been somewhat "puffed up" when wearing their dark-colored, double-breasted uniforms with those shiny brass or nickel-plated buttons. Then there were gleaming metal cap badges that proclaimed CONDUCTOR. These men took pride in being officially in charge of an electric car, and they were not about to play "second fiddle" to motormen.[102]

Even though the streetcar motorman Casper Jackson failed to find employment on that never-to-be built Hoosier State interurban, he surely could find a job on one of that state's burgeoning network of traction roads. If and when he did, he may not always have been happy. Throughout the country interurban roads became notorious for their poor pay; wages might be from 20 to 40 percent less than compensation given to comparable steam railroad employees. Interurban workers, however, generally fared better financially when compared to their counterparts on street railways. Although operating employees had a clean work environment, the experience itself might have its drawbacks. Companies often demanded long days, and perhaps there was no seasonal slack in their work routine. Employees assigned to freight operations, especially with LCL service, found that their days or nights involved lifting and moving a vast array of items: "boxes, cartons, crates, bundles, sacks, shooks, milk cans, baby chicks, egg Pullmans, bread and cake fibre boxes." Then there were the much heavier and bulkier shipments. This was one: "Kitchen coal ranges – waybill called for 1100 pounds – damn crate weighed that much," complained an interurban conductor. And enforcement of the book of rules may not have been too popular with men in train service. Motormen, for example, were not thrilled about the possibility of being penalized for wasting power by starting and stopping too quickly. The Waverly, Sayre & Athens Traction Company went so far as to print a pamphlet, DON'TS for Motormen, that listed 83 "don'ts," ranging from "Don't gossip in and around your car while you are on duty or in uniform" to "Don't fail to run slow around curves and through switches, so that your trolley will not leave the wire." Companies made specific demands on conductors that may not have been well received. The Mesaba Railway in Minnesota required its conductors (at their own expense) to wear a coat jacket fitted with multiple pockets, and it demanded that these pockets be used in this fashion: "Coat: right upper pocket: unfilled ticket and coupon envelopes; right middle pocket: punch; right lower pocket: half dollars; left upper pocket: pass pad; left middle pocket: tickets; left lower pocket: hat checks; inside upper right pocket: timetable, tariff sheet and excess baggage checks; inside upper left pocket: filled pocket envelopes." Most interurban managers did not want their employees to unionize, fearing that their inevitable demands would be financially damaging. However, they objected less to workers who joined locals of the steam railroad brotherhoods for "fraternal benefits." These major and minor issues triggered labor unrest. Strikes and work stoppages among interurban employees, particularly those in train service, were widespread. Usually, though, management emerged victoriously.[103]

Take the case of employees on the Kewaunee & Galva Railway (previously Galesburg & Kewaunee Railway) that connected the western Illinois towns of Kewaunee and Galva. Growing unhappiness with management expressed by motormen, conductors, and fellow workers prompted these men in 1910 to join a national union, the Amalgamated Association of Street and Electric Railway Employees of America (AASEREA). Soon their union spokesmen sought to resolve their differences with management on three issues: wages, permitting motormen on Kewaunee town runs to sit on stools, and free transportation for employees on all lines. With a threatened strike scheduled for May 1, 1910, a company lawyer engaged the Illinois State Board of Arbitration to mediate the dispute. Although employees struck, the arbitration process began almost immediately. Even though a representative from the national union convinced strikers that mediation was the best course of action, the men were suspicious of a state board that they felt was pro-corporation and anti-worker. Amazingly, within a day the board announced its decision. Wages would be increased for both those assigned to streetcar service and those who operated interurbans. Beginning wages for local line employees would be eighteen cents per hour. After six months there would be an increase to twenty cents, in another six months to twenty-one cents, and then in another six months to a maximum of twenty-two cents. Interurban workers would be granted two cents an hour more than their local peers. Others would also receive pay increases: car repairers twenty-two cents per hour, powerhouse engineers twenty-two cents, and electricians twenty-five cents. Overtime pay would amount to one-and-a half times that of regular pay levels. Even though the wage package was hardly magnificent, workers claimed victory. But the board demanded that local motormen stand for most of their runs. Five days after the walkout began, service between Kewaunee and Galva resumed. Labor peace continued, but that would not be the case on many other interurbans.[104]

A more protracted and bitter walkout took place on the San Francisco–Oakland Terminal Railway, known as the Key System, a Bay Area traction road that had characteristics of both an interurban and suburban trolley. On October 1, 1919, a nasty strike began, led by carmen and joined by train crews, members of the AASEREA. Workers demanded significant wage increases and the eight-hour day. When these men initially refused arbitration, management brought in strikebreakers to restore operations. Violence erupted. Six days into the strike the *San Francisco Chronicle* reported that there were "continuous battles between the police and armed non-union men on one side and mobs of strike sympathizers on the other." This confrontation led to five persons being shot, although none sustained life-threatening wounds. It did not take long before additional Key System employees joined the walkout; electrical workers left their jobs at the shops and power houses. With more men "hitting the bricks," labor and management agreed to talk. Their discussions led to an agreement to submit the disputed matters to an arbitration board, and service resumed. But the ultimate decisions of the board did not favor the strikers. It would take years before Key System employees got meaningful wage increases and that coveted eight-hour day.[105]

Not long after World War I, tensions throughout the nation developed between labor and management. Better wages during the war years led to pay cuts in the early 1920s when the country endured the so-called forgotten depression. It would be in 1922 that steam railroads slashed wages and made dramatic work-rule changes that triggered a bitter shopmen's strike, the worst for the industry in the twentieth century. This unrest resulted in extensive physical violence, property destruction, and curtailed train operations.[106]

During this period interurban workers on various lines also experienced pay cuts and went out on strike. This occurred on the Grand Rapids, Grand Haven & Muskegon Railway. In 1921 the company reduced wages for motormen and conductors by five cents an hour. Although these employees did not like the announced pay scale, they grudgingly accepted it. Then in June 1922 they learned that their wages would be reduced by an additional five cents. That was too much for these one hundred or so trainmen; they joined the AASEREA and left their posts. While management tried to maintain passenger service with "scabs," it shortly hammered out an agreement with union representatives. Workers would have a two and one-half cent wage reduction instead of five, and their union would be recognized.[107]

While the snarl level reached dangerous heights on the Key System and other interurbans, there were companies where labor peace reigned. Acts of corporate noblesse oblige may have been the reason. On the Southwest Missouri Electric Railway, for example, management embraced a policy of employee welfare. In 1901 it organized the Electric Railway Club, "an employee benefits association for fraternal and social purposes." Membership was not compulsory, but those who joined paid a dollar admission fee and monthly dues of fifty cents. In case of disability, benefits of a dollar per day were paid for a period of sixty days after the first five days of disability. In 1909 the interurban president personally and board of directors jointly contributed $10,300 to build a three-story concrete Tudor-style clubhouse next to the road's car barn in Webb City for "the enjoyment of the company's employees and their families." This proved to be a sound investment that generated much good will.[108]

What took place on the Southwest Missouri Electric Railway was hardly unique in the annals of interurban labor-management relations, or for that matter in other contemporary American businesses, ranging from mining to textiles. During the era of the World War the Southern New York Power & Railway Company helped to underwrite the costs of a "beautiful club house known by all as Tammany Hall." Located in Hartwick, the road's operational center, this building for employee events contained a large auditorium "designed to serve as a gymnasium with a wide stage for theatrical productions and was the location of many banquets, dances, productions and other social affairs." But the Southern New York provided more than a venue for social functions. Earlier the road introduced an employee self-help organization, the Employees Mutual Benefit Association (EMBA). For a monthly fee of fifty cents members received a weekly sick payment of $7 that, if needed, would last for thirteen weeks. When an EMBA member died, a $100 death benefit went to beneficiaries.

The Southern New York was mostly a road of happy or at least peaceful workers.[109]

In 1911 an interurban executive commented in general terms on company-sponsored worker benefits: "Many companies have established quarters at car barns and terminals which are conveniently fitted up with toilets, wash basins and individual lockers and contain reading rooms with comfortable chairs, and files of the popular periodicals and transportation journals." No one denied that such "perks" advantaged companies. "These provisions give the employee an opportunity to relax during his spare or waiting moments without visiting adjacent saloon or pool rooms and getting into company which is more or less demoralizing. It also enables the company more easily to find its men if needed unexpectedly."[110]

There was no corporate welfare programs for those men who built interurbans. During the construction phase some of the worst disputes, albeit usually of brief duration, occurred. Laborers might not be paid on time; indeed, that was often the bone of contention. When the Oneonta, Cooperstown & Richfield Springs Railway was extending track north from Richfield Springs to Mohawk, New York, in spring 1903, laborers were not compensated for the month of May and were told by the company to stop work until they could be paid. After a week passed without any indication that their wages were forthcoming, a group of angry men blocked the track near Richfield Springs, preventing a southbound car from proceeding. Management responded. It dispatched a car with law enforcement officers to reopen the line, but the determined workers blocked their efforts. Finally after two trouble-filled weeks the interurban raised the money for both back and future wages that allowed construction to continue.[111]

Other factors that explain sporadic labor unrest among construction workers may have come into play. General working conditions might not have been tolerable. Laborers usually lived in temporary tent or shanty camps, which may have lacked an adequate supply of clean water and good sanitation and were perhaps placed in remote locations. Moreover, the local population may have wanted the interurban, but they resented having in their midst what seemed to be hardened laborers who drank, fought, and used bad language (if they spoke English at all). Thefts of poultry, eggs, or something else may have heightened tensions. Even the eating habits of immigrant workers may have been annoying. When the Elmira, Corning & Waverly was under construction, the workers were Italians, having recently arrived from the Old Country. "They had not assumed American ways – nor we Italian – and their kettles of continually boiling spaghetti and macaroni caused some shock to local residents." Fortunately for this Empire State interurban, no unrest occurred along the emerging right-of-way.[112]

Shop and maintenance employees performed a range of tasks. In late 1947 workers on the Chicago, North Shore & Milwaukee Railway paint a recently acquired freight motor from the Oregon Electric Railway, a road that had dieselized shortly after World War II. Unfortunately, this piece of secondhand equipment, which became North Shore Line No. 458, performed poorly.

Author's collection.

Yet some immigrant construction and maintenance workers seemed largely satisfied with poor living conditions and low wages. That appears to have been the case with Mexicans. The political upheaval associated with the decade-long Mexican Revolution, which erupted in 1910, prompted thousands of able-bodied men to seek work north of the border. The Pacific Electric, for one, took advantage of this usually docile and cheap labor for line expansions and track maintenance. These men, who probably at best spoke a broken English, were willing to live in inferior company-owned housing and to accept meager wages. In 1910 the average Pacific Electric laborer made $1.50 for a ten-hour day although the national average stood at between $2.50 and $3.00. Still these Mexican workers lived in a relatively safe environment and earned more than they had back home.[113]

Employees at the upper echelons were much better paid and often better educated, some having had formal professional training. Those who were charged with maintaining operations might have earned engineering degrees from such institutions as the Massachusetts Institute of Technology, Purdue University, and the University of Illinois. At that latter institution the Department of Electrical Engineering offered a degree in electric railway engineering and owned a Jewett-built test car that operated on the Illinois Traction System for "hands-on" instruction. Office workers might be graduates of those small proprietary business colleges that flourished throughout the country, or perhaps had taken business classes in an academy or high school. Top officials themselves might have had a technical, liberal arts, or professional background.[114]

No different from other businesses, there was mobility of personnel. The advertising section of the *Electric Railway Journal* contained numerous "Position Wanted" and "Positions Vacant" listings. This one appeared in the issue of June 10, 1911: "Young Civil Engineer, at present engaged on interurban construction, wishes position in the operating department of an interurban road; experienced on steam, interurban and city lines. Familiar with train-orders, telephones, signals, car equipments and tariffs. References on request." Biographical sketches of ranking interurban officials show that their careers often paralleled their steam railroad counterparts, moving from road to road and climbing up the corporate ladder.[115]

PUBLIC CONCERNS

The Interurban Era coincided with the national progressive reform movement, a great housecleaning escapade that lasted from roughly the late 1890s through the era of World War I. The public, especially vocal consumers, lashed out at what they considered to be acts of corporate arrogance, being troubled by poor or unsafe products and services, tax dodging, and political corruption. Frequently they aired their wrath against the quasi-public corporations, concentrating on gas, water, and traction concerns. Street railways, though, rather than interurbans, took the brunt of their rage. Still, some public unhappiness existed with these intercity electric roads.[116]

Although issues that involved citizens versus interurbans varied widely, a common bone of contention involved street operations. Some urban dwellers disliked the physical appearance of a street railway or interurban and fought efforts to grant franchises that allowed such construction. As early as the 1850s residents of the fashionable Chestnut and Walnut Streets in Philadelphia strenuously objected to a horse-car line in their neighborhoods, believing that streetcars would "invade, vandalize, and vulgarize our choicest streets or public spaces." These individuals were early examples of the NIMBY, or "not in my back yard," syndrome. When the Portsmouth, Kittery & York Electric Railroad was under construction in the late 1890s, there were those in York who fussed about overhead wire and track in their midst. "There is some question of the picturesqueness of a trolley line," commented the *York Courant*. "How will it beautify the streets as well as add to the comfort of the lovers of carriage riding? The beauty of its square, painted poles that line the streets with tiresome regularity; all provided with their square iron fish rod overhanging the tracks, with its copper fish line, connected with pure soldering to that of the next pole. Its occasional turnouts and suspended network of wire; and beneath all the gracefully 'kinked' track, large and awkward frogs and switches." Nevertheless, these Maine NIMBYs failed to prevent this rural trolley from occupying the principal thoroughfares of York and neighboring communities.[117]

Interurbans did operate on thousands of urban streets. Some utilized existing street railways, paying rent to host companies, but others owned their own track. It was also common to have interurban roads provide local city service. The operational details were usually incorporated into the franchise agreements. Some communities were harsh and others lenient in what they required. If the latter occurred, there might have been a "franchise grab" where traction lobbyists, with "their pockets lined with gold," got what they wanted from municipal office holders; bribery of officials was hardly unknown.

Typical of more restrictive requirements was the 1904 agreement imposed by Indianapolis officials on the proposed Indianapolis, New Castle & Winchester Traction Company. In this case the city engineer recommend that "certain stipulations be made as to paving between tracks, reduced fares to city passengers, and payment of a sum per annum for use of the streets." It was also common to require laying specialty T-rail that weighed 60 pounds per yard or heavier, placing tracks as nearly as possible to the center of the street, thus allowing horse-drawn vehicles adequate parking space along commercial thoroughfares, and controlling car speeds and times of operation. Usually the traction company had to maintain all or portions of the street. This became an ongoing concern of residents and the scourge for many an interurban company, especially as their revenues declined.[118]

Occasionally, a physical clash erupted between a community and an interurban over the placement of tracks in streets. Such a happening took place in Waukesha, Wisconsin. The Milwaukee Light & Heat Traction Company (later the Milwaukee Electric Railway & Light Company, or TM) sought a double-track extension into the commercial core of Waukesha so that riders need not board or alight in front of a row of saloons near the Soo Line depot at Broadway and East Avenues. Members of Common Council, however, voted to limit the company to a single line. The consensus was that farmers required ample room to hitch their wagons in front of stores and other businesses. The interurban then took legal action to enjoin the town from enforcing its decision, but soon it decided to take matters in its own hand. In the wee hours of Saturday, July 1, 1899, crews began to install the double track. An observant resident, who knew that construction was illegal, rang the fire bell, and the alarm brought firefighters and other citizens to the track-laying site. Realizing what was happening, anti-traction forces had the fire hoses turned on the workers; the "Railway Riot" was in full swing. Some of the laborers for the TM saw friends in the crowd and decided to switch sides and proceeded to rip up the tracks, but their foreman stopped them. When the company hurriedly rounded up replacement workers, the enraged town fathers ordered that their big steamroller be placed in the path of the track. But they lost. Court intervention permitted completion of the extension down Broadway, leaving angry residents, especially merchants.[119]

Less restrictive requirements appeared. The town fathers of Columbus, Kansas, who may or may not have represented the wishes of their constituents, were so anxious to accommodate the Joplin & Pittsburg Railway that they essentially gave the company carte blanche to use streets as it wished. The major stipulation in the franchise involved only a small annual tax: "The grantee shall pay to the said city on the first day of July, following the completion of said railway, the sum of $25.00, and each succeeding July thereafter the sum of $25.00 in lieu of franchise tax, occupation tax, car tax or any tax of special levy against the grantee or its property until the population of said city shall exceed five thousand, and then ten dollars addition for each one thousand population above said five thousand." No progressive ad valorem taxes employed here.[120]

Residents, whether pro- or anti-interurban, frequently complained about passenger and freight equipment running too fast over streets. Their fears were real. A speeding car could strike pedestrians, frighten horses, or cause other harm. In Holland, Michigan, the local constabulary took action against the crew of a fast-moving car of the Grand Rapids, Holland & Lake Michigan Railway. "Marshall Kamferbeek arrested two of the Interurban motormen Tuesday on the charge of exceeding the speed limit of 14 miles an hour on Thirteenth Street," reported the local newspaper. "He timed the cars and found that despite his warnings the motormen were sending them along at the rate of 17 to 20 miles an hour. The men were arraigned before Justice Van Duren and upon pleading guilty were assessed fines and costs amounting to $7 each."[121]

Municipal ordinance after municipal ordinance controlled interurban freight operations in various ways, all supposedly designed to protect the public and enhance the quality of community life. In the 1930s a traction enthusiast, who rode with the crew of an overnight Indiana Railroad freight, elaborated on these restrictions. "We would drop a car at Muncie and pickup a load at Hartford City, always observant of the six-car consist limit. The towns and cities along the traction lines had ordinances limiting the length of trains." He went on to say, "Some had ordinances against using the air horn; others had rules to the effect that the bulk of the train had to be left outside the town while the crew did their work with the freight motor." Communities might limit the frequency of movements. An ordinance in Detroit restricted freight operations to a single unit on city streets and at intervals of at least two hours apart in each direction. There were also requirements that verged on the silly. One involved disguising a freight car or trailer as a passenger car; citizens objected to what they considered to be visual pollution. In 1910 the Philadelphia & Easton Electric Railway was forced to gussy up its gondola car that hauled coal and fly ash, being fitted with a roof and striped side curtains. In the early 1930s some residents in Milwaukee who lived adjacent to the tracks of the TM fretted about vibrations caused by passing freight trains, objecting to the sensation and fearing structural damage to their homes. These discontents obtained a court order that required the interurban to limit freight space to not more than a quarter of the total area of each car that moved over a city street.[122]

Night freight operations could be irritants as well. Even though interurbans followed the letter of the law, people, especially those staying in downtown apartments and hotels, likely were annoyed by their loading and unloading activities and by any interline transfers of equipment. During these switching activities conductors might blow shrill police whistles to signal motormen rather than use hand lanterns or fusees. The groaning of traction motors and the banging together of couplers added to the irration.[123]

Public safety sparked anti-corporate feelings, leading to regulatory changes and becoming an ongoing concern. All forms of transportation have had their signature disasters. For steamboats it was the explosion of the *Saltana* near Memphis, Tennessee, on April 27, 1865. The ensuing fire and sinking killed about 1,800 of the 2,027 onboard. For Great Lakes steamships it was the SS *Eastland* disaster of July 24, 1915, a boat that capsized in the Chicago River, drowning 844 passengers and crew members. For steam railroads it was the July 9, 1918, head-on crash outside Nashville, Tennessee, of two speeding Nashville, Chattanooga & St. Louis Railway passenger trains. One hundred and one railroaders and riders died, and more sustained serious injuries.[124]

The deadliest wreck on an American interurban took place on Wednesday, September 21, 1910, when two cars running over the Fort Wayne & Wabash Valley Traction Company collided on a sharp curve near Kingsland, Indiana, 18 miles south of Fort Wayne. So terrific was the impact that the crash was heard 4 miles away, causing some people to believe that there had been a dynamite explosion. The collision killed forty-one passengers and badly injured others. Unfortunately the maimed did not receive immediate medical attention; it took about ninety minutes before physicians could reach the mangled cars. "That anything alive could have survived that terrible sweep of splintered wood and twisted steel is a miracle," reported a journalist.[125]

Reasons for the Wabash Valley tragedy were similar to those for other interurban accidents. The primary cause was the failure to heed a train order, which was critical on a single track line that lacked block signaling. There was more. A motorman and a conductor on one of the two cars had

"The Cars Came Together on a Sharp Curve."—News Item.

The tragic interurban accident that occurred on September 21, 1910, near Kingsland, Indiana, made front-page copy for scores of daily newspapers, mostly in the Midwest. An artist for the *Chicago Daily News* created "The Grim Reaper's Sickle," a somewhat scary rendition of the event.

Author's collection.

been hired even though they had had poor work records, and they continued to receive demerits while in company service. An investigation conducted by the Indiana State Board of Railway Commissioners revealed that over a period of time seventy-two motormen and conductors on the Wabash Valley had either quit or been fired for serious rule violations due to drunkenness, insubordination, incompetence, ignoring train orders, or overrunning meeting points. Some employees were poorly trained, having been promoted to interurban assignments directly from street railway service. Moreover, since traction lines commonly strove to keep labor costs to a minimum, they employed "trains crews that are mostly green country boys, hired because they work cheap and do not form unions, and put into important service without proper apprenticeship."[126]

Public reaction to the Kingsland disaster echoed responses to other interurban wrecks: shock, sadness, and anger. Bluffton, home to nineteen victims who had boarded the doomed special northbound car for a fair in Fort Wayne, was a community in distress. Two days after the accident Mayor Frank Smith asked that all businesses and schools close after 1:00 PM that Friday in respect for the victims. Residents complied. "The town is in mourning and business is practically at a standstill," recounted a press report. "There is hardly a home here that is not affected, either through the loss of members of the family or dear friends." The tragedy prompted Fort Wayne resident Mrs. Birdie Tomlinson to write and have published *The Kingsland Wreck*, a piece of sheet music that contained this chorus:

> Alone in this world of sorrow, now I am left to roam,
> No one to comfort or cheer me, only a broken home,
> That's why I'm sad and lonely, loved ones I long to see,
> Voices I now hear calling, calling for you and me.[127]

Pressured by public outrage, the Indiana General Assembly, on the recommendation of Governor Samuel Ralston, a progressive Democrat, replaced the railroad commission with a public service commission that had enhanced powers to supervise rates and services of all steam and electric railroads. In 1913 and 1915 the legislature gave the regulatory body greater authority over railroad safety provisions, including recommendations for installation of signaling devices on major intrastate interurban routes.[128]

Although the Chicago & North Western Railway, a steam road, coined the "Safety First" slogan, interurban companies repeatedly sought to comfort any public fears by proclaiming in their literature and advertisements that they could expect an uneventful trip. "'SAFETY FIRST' is the best phrase in the Interurban vocabulary," proclaimed the Kansas City, Clay County & St. Joseph Railway, "and at *all times* this motto is practiced as well as preached."

Even in the waning years of the Interurban Era safety issues continued to command attention. In November 1936 Boake Carter, a provocative radio commentator, blasted the North Shore and South Shore lines for "the use of WOODEN coaches for traction service." He told his national CBS radio audience: "Inasmuch as the North Shore R.R. Co. equipment is much the same [as the South Shore], and that it was one of the [North Shore] trains that crashed into a standing 'L' train in Chicago a couple of weeks ago [October 21, 1936], splintering a **WOODEN** [L] car to matchwood, killing many and injuring many more – we grew interested in South Shore R.R. operations as we rode along. And after asking many questions and making observations we found that many more passengers were riding these trains because of lowered fares, but added revenue was certainly not coming back in better wages, better working conditions, or better trackage or equipment." His expose continued: "Repeated requests have been made to the receiver of this line [South Shore] for installation of shatter proof glass – for the safety of the traveling public, but the answer has been for 18 months the same: 'The cost would be prohibitive.' Yes, so is the cost prohibitive when it comes to throwing old antiquated WOODEN CARS away and substituting steel ones. And then some time a tragic accident happens – and the cost runs into millions and lives are lost forever."[129]

Boake Carter, however, got his facts garbled. At the time of his broadcast the North Shore Line was in the process of leasing its remaining wood-bodied passenger cars to the Chicago, Aurora & Elgin. However, they returned to the North Shore in 1946, but soon went back to the CA&E, where most continued in service until 1953. The South Shore had only one wooden car, a former passenger unit that handled daily newspaper deliveries, and it would be scrapped in 1941. Still, there continued to be a concern about equipment safety, highlighted by the absence of protective glass or by badly worn wheel flanges.[130]

State legislators and regulators had to deal with public complaints other than matters of safety. Generally, they involved poor service and inadequate station facilities. Although rate controversies popped up, they were less common than those affecting steam railroads because ticket, express, and freight prices were usually lower.

Complaints about inadequate service varied. Some involved cars that operated too slowly. Because of poor power supply, portions of the lines owned by the Eastern Ohio Traction Company (EOT) had reduced speeds. It was reported that a one-horse sleigh beat a car running between Hiram and Chagrin Falls and that Hiram residents mockingly contended that EOT really stood for "Every Other Thursday." Then there were common complaints about equipment capacity, particularly on those roads that served a commuter clientele. An interurban might dispatch a car with too few seats, forcing passengers to stand where "compression is the issue." In 1907 management of the Falls Rivet and Machine Company, which operated plants in the Ohio towns of Kent and Cuyahoga Falls, complained to the state railroad commission about the service provided to its employees by the Northern Ohio Traction & Light Company. Said the official report: "It appears from the evidence that at the time the complaint was filed and during several months prior thereto, the car of defendant company which leaves Kent [for Cuyahoga Falls] at 5:30 PM on Monday, Tuesday, Wednesday, Thursday and Friday daily carried passengers greatly in excess of its seating capacity; that the seat capacity of said car is forty." Commissioners ordered the interurban to deploy cars "with seating capacity of not less than seventy persons, and continue to furnish such car or cars until the average daily number of passengers carried on that run decreases to a point that will justify vacating or modifying this order."[131]

A year after the Northern Ohio Traction & Light case, Ohio regulators dealt with a complaint from citizens of Summerford, a Madison County village of about 350 residents. The concern involved the absence

Residents of the coal-mining town of Hiteman relied on the Albia Interurban Railway for business, shopping, and pleasure after its opening in 1908. The Hiteman terminal was modest yet functional, and in this ca. 1910 photograph a car has just arrived from Albia.

Author's collection.

of a depot on the Ohio Electric Railway line that ran between Columbus and Springfield. The commission spelled out why the community was unhappy. "There is no other railroad passing through or near Summerford, and it appears that it is the most convenient point for residents of quite a large territory surrounding the village to take advantage of defendant's line in reaching London [county seat], Columbus and Springfield and elsewhere as occasion demands." The report noted, "The evidence shows that from forty to fifty people entrain and detrain at Summerford daily to and from various points on defendant's line, many of whom live at other villages or in the surrounding county and drive to said village to take advantage of defendant's line to reach their destination." Since state law stated that "every railroad [including an interurban] is hereby required to furnish reasonably adequate facilities," Summerford got its desired depot. Patrons, whether village residents or not, would have a conveniently located, enclosed, and heated waiting space.[132]

Although disgruntled traction patrons customarily took their grievances about rates to regulatory bodies, alternative actions occurred. In 1909 the recently opened Albia Interurban Railway encountered a boycott from residents of Hiteman, a coal-mining town of approximately 2,500 residents that lacked steam passenger service. They demanded the fare over the 8-mile route to Albia be reduced from twenty cents to fifteen cents and that the round-trip charge be set at thirty cents. The ploy worked. Fearing the economic loss of shoppers who stayed home, Albia merchants successfully pressured management to bring about that fare reduction. In this case there was no need to take the matter to the Iowa Railroad Commission.[133]

As the interurban era came to a close, the number of complaints increased. In the late 1920s residents of greater New Orleans took aim at the sole interurban in Louisiana, the Orleans-Kenner Electric Railway, a small electric road that extended on a private right-of-way along the Mississippi River on the north side of New Orleans to the town of Kenner. This company, which had initially planned to build to Baton Rouge, also provided electric power to customers along its route. In November 1927 the Seventh Ward Civic Improvement League of Jefferson Parish blasted the company for its recent fare hikes and obsolete equipment and also complained about high electricity charges and deposits for electric meters. Little happened. Then the interurban folded in 1930, and the New Orleans Public Service Company took over the power business.[134]

The hundreds of interurban companies cannot be collectively singled out as chronic wrongdoers – they caused fewer concerns than other quasi-public corporations. After all, these electric roads needed public good will, depending heavily on passenger revenues, although as the industry declined, freight traffic gained greater importance for the surviving roads.

It was the exceptional interurban that did not try to keep patrons happy. Companies in newspaper advertisements, public timetables, and other outlets expressed their determination to be good citizens. In fact, their collective outreach was much stronger than their steam road cousins'. "The company desires to provide a service both safe and satisfactory to its patrons – one which will merit their continued patronage," announced the Kendallville, Indiana–based Toledo & Chicago Interurban Railway in a 1912 timetable. "We at all times invite fair minded criticism of our service, and welcome practicable suggestions for its betterment. We desire an opportunity to investigate and adjust any personal difficulty you might have with the Company. In short, as public servants, we wish to operate this road to the satisfaction of the public, and will promptly and cheerfully undertake to correct any mistakes made by the management or employees." In the same vein the Buffalo & Erie Railway told readers of a 1925 schedule: "It is the earnest purpose of this road to furnish this community with the best transportation possible and to welcome any suggestions for improvement from our patrons." And the Cleveland, Southwestern & Columbus Railway adopted this straightforward motto: "The Public Be Pleased." This was a far cry from what William Henry Vanderbilt of the New York Central Lines allegedly proclaimed in the 1880s: "The Public Be Damned!"[135]

Betterments involved various upgrades. Larger roads, with their greater incomes, regularly updated equipment and facilities. For passenger equipment this meant steel replacing wood and improved interior amenities that ranged from electric fans and more comfortable seating to food and beverage services. Although the signature station for the industry was the multistory Interurban Terminal Building and attached train shed in Indianapolis, some companies erected substantial and attractive depots, either initially or as replacement structures. As these were usually of brick construction, especially important if the building contained an electrical substation, the enhanced beauty surely pleased civic boosters and travelers alike. And in order to speed up "limited" cars and to expedite freight and express shipments, some interurbans built "cutoffs" or belt lines to mitigate certain urban choke points.

The Milwaukee Electric Railway & Light Company is one firm that erected eye-appealing structures. Its headquarter offices were located in its stunning four-story Public Service Building that opened in 1905 at the corner of Second and Sycamore (later Michigan) Streets in downtown Milwaukee. But this was more than an office facility. The first floor served as the interurban terminal, with ticket office, two waiting rooms, restrooms, lunch counter, and newsstand and thirteen tracks, three of which were inside and ten outside. Although the company initially utilized ticket offices and waiting-room space in storefront buildings in various communities along its 198-mile system, these facilities were often replaced with substantial stations with off-street trackage. Even at rural stops, the road erected attractive shelters. "These were not the flimsy 'lean-to's' which came to disfigure the countryside on other interurbans," noted a company historian. "The standard TM shelter was a sturdy structure with a peaked roof which had just enough line to give the appearance of a circus tent."[136]

If the industry had not collapsed, other betterments designed to enhance patrons' interurban experiences would surely have occurred. The few remaining roads commonly did just that, usually through equipment upgrades and line relocations. Unlike steam railroads, the mostly short-lived passenger interurbans lacked the luxury of time (and usually resources) to create the best possible physical plant and service.

HOOSIER TRAVELER

PUBLISHED NOW AND THEN FOR PATRONS OF THE INDIANA RAILROAD SYSTEM

Number 1

Modern Electric Cars Introduce New Era in Swift, Comfortable Transportation

THIRTY-FIVE luxurious new electric rail coaches of the Indiana Railroad System mark a new era in electric railway transportation for Hoosierland.

Nothing like these new cars has ever before been offered the traveling public in Indiana. They mark a complete new step—a new conception—in effortless, fast, safe transportation.

Representing an investment of $980,000, these cars were built only after an exhaustive study of tomorrow's needs. Their completeness is the result of long experience in the electric transportation field and of careful research under actual operating conditions.

Every item and appliance used in building these cars was first proved, tested and subjected to strain and question. They are not an untried experiment, but a proved and tested engineering product. Railway officials and operators know exactly how they will perform under every operating condition to which they may be subjected.

Greater Speed

Answering the modern demand for quick, safe transportation, the 35 new deluxe cars have been equipped with specially designed and constructed motors, capable of driving them at speeds of 70 miles an hour and more.

In addition to the powerful motors, a streamlined exterior with rounded contours reduces wind resistance and adds to the speed of the cars. They have a remarkably rapid pickup after a stop and soon reach full speed.

Observation Lounge Available to All Without Extra Charge

SAYING GOODBYE 3

PLEASING PEOPLE

No major American enterprise has risen and fallen so rapidly as did the electric interurban. Although the business was relatively stable through the era of World War I, a noticeable decline set in by the early 1920s and became strikingly apparent later that decade. Toward the end of the 1930s the industry was in shambles. Mileage stood at 15,470 in 1918, dropped to 12,308 in 1928, and plunged to 4,613 by 1938. Although a few electric roads operated into the post–World War II period, mostly as freight carriers and often dieselized, what might be considered the "typical" interurban had already vanished. Interurban historians George Hilton and John Due contend that by 1933 such roads had largely disappeared. The culprits were the automobile, the truck, the "Good Roads" movement, the lack of proper maintenance and betterments, and the Great Depression.[1]

The weakest passenger interurbans failed quickly, and healthier ones had to fight for their survival, usually by employing innovative equipment and services. Some roads acquired lighter, faster, and smoother riding cars, or they upgraded older rolling stock. In 1927 the Northern Ohio Power & Light Company (NOP&L), successor to the Northern Ohio Traction & Light Company, lauded its replacement cars built by the G. C. Kuhlman Car Company. The NOP&L reminded the public in a richly illustrated folder about its "Deluxe Electric Line Chair Car Service." The promotional copy read in part: "Lighted Steps Provide Against Accidents; Individual Plush Seats That Make Riding a Comfort; Rubber Flooring Helps Eliminate Noise and Adds to Sanitation; Wide Windows Give Passengers a Splendid view; [and] Lighting That Makes Reading Easy." That same year the Northern Texas Traction Company distributed a brochure that promoted its *Crimson Limited* between Dallas and Fort Worth. "Today we dedicate to the service of the public the 1927 model 'Crimson Limited.' This train is the result of a country-wide study of the best in

In 1931 the Indiana Railroad System announced in the inaugural issue of its *Hoosier Traveler* the purchase of "thirty-five luxurious new electric rail coaches" built by Pullman and American Car and Foundry. Recently the company's parent, Insull's Midland United Corporation, had consolidated what it believed to be the state's viable traction properties into a single company. As for its new rolling stock, the railroad said, "The investment of such large sums [of money] implies a substantial faith in the future of the territory served by the lines between Fort Wayne, Indianapolis and Louisville." But in 1933 the interurban fell into receivership, and in 1941 its last routes were abandoned.

Author's collection.

intercity passenger transportation. We have aimed to incorporate in it the most advanced ideas, and thereby offer our friends and patrons the last word in travel – comfort, luxury of appointment and general attractiveness, combined with the same safety, speed and dependability which have been watchwords of our service for twenty-five years."[2]

During these twilight years the epitome of better equipment came with formation of the Cincinnati & Lake Erie Railroad (C&LE). This company, which officially opened on January 1, 1930, combined several failing interurbans that once had been part of the expansive Ohio Electric Railway. The core component was the former 216-mile Ohio Electric main line between College Hill (Cincinnati) and Toledo, and it also controlled a connecting 45-mile route between Springfield and Columbus. Its head, Dr. Thomas Conway Jr., an industry consultant and former finance professor at the Wharton School of the University of Pennsylvania, believed that a profitable passenger market existed for a modern interurban that linked not-too-distant urban centers. The C&LE invested in multiple lightweight (steel and aluminum), low-level, high-speed cars built by the Cincinnati Car Company, an order that consisted of ten coaches and ten coach-observation cars. On June 29, 1930, Conway, a public relations wizard, showed off these state-of-the-art cars, known as "Red Devils" because of their Tuscan red paint scheme and speed, to 150 members of the news media from Ohio and Michigan before they entered revenue service. The editor of the *Deshler* [Ohio] *Flag* was one who liked what he saw. "The cars are so constructed that there are no blind partitions to shut off any part of the view. One can look safely too, as both the front and rear ends of the car are completely enclosed with glass of the non-shatterable type, and flying glass and splinters are a thing of the past. Big, comfortable, low sitting individual chairs with individual head rests greet one upon their first entrance to the car." This newspaperman added, "The observation compartment is especially well equipped. Big comfortable overstuffed davenports and chairs make for very comfortable riding. A writing desk is placed on each side of the aisle and two small tables with small table lamps finish out the luxurious fittings."[3]

Always a publicity hound, Conway came up with an imaginative way to increase awareness of the smart rolling stock that would whisk riders in comfort over C&LE rails. On July 7, 1930, the interurban staged a highly publicized race between a rather slow biplane and car No. 126 on the "Moraine Flats" south of Dayton. This "Red Devil" outdistanced its aerial competitor by a car length, racing along upgraded track with a strong power supply and reaching a speed of nearly 100 miles per hour. The stunt worked. Theater audiences may have been startled by what they saw. They surely were intrigued at this air-interurban contest as they watched this Pathé News Weekly film footage, complete with sound, from the vantage

points of several well-placed trackside cameras and one in the plane's cockpit. Others read about this event in newspapers and magazines.⁴

Dr. Conway was not the only showman in the contemporary transportation world. William Appleyard, founder of Vermont Transit Company, attracted Pathé News cameramen to Burlington, Vermont, for the August 4, 1929, celebratory burning of a streetcar to signify the end of local traction and the beginning of replacement bus service.⁵

Less spectacular than the Cincinnati & Lake Erie's race, yet also associated with aviation, was one of the most creative passenger-generating schemes attempted by an interurban. Beginning on May 5, 1928, the Cleveland, Southwestern Railway & Light Company (Southwestern) offered riders at selected stations the convenience of purchasing tickets for connecting flights on Stout Airlines, a recently launched commercial air carrier that linked Cleveland with Detroit and later Chicago. Unfortunately for the failing Southwestern, few travelers opted for a combined interurban-air journey. In addition, the Southwestern briefly sold excursion tickets for a 50-mile sightseeing flight from Cleveland in a Ford

When new in 1930, the "Red Devil" cars, which sped along the Cincinnati & Lake Erie Railroad's lines between the Ohio cities of Cincinnati and Toledo and Springfield and Columbus, looked sharp and elegant. But as this Buckeye State interurban encountered hard times, these Red Devils showed signs of wear. On September 22, 1937, car No. 121 prepares to leave Lafayette Street station in Toledo for Springfield, Dayton, and Cincinnati.

Krambles-Peterson Archive.

Tri-Motor airplane. A more successful interurban-airline joint-ticketing arrangement involved the Chicago, North Shore & Milwaukee Railroad (North Shore Line) and airlines serving Midway Airport in Chicago.[6]

The motor bus became a more common response to modal competition. It might be coordinated interurban and bus service. Actions taken by the Toledo & Indiana Railroad (T&I) represent this strategy. The T&I, which failed in its plan to build a connection between the Ohio and Indiana interurban networks, began in the mid-1920s to provide patrons direct bus service from its end-of-tracks at Bryan, Ohio, to Fort Wayne, Indiana, and other destinations. Later in the 1920s and early 1930s it became increasingly common for surviving interurbans to operate their own bus subsidiaries. Such carriers as the Cedar Rapids & Iowa City, Milwaukee Electric Railway & Light, Pacific Northwest Traction, and Sacramento Northern took to the highways. Bus technologies had advanced greatly, and the network of roads continued to improve.[7]

Notwithstanding efforts by interurban companies to attract and retain riders, their improvements hardly guaranteed success. Even with luxury passenger equipment the Northern Ohio closed its last routes in 1932, and the Northern Texas Traction shut down two years later. Those deluxe "Red Devils" of the C&LE, though, ran along its Springfield to Toledo line until 1937 and disappeared from its remaining trackage in 1939. (Yet several ex-C&LE cars were sold to other interurbans.) Americans, it seems, would rather drive their automobiles, explaining why car ownership, including new and used models, soared during the 1920s. A national survey in 1927 revealed that 55.7 percent of the 27.5 million families in the country owned automobiles and that 2.7 million of these families owned two or more cars. Liberal credit terms bolstered sales, especially for used vehicles, as did cheap gasoline. Automobile owners liked the freedom to take their business, shopping, or pleasure trips whenever they wished, with no need to consult a traction timetable. Americans preferred the privacy of the car – especially true for females who objected to acts of male harassment. And in their automobiles they could carry bags and packages with less effort than they could on any piece of interurban equipment. In the 1929 *Middletown* study of Muncie, Indiana, a community that had excellent interurban service, sociologists Robert and Helen Lynd chronicled this love affair with the "tin lizzie." They found a working-class woman who vowed to "go without food before I'll see us giving up the car," and another woman who said that her family would rather "do without clothes than give up the car." "The Age of Automobility," with more than 20 million cars on the road, had arrived in Hoosierland and the nation.[8]

In a similar fashion, farmers and others who relied on interurbans to transport less-than-carload (LCL) shipments and livestock found that trucks better served their transportation needs. A farmer might buy a

By the 1930s most surviving interurbans either operated their own bus subsidiaries or coordinated with nonaffiliated bus companies to connect with their routes. Although the Cedar Rapids & Iowa City (CRANDIC) owned a bus division, it worked with other bus firms. On May 13, 1939, car No. 109 is stopped in front of its Cedar Rapids station at 4th Avenue SE and 2nd Street.

John F. Humiston photograph, author's collection.

new or used truck or hire the trucking services of a local hauler, perhaps a creamery operator, sale barn owner, or neighbor, and reach his destination on his own schedule and in a timely fashion over all-weather, farm-to-market roads. As automobile registrations spiked so did those of trucks, increasing from 605,496 in 1918 to 3,294,409 in 1928 to 4,475,577 in 1938.⁹

In what turned out to be a largely futile effort to survive, several interurbans offered innovative freight choices, supporting the notion that from adversity often springs innovation. Several examples stand out. In 1928 Lake Shore Electric, Northern Ohio Power & Light, Ohio Public Service, Penn-Ohio, and Toledo & Indiana banded together to launch their jointly owned Electric Railways Freight Company. The firm offered customers joint billing and freight handling, and a subsidiary, Elway Transit, provided customer pickup and delivery. The forwarding firm sold speed and just-in-time delivery, and some shippers gladly paid a premium price for this service. Although a financial flop, the Lake Shore Electric Railway, acting independently, caught the public's eye in September 1930 with introduction of the Bonner Railwagon, a concept invented and refined by Toledo banker and entrepreneur Colonel Joseph Bonner. In 1919 *Popular Science Monthly* lauded Bonner's creativity, explaining that "freight of less than a carload may be moved direct from the point of origin to the destination warehouse or wholesaler without rehandling!" But it took the Lake Shore Electric to embrace it. From several suppliers the company purchased six 10-ton, 18-foot truck trailers that could be hauled on specially

The Great Depression affected one of the Midwest's early interurbans, Stark County Electric Railroad, named for the Ohio county that it served. Although for years this company had been strong financially, it slipped into receivership in 1932. O. K. Ayers, its receiver, made clear when he assumed his duties that the public must patronize the line if low fares and service were to continue. Notwithstanding his pleas, the company quit in 1937. Just as the Stark County Electric struggled during the Great Depression, so did another Buckeye State interurban, Columbus, Delaware & Marion Electric Company. The company's message to the public, which appeared in its public timetable for June 19, 1933, three months after it entered bankruptcy, was direct: "Your Interurban **Use IT**." That fall, however, the road shut down.

Author's collection.

designed 55-foot flatcars and also operate on roads, giving shippers convenient door-to-door service. As it announced: "Co-ordinated highway-railway freight service. Express Freight Service at Truck Rates. Railwagons – semi-trailers that travel equally as well over the highway as over the railway – are now in operation between Cleveland and Toledo over the Lake Shore Electric Railway System. Railwagons are virtually side tracks on wheels." This imaginative offering, however, was short-lived. By

Management of the struggling Lake Shore Electric Railway did what it could to promote its novel Bonner Railwagon service. This included placing an advertisement in its February 22, 1931, public timetable.

Author's collection.

1932 a perfect storm killed the Bonner Railwagon: regulatory problems, unregulated truck competition, and a deepening depression. Two other Midwestern interurbans, North Shore Line and Chicago, South Shore & South Bend Railroad (South Shore Line), fared better with truck trailers-on-flat cars (TOFC). The former introduced "Truck Ferry Service" in 1926, and the latter followed a year later. In fact, the North Shore Line became the first American railroad to provide such service, creating the prototype for the TOFC business. In the mid-1930s two financially strapped steam roads, Chicago Great Western and New York, New Haven & Hartford (New Haven), followed suit by adopting this "piggyback" concept. A more common form of electric railway intermodal service involved various types of containers that could be transferred between rail cars and trucks. The Rockford & Interurban Railway was one such provider. The same year that the North Shore Line began its "Ferry Truck" operations, this struggling Illinois traction road introduced a door-to-door containerized express service. It did so by using special truck trailers and removable freight bodies that could be placed on company flatcars. The waning industry also took pride in the introduction of equipment that revolutionized perishable food shipments, the mechanically cooled refrigerator car. "Reefers" had been used for decades, but they required block ice that needed to be replenished at regular intervals. In 1924 the Northern Ohio Traction & Light introduced a freight car equipped with an insulated body and electrical refrigeration units. The result pleased the Cleveland Provision Company, a wholesaler that distributed meat and dairy products throughout northeastern Ohio. A few years later the North Shore Line provided similar cars to transport dairy products from Wisconsin to the Chicago market.[10]

Whether an interurban embraced innovative practices or not, companies generally provided service as best they could until their last passenger cars and freight motors rolled out of their carbarns or yards. Some roads, including the Indiana Railroad, maintained their equipment and physical plants until the end and dispatched roughly the same number of trains as they or their predecessors had done from the beginning. "A timetable from the THI&E [Terre Haute, Indianapolis & Eastern which became part of the Indiana Railroad in 1931] was really not that changed from its opening to its abandonment."[11]

THE STING OF ABANDONMENT

Innovations and good customer service could not save the vast majority of interurban companies. A human tragedy followed. Most apparent was the loss of jobs for individuals employed by a faltering or abandoned traction road, which was especially painful as the Great Depression deepened and national unemployment soared. By 1933 approximately one in four wage earners in the country, totaling some 13 million workers, lacked a full-time job. That year the gross national product had fallen to half its 1929 level, and newly elected New Deal politicians, led by President Franklin Roosevelt, were just beginning to roll up their sleeves to get Americans back to work. But economic recovery took time, and for many it was not until the era of World War II that they found steady, good-paying jobs.[12]

Abandonments that coincided with hard times made life difficult for out-of-work interurban employees. Often they had hired out during the construction period, mostly prior to 1907. Assuming that many were then in their late teens or twenties, these men were now in their forties, fifties, or older, and not the age that employers would usually want. Even if they had worked twenty years, twenty-five years, or longer, they were not likely

On the eve of the Great Depression the Southern Ohio Public Service Company, originally Columbus, Newark & Zanesville Electric Railway, abandoned operations. On February 15, 1929, a Zanesville photographer recorded the last car to leave his hometown. Likely the motorman (*left*) and conductor (*center*) are about to join the ranks of the unemployed. Perhaps the local druggist (*right*) had sold tickets for the defunct interurban.

Author's collection.

covered by a pension, and there were no government-sponsored social security or railroad retirement programs either.

In a remarkable display of human kindness, Bowman Elder, who in 1933 became the receiver of the bankrupt Indiana Railroad, successor to the properties of the Union Traction Company and manager of additional Hoosier State interurbans, protected jobs by slowing down the liquidation process. But after January 1941 what had once been dubbed the "Renaissance Interurban" was no more. In a 1996 interview with Robert C. Post, publisher of *Railroad History*, transit executive and consultant George Krambles, who joined the Indiana Railroad in 1936 following graduation from the University of Illinois, shared these thoughts about employees during the final years: "They [Elder and his associates] kept going, not with a feeling that they were suddenly going to blossom into a financial success, but mainly because they had several hundred employees, even at the end. There were more than a thousand when I went down there. And these were men who were raising families and sending kids to school on salaries of forty cents an hour. To cut things off would have left most of them with no place to go. So they tried to keep it together to preserve their jobs."[13]

Even with that corporate concern, dismissed or soon-to-be discharged workers of the Indiana Railroad experienced mental anguish. Dick George, a traction enthusiast, recalled that "Shorty" Harrington,

SAYING GOODBYE 135

who worked as senior motorman on the *Dixie Flyer* between Indianapolis and Louisville, told him when service was about to end, "I don't know what I am going to do."[14]

Not all displaced interurban employees joined the ranks of the unemployed or underemployed or took low-paying jobs with New Deal relief agencies, usually the Civil Works Administration or the Works Progress Administration. There were those who possessed transferable skills and were able to move into other positions. One was H. K. Ferrell, an electrician for the Kansas City, Clay County & St. Joseph Railway. Although he found himself jobless when this interurban shut down in March 1933, he quickly found employment maintaining airplane navigation beacons, and later he used his expertise for electrical contractors and builders. And Dick George remembered that a few former Indiana Railroad employees found jobs as drivers or mechanics with an affiliated bus company, Indianapolis & Southeastern, possessing skills that could be used in transportation or other businesses. When the Illinois Terminal Railroad dispatched its last passenger cars, veteran motorman C. J. Kempfer turned to farming near his home in Sparta, Illinois, telling a newspaper reporter, "I've seen the handwriting on the wall. People don't ride this line like they used to."[15]

Investors and owners alike felt the financial sting of abandonment. During those heady years of the industry, many individuals acted on their own or followed the advice of others to buy stock and bonds, whether for speculation, long-term growth, income, or community betterment. Some could afford their financial losses, but others could not, especially during hard times. An Indianapolis lawyer recalled that while settling the estate of a widow of modest means, he found in her bank lockbox "a stack of securities from various electric interurbans. The woman and her family had lost thousands [of dollars]."[16]

While no one likely shed a tear for the major players of those syndicates who, if they had retained their holdings, found their shares worthless, smaller owners probably could not afford the financial collapse, and they suffered. Writer Carl Van Doren, whose father, Dr. C. A. Van Doren, an Urbana, Illinois, dentist, had a substantial financial and emotional stake in the 26-mile Kankakee & Urbana Traction Company, offered this poignant commentary about the final years:

> My father at that time was deeply troubled. The last of his enterprises, an electric road that would run north and south through Urbana, was still in its earliest stage; yet even then he may have had more qualms about it than he was ever to confess. The line would compete not only with the Illinois Central railroad, which it paralleled, but with automobiles and trucks – more numerous every year, and destined in the end to bankrupt this little Kankakee and Urbana Traction Company of which he was president. People put money into it because he asked them to; they believed in him as he believed in it, for his initial faith in it was very strong; and thoughts of these

people were to rob him of much sleep before he died. The railroad never did prosper, though it ran for years; not so far as Kankakee whose name it bore but at least as far as Paxton, which scarcely qualified as a terminal point. We all witnessed the dismal, slow disaster without any power to stop it on our part. It was eventually, in combination with the agricultural depression of the 1920s, to take away from him whatever wealth he had; my mother, by buying a few houses and renting them, and by renting rooms in her own house to university [of Illinois] people, saved them both in so far as they could be saved. All of this was a heart-rending spectacle.[17]

Abandonment of the "University Route" in 1926 surely affected more than its investors, managers, and workers; it probably hurt regular riders. Not everyone in its service territory owned an automobile, and passenger trains on the largely parallel Illinois Central were less convenient and more expensive.

There were losses that may not have received any public attention. Such occurred when the Kansas City, Leavenworth & Western Railway folded in 1938. Shortly after its abandonment an official from the Kansas State School for the Blind in Kansas City, Kansas, a facility located on a campus about a block from the interurban line, lamented the end of hourly cars. When service existed, sightless students frequently relied on the distinct air whistles of the cars to regulate their activities, serving as a sort of striking clock.[18]

Throughout the collapse of the industry, efforts were made to keep some troubled roads running. An example of that "Save the Interurban" spirit involves the final years of the Kansas City, Clay Country & St. Joseph Railway (KCCC&StJ). This superbly engineered and well-built road, which opened late in the construction period, ran between the commercial cores of Kansas City and St. Joseph, a distance of 51 miles, and operated a 28-mile line between Kansas City, Liberty, and Excelsior Springs, Missouri. Although earnings had been good prior to 1929, the onset of the Depression caused a sharp drop in revenues. Forced into receivership, management opted not to reorganize but to abandon. But as the "Excelsior Springs Route" was near death, efforts began to continue operations. In January 1933 a citizens' committee, consisting of merchants and other businessmen, formed to preserve service. To encourage public support, backers emphasized that many residents relied on the interurban for commuting, shopping, and business, and more than one hundred heads of families would be out of work. Abandonment, they believed, would also lower real-estate values. Soon committee members promoted the sale of small lots of stock in a company that they hoped could purchase and operate the interurban. "Therefore let everybody subscribe for as much stock as he possibly can. It is not charity. It is not a gift. It is an investment that will be a definite help to our community, our country, our business and ourselves." But the committee's efforts failed. Observed the *Excelsior*

Employees of the Lake Shore Electric Railway were kept employed as long as possible after abandonment. In summer 1938 they load ties as dismantling occurs on the Cleveland–Lorain section of the main line.

Author's collection.

Springs Daily Standard, "Too many other means of transportation were available that many businessmen here felt that whether the line ran or not would not make any difference."[19]

As one group seeking to save the KCCC&StJ dissolved, another appeared. Although service had been suspended on March 11, 1933, Benjamin M. Achtenberg, a Kansas City lawyer and former St. Joseph resident, spearheaded a group of interested citizens, mostly suburbanites and former employees, to revive the interurban. After studying area freight needs, Achtenberg proposed to make the property profitable by introducing a container service. "Merchandise would be locked in huge boxes and put onto a flat car and later lifted off to a truck for delivery." He also planned to revitalize the passenger sector by replacing the original cars with lightweight ones that required only a single crew member, thus reducing operating expenses. The major obstacle to the revitalization plans centered on raising the $150,000 needed to purchase the road. As in the earlier crusade to save the KCCC&StJ, the Achtenberg organization marketed stock in small amounts, $5 and up, but the money raised proved disappointing. And an effort to secure a $100,000 loan from the federal government's recently created Reconstruction Finance Corporation came to naught.[20]

Nevertheless, backers of what was officially the Kansas City, St. Joseph, Liberty & Excelsior Springs Railway Company petitioned the Missouri Public Service Commission for permission to reopen. Regulators, however, heard strong opposition from representatives of five competing steam roads who argued that the moribund company no longer served a public need. Yet in July 1934 the commission granted the reorganization group a certificate of convenience and necessity. During that same month the bankruptcy judge ordered the property sold so that operations could be resumed.[21]

In August 1934 the bidding took place. To the disappointment of many former patrons and employees, the quest to save the interurban failed; insufficient financial backing was the culprit. The highest bidder was a Chicago salvage firm, and a unit of the Union Pacific Railroad acquired the bus subsidiary Kansas City, Clay County & St. Joseph Auto Transit Company. Then during the fall months of 1934 wrecking crews dismantled the line (which provided temporary employment for a few former employees), and the interurban rolling stock and other assets were either sold or junked. Achtenberg personally managed to purchase the right-of-way for $500, "still hoping that he could eventually restore the line in some form." That, of course, did not happen.[22]

REMEMBRANCES

It is wrong to suggest that a strong wave of nostalgia swept across America as interurbans one after another disappeared, but in many communities people commemorated their demise. Perhaps they boarded the last scheduled car or wrote a local newspaper to share their thoughts, nearly always of sadness. Perhaps, too, reporters covered these events, and maybe their bosses wrote farewell editorials that lamented the end of service or hoped that service might someday return. "As almost everyone does in looking at the past, there is a tendency to look at the electric interurban railways through a lens of nostalgia and perhaps with a little wishful thinking," opined William D. Middleton, a prolific writer of traction books and articles.[23]

Representative of this saying-goodbye phenomenon was "Last Car Passes on Southwestern," a piece from *Cleveland Plain Dealer* reporter Roelif Loveland. On February 28, 1931, he witnessed the final day of service on the Cleveland, Southwestern Railway & Light Company, once the second-largest interurban to radiate out of Cleveland. Abandonment ended what residents called the "Green Line," a name derived from the dark green color and gold lettering that for years distinguished its cars and also its public timetables and promotional literature. Loveland closed his coverage with this short poem:

> Oh, the trucks and the buses and the automobiles
> Have killed the merry rumble of the "Green Line" wheels.
> They grabbed up her fares; on her freight they fed –
> Shed a tear, Old Settler, The "Green Line"'s dead.[24]

Immediately prior to World War II and after, organized groups of traction fans took to the remaining rails. On Sunday, December 15, 1940, members of the Central Electric Railfans' Association have chartered an Indiana Railroad car, which is traveling south from Fort Wayne and about to cross the Erie Railroad at Kingsland, Indiana.

John F. Humeston photograph, author's collection.

Remembrances took still another form with the growth of railroad enthusiast groups. In the 1930s traction lovers might have held membership in the steam road–oriented Railway & Locomotive Historical Society (R&LHS), Rail Enthusiasts, or Railroadians of America, but they also launched their own organizations, either local or regional in scope. Two pioneer electric traction clubs, the Lancaster (Pennsylvania) Railroad & Locomotive Historical Society (unrelated to the R&LHS) and the Interstate Trolley Club, with members in greater New York City and Philadelphia, which appeared in 1933 and 1934, morphed into the much larger National Railway Historical Society (NRHS). The event led to formation of what became the country's premier railfan organization, taking place on August 18, 1935, with a "farewell" excursion over the soon-to-be abandoned Washington, Baltimore & Annapolis Electric Railway. Participants decided that merger and expansion under a new organizational structure made sense.[25]

Yet the NRHS was not the ideal organization for "juice" fans. While members shared much in common with all fanciers of the steel rail, the organization became dominated by those enthusiasts whose first (and often only) love was the iron horse. A desire for separation took place. In August 1934 the Electric Railroaders' Association (ERA), started in New York City; it grew rapidly to about five hundred members and focused on preserving the history of electric railways, both streetcars and interurbans. Later on, traction fans in the Chicago area became acquainted, helped by a 1937 NRHS sponsored trip on the Toledo, Port Clinton &

It is September 8, 1946, and members of the Illini Railroad Club tour the Illinois Terminal facilities in Decatur, Illinois. At this time it was customary for railfans, both electric and steam, to dress up for their sponsored outings, although some appear to be somewhat disheveled.

Author's collection.

Lakeside Railway, a few years before that Buckeye State interurban ended passenger service. Then in May 1938 these enthusiasts sponsored their own outing. Read a notice in *Railroad Magazine*, a nationally distributed publication that allowed personal communications at no charge to fans:

> The Electric Railroaders' Association in Chicago is planning a jaunt over the Gary–Valparaiso line of the Gary Rys., to include 100 miles of travel, part of the trip over right-of-way and track of the defunct New York–Chicago [sic] Air Line, etc. Fare will be about $1; address Frank E. Butts, 1118 East 64th Street, Chicago, Ill., before April first.[26]

Success of the Gary Railways trip resulted in the formation of the Central Electric Railfans' Association (CERA), a group separate from the ERA. Explained George Krambles, a long-time member, in 1940, "In a

On July 26, 1953, the Iowa Chapter of the National Railway Historical Society sponsored an excursion special over the Fort Dodge Line between Fort Dodge and Des Moines using cars Nos. 62, 64, and 74.

George Niles photograph, author's collection.

SAYING GOODBYE 141

conference one sultry afternoon in early July 1938, the name of the new group was selected from twenty proposed and we believe the term *Railfan* was coined to meet our requirements; at least, it was independently arrived at and adopted into the new club's name: *Central Electric Railfans' Association*."[27]

What became the hallmark of the CERA were its publications, becoming more sophisticated over time. Initially its "Bulletins" were printed handouts distributed to members on fan trips in which the history and other facts about the outing were described. A mimeographed schedule was also produced. Eventually these publications, which numbered in the scores, became heavily illustrated, book-length histories of a particular interurban, electric traction in a state or region, or equipment types.

Other traction aficionados and organizations produced a variety of publications. Notable was the appearance in the mid-1940s of *Interurbans News-Letter* and *Interurbans Specials*, founded by California traction buff Ira Swett, later becoming the Interurban Press and the affiliated *Interurban Films*. Another noteworthy event occurred in 1952 when a split of sorts took place within the ranks of the Central Electric Railfans' Association that led to creation of the Chicago-based Electric Railway Historical Society (ERHS). Supporters of this incorporated group, unlike some CERA members, wanted to collect and preserve urban traction cars. "The idea was to use the proceeds from the sale of Bulletins to help finance equipment acquisitions." The Swett and ERHS groups produced low-cost company and equipment histories, containing text and illustrations, and aimed at the enthusiast market. Swett's works, though, were not only historical; they promoted modern electric railway technology. Similarly, several small publishers who liked traction contributed to the growing number of interurban-related titles. Donald Duke was one. Not only did he write manuscripts for his Golden West Books, including *Pacific Electric Railway* and *West Coast Interurbans: California*, but he published the studies of other traction authors. As he said, "Traction books sell pretty well, at least that has been my experience over the years at Golden West." That was an understatement; his multivolume series on the Pacific Electric sold more than 70,000 copies. As with non-traction rail publications, scores of self-publishing authors appeared, usually focusing on a single and perhaps obscure interurban company. Academic presses later joined the parade of publishers, with Indiana University Press and the Johns Hopkins University Press being the most active.[28]

And who were these purchasers? Resembling their cousins the steam/diesel road fans, traction (streetcar and interurban) enthusiasts came from all walks of life. Said a veteran "juice" buff: "Ditch diggers to doctors." Fewer women, though, belonged to traction organizations. The probable reason was that these male members were often single, and "they had alternative life styles." Since the vast majority of railfans are collectors, whether books, hardware, photographs, or timetables, the genre gained a reputation for "wildness." Especially on last runs, traction fans might take home signs, marker lamps, or anything that "wasn't nailed down." When enthusiasts descended on the York Railways in Pennsylvania on February 4, 1939, to commemorate its final day of operations, they "practically stripped the cars of anything that they could pry loose as a souvenir." Then there were the traction characters. One memorable fan was John Alden, a well-to-do bachelor from Washington, D.C. Not only did he wear fancy western attire, including leather pants and boots (no traction uniform or cap for him), that made him stand out on any trip, but he usually carried with him a polished brass air whistle that he named "Susan Louise." Alden would ask an employee of the host interurban or trolley museum or a fellow rider to climb up on the car and temporarily replace the existing whistle with his beloved Susan Louise. Most complied.[29]

It would be the trolley enthusiast, whether in an organized group or not, who joined those who wanted to participate in last runs. It also was not uncommon for individuals who had ridden a road during its opening day to be part of the farewell crowd. These were often sentimental events. Shortly before the March 1, 1946, abandonment of the Salt Lake & Utah Railroad, "The Orem Road" that linked Salt Lake City with Provo and Payson, Utah, Ira Swett wrote these thoughts for his *Interurbans NewsLetter*: "As the time neared for the last car to pull out, old-timers recalled their interesting experiences of the third of a century the Salt Lake & Utah has been operating. Only in memories will traditions and experiences of the Orem Line's golden years remain. All these, the days when snow stopped the trains, when accidents marred the cars' records, when vaudeville actors hired special trains, and much more occupied their thoughts during the final hours of the SL&U."[30]

Sentimental feelings could take a bizarre twist. When the Missouri & Kansas Interurban dispatched its last run on July 9, 1940, between Olathe, Kansas, and Kansas City, Missouri, the observance got out of control. "There was genuine sorrow by many at the passing of the last passenger trolley link between Kansas City and one its suburban areas," wrote Elizabeth Barnes in the *Johnson County Herald*. "And there were those, too, who marked the demise of the electric line with boisterous rioting." By the time the packed car reached downtown Kansas City and had returned to Overland Park, Kansas, "a virtual wreck had been made of its interior. Windows had been smashed by the merrymakers, seats had been torn out, fixtures had been destroyed, and advertising placards had been scattered over the floor." It was a day to remember.[31]

While not a traction fan special, members of the Illini Railroad Club and other enthusiasts join the throng of people who rode the last Chicago, North Shore & Milwaukee *Electroliner* from Chicago to Milwaukee in February 1963. In the crowded tavern-lounge car conductor John Horachek talks with Maurice Klebolt, Illinois Railroad Club president. For the next fifty years Horachek and other former North Shore Line employees relished their annual employee reunions.

John Gruber collection.

The few remaining interurbans that survived into the 1950s attracted considerable attention when they ended their passenger operations, although usually (except for the North Shore Line and the Chicago, Aurora & Elgin) they continued as freight haulers. A quintessential closing took place on March 3, 1956, when the Illinois Terminal (IT) ran its last car between Springfield, Illinois, and St. Louis.[32]

The Illinois Terminal (previously Illinois Traction) was a distinct Midwestern interurban. The company benefited from a strong carload freight business and even during the Great Depression remained an active passenger carrier. Following Pearl Harbor the crush of wartime riders forced the company to buy fifty-six old coaches that had once served the Sixth Avenue Line of the Interborough Rapid Transit in New York City, pressing them into service to transport workers from Springfield and Decatur to two U.S. Army ordnance plants located in the intermediate town of Illiopolis. In 1945 IT wartime traffic peaked at a whopping 8.6 million passengers. Remaining optimistic about the passenger sector, management announced in 1946 that it had placed a nearly $1 million order with St. Louis Car Company for eight lightweight streamlined passenger cars. Then in 1948 and 1949 these "Liners" entered service on the road's St. Louis–Decatur and St. Louis–Peoria routes. A news release read in part: "The three-car units, to be known as the 'Mound City' and the 'Fort Crevecoeur' will accommodate approximately 115 passengers. The two-car unit, which consists of a motorcar and parlor-dining car, will seat 92 persons, and will be named the 'City of Decatur.'" When the equipment went on exhibit in sixteen towns and cities between October 25 and November 1, 1948, nearly 15,000 people came for a look. This capital investment, however, failed to pay off, forcing the company in the mid-1950s to win regulatory permission to withdraw the remaining "Liners."[33]

Word of the last day of long-distance passenger operations on the Illinois Terminal spread rapidly through the fan community and in towns and villages along the 102-mile route. By late February 1956, the Illini Railroad Club, an independent enthusiasts' group dominated by traction buffs and headed by Champaign resident Maurice Klebolt, announced its plans to commemorate the event. Area newspapers reported that anyone could accompany club members, and there was an incentive to do so. An individual who paid $7 would receive a round-trip ticket, box lunch en route, and side trip from St. Louis to the IT shops at Granite City, Illinois.[34]

The big day came on Saturday, March 3, 1956. By 10:00 AM in Springfield about 175 railfans who hailed from throughout the Midwest, and others, too, had boarded the last train for St. Louis, and more followed the route in their automobiles. IT management cooperated with the wishes of the Illini Railroad Club. Rather than using its newest equipment, the three-car train consisted of its oldest cars, dating back to the 1910s. Club members draped black cloth on the lead car and placed a black wreath around its headlight. This trip, though, had an air of informality. The crew allowed fans (and anyone else) to detrain at selected locations and then backed up the cars and sped past the onlookers, who had cameras ready for the cherished "photo run by." Throughout the trip, according to a St. Louis reporter, "townspeople crowded streets around stations just to see the last train go through. Passengers were picked up along the way on the trip to make this sentimental journey." It seemed to be more of "a happy than a sad day" for those who stepped off the cars in St. Louis at 4:15 PM. Later a fast night ride was made back to Springfield.[35]

Five years before the Illinois Terminal ended its Springfield to St. Louis service, a similar event took place on the Milwaukee Rapid Transit & Speedrail Company, successor to the Milwaukee Electric Railway & Light Company. On the evening of Saturday, June 30, 1951, the last scheduled car left the Public Service Terminal in Milwaukee for the run to Waukesha. Differing from the IT trip, this was a somber event, "a day many dreaded." Explained the company's historian: "Riders on that final run spoke little. Most seemed bewildered; those who did speak expressed anger and hurt. A way of transportation that had been a part of their lives for half a century was coming to an end – and there was nothing they could do about it."[36]

It did not take long before much of the interurban infrastructure disappeared. Take rights-of-way and structures. If a traction road had

Although the Cleveland, Southwestern Railway & Light Company, previously Cleveland, Southwestern & Columbus Railway, closed in 1931, some structures remained. By the 1980s the attractive former brick depot and substation at Chippewa-on-the-Lake, located in Medina County, Ohio, had become a storage facility.

Author's photograph.

operated on a private right-of-way (rather than on or alongside a public road), adjoining property owners frequently took possession, either as the result of the original land agreement or by purchase. In some cases this strip became chocked with weeds, brush, and trees. If the former interurban remained in the power distribution business, it might retain (and maintain) the right-of-way for its pole lines. Buildings shared similar fates. Some were outright abandoned, but others found adaptive uses, paralleling what happened to hundreds of unwanted steam road depots. These remnants of the interurban era might become a business, office, or storage facility. Because of the danger of electrical fires traction companies commonly had employed brick construction for their substations, which were often attached to masonry depots that featured the customary interior spaces of office, waiting room, and freight house. This sturdy construction made discarded interurban structures longer lasting then wooden ones, and rarely were they moved offsite as were the frame combination depots of steam railroads.

Not surprisingly, thousands of pieces of rolling stock went to their graves, becoming so much charred wood and scrap metal. Some cars were recycled into cabins, chicken coops, storage sheds, diners, or other commercial businesses. Two former cars of the Cincinnati, Georgetown & Portsmouth Railroad found renewed life in the southern Ohio town of

The Northern Ohio Railway Museum, located in Seville, Ohio, near Chippewa Lake, is a street car and interurban museum that has struggled. It was launched in 1965, and its dedicated volunteers have been slowly collecting and restoring rolling stock and constructing a piece of demonstration track laid on the former Cleveland & Southwestern Railway right-of-way. This 2003 photograph reveals the modest progress that these traction enthusiasts had made.

Author's photograph.

Bethel. The woman who purchased these cars when the interurban folded had them placed on a corner lot in a residential section. Then she hired carpenters, who, according to a student of this interurban, "removed the vestibules, built a roof over the two cars, a porch was built where the vestibules had been and the seats removed and presto, she had a well lighted, one room, grocery store!"[37]

Pieces of operable and restorable rolling stock have also survived, and traction enthusiasts have done much to preserve these relics of a past era. Since the late 1930s a variety of electric railway museums have appeared, ranging from the large and prosperous to the small and struggling. Popular ones include the Connecticut Trolley Museum in East Windsor, Connecticut; Illinois Railroad Museum in Union, Illinois; Interurban Railroad Museum in Plano, Texas; Minnesota Streetcar Museum in Minneapolis, Minnesota; Orange Empire Railroad Museum in Perris, California; Shore Line Trolley Museum in East Haven, Connecticut; and Western Railroad Museum in Suisun City, California.

The oldest and one of the most important is the Seashore Trolley Museum in Kennebunkport, Maine, founded in 1939 by a handful of traction buffs who learned that summer car No. 31 of the Biddeford & Saco Railroad could be acquired because of the company's decision to replace electric traction with motor buses. The price for the open car was $150, and

Traction buffs were not about to allow summer car No. 31 of the Biddleford & Saco River Railroad to be junked. Their efforts in 1939 led to a successful restoration and the founding of the Seashore Trolley Museum in Kennebunkport, Maine.

New England Electric Railway Historical Society collection.

ten individuals contributed $15 each for the purchase. A strip of land, once used by the Atlantic Shore Line interurban, was rented (later purchased), and No. 31 was moved and restoration work begun. "This is the way we started, with one car, with no great thought we were going to have more cars or that we would develop into a museum of any size" explained a founder. More equipment followed, and in 1941 these dedicated enthusiasts established the New England Electric Railway Historical Society, a non-profit educational foundation. The collection grew, and the museum became well known for its diversity of interurban passenger cars, freight motors, and other traction rolling stock.

For some older Americans memories of the interurban era linger. Byron Olsen, a retired railroad attorney from St. Paul, Minnesota, who early in life fell in love with traction in the Twin Cities, recalled the final days of passenger service on the Fort Dodge, Des Moines & Southern Railway (Fort Dodge Line), one of the enduring midwestern interurbans. Toward the end of his junior college career at Grand View College in Des Moines he and two friends took a ride on the this electric road, and more than sixty years later he recounted that experience:

> But in spite of the almost daily reminders of the living Fort Dodge Line, I never got around to taking a ride until the end of my Des Moines college days. I was too wrapped up in college. Finally my second year concluded and I made ready to return home. My next two years of college would be at the

University of Minnesota. I had to stay in Des Moines an extra week to finish up a school bus job I had. So I rounded up a couple of buddies who turned out to be interested in an interurban ride, and away we went!

We departed from the depot by the Capitol for a ride to Boone. The car assigned was one of the lovely Fort Dodge Niles cars, which had undergone a modernization which had revised the roof contour and eliminated the clerestory windows, and had covered the arched stained glass upper side windows. Yet I thought the cars were still imposing and handsome. A sunny yellow livery adopted in the forties brightened the appearance considerably. With dark green trim, it reminded me of my home town Twin Cities Lines streetcars. Our car No. 82 still carried its winter snow plow pilot, and with its locomotive bell and air horns on the roof, presented an appropriately imposing appearance. The conductor was in full railroad uniform, and as I recall, the motorman had proper engineer attire.

We backed east a short way to a loop to turn the car, still near the Capitol Hill. Then we headed first east and then turned north through the Des Moines east side industrial and suburban area. Once out in open country, it was a true interurban experience. There are few transport vehicles that roll as effortlessly as an electric railroad vehicle geared for higher speeds. It was quiet yet fast as only an interurban can be.

The conductor recognized that we were out for a joyride, not a destination. Soon the three of us found ourselves in the forward baggage section at the right front and center forward window positions. Ringside seats, as it were. Like similar Illinois Terminal interurbans, the motorman's cab on a Fort Dodge interurban was located at the left front of the car. It was walled off, but the motorman soon established communication with his baggage room passengers.

There was very little passenger business taken aboard which probably reflected the norm by 1954 any day of the week. A gray haired lady boarded at a gravel road crossing along highway 69 between Boone and Ames. Ames was reached via a branch line and the Fort Dodge main turned northwest toward Boone before we reached Ames.

Our interurban car was clean and comfortable, and rode well. The route was mostly tangent track, neither hilly nor curvy. As we approached Boone, we crossed US highway 30 and the nearby Chicago & North Western Chicago-Omaha main line on a bridge to separate us from the real railroad route. Soon we slowed for entering Boone and proceeded downtown. Boone was approximately midpoint between Des Moines and Fort Dodge, and was the site of a Fort Dodge yard and shop facilities.

By then, we had learned that we could stay aboard car 82 and continue to Fort Dodge. We could still make it back to Des Moines by the end of the day on a returning train. And this would enable us to travel across the Fort Dodge's great scenic attraction, a more than 100 foot high steel trestle crossing a tributary of the nearby Des Moines River. It was a favorite photo stop on railfan excursions.

Unfortunately, I wasn't very adventurous in those days and we declined to take advantage of this opportunity. Only a few days later, spring flooding on the Des Moines River would wash out several parts of the line and flood the powerhouse, just a few miles away at Fraser. Although the Fort Dodge would be rebuilt and operate electric interurban service for a few more months, by the end of September the next year, it would be all over. For years afterwards, I savored this trip and kicked myself for not riding the Fort Dodge more when I had the chance.[38]

Byron Olsen missed his chance to experience the great scenic attraction on the Fort Dodge Line, the high bridge span over the valley of the Des Moines River north of Boone, Iowa. About the time of Olsen's trip, car No. 82, which he also rode, crosses this impressive steel structure.

George Niles photograph, author's collection.

SAYING HELLO AGAIN

Only the South Shore Line survived as a passenger carrier into the twenty-first century. Although "America's Last Interurban" came close to shutting down in 1977, Indiana lawmakers passed legislation in 1978 that enabled four counties through which the line operated – LaPorte, Lake, Porter, and St. Joseph – to form the Northern Indiana Commuter Transportation District (NICTD) and service was saved. In time this public authority made substantial improvements, including new multiple-unit electric cars and nonmotorized trailers, a computer ticketing system, and a line extension to the Michiana Regional Airport in South Bend. Upgrades and improved service continued. In 2015, for example, the South Shore introduced an express train from South Bend to Chicago, covering that distance in less than two hours. Said the NICTD's general manager, "This certainly is the wave of the future for this railroad. It's what people want and it's what the strategic plan can deliver."[39]

While the South Shore Line became a poster child for the contemporary interurban, other urban areas witnessed the preservation and upgrading of their suburban electric operations, including the Shaker Heights Rapid Line of the Greater Cleveland Regional Transit Authority and the Red Arrow Lines of the Southeastern Pennsylvania Transportation Authority. Just as old street cars have been restored and new ones have reappeared in a number of cities, including Atlanta, Memphis, New Orleans, Seattle, and Washington, D.C., interurban-like operations, renamed "light rail," have also been built. The prototype is the "San Diego Trolley" (a misapplied term), which began its operations in 1981 and came to link this southern California metropolis with El Cajon, La Mesa, National City, San Ysidro, and other nearby communities. Significantly the San Diego Trolley (San Diego Metropolitan Transit System), MetroLink (Bi-State Development Agency) in metropolitan St. Louis, Bay Area Rapid Transit (BART) in greater San Francisco, and others share characteristics with urban trolleys – street running, grade crossings, and the like – but they also extend into the countryside and serve additional municipalities. There are instances where light-rail cars operate on former steam and interurban rights-of-way and use other pieces of preexisting railroad infrastructures. These lines might also parallel a former interurban or serve the same transportation corridor.[40]

The reasons are varied for the surging popularity of light rail. As with contemporary streetcars, the public likes light-rail rolling stock because it is clean and attractive. These cars are modern and sleek, featuring plastics, stainless and painted steel, and transparent glass. In these environmentally conscious times most riders appreciate quiet and odor-free equipment that is seemingly "green," leaving few if any "carbon footprints." And everyone enjoys the convenience of frequent service. Light-rail systems, which by 2015 totaled about 1,500 miles, have stimulated urban and suburban redevelopment and growth and have provided commuters and other riders alternatives to congested roadways, automobile wear-and-tear, parking costs, and gyrating fuel prices. Politicians and developers sense opportunities to revitalize neglected urban neighborhoods and the promise of transit-related economic growth, including enhanced real-estate values. Urban boosters like to brag about their light-rail systems, suggesting that they demonstrate that their cities are forward-looking and "big league." "What is past is prologue" may not ring true, but some progressive cities are rebuilding systems that they walked away from decades ago. Unquestionably, the reasons for a gestating second interurban era strikingly resemble why electric intercity traction first appeared. Yet the electric interurban fury that once gripped the county is not likely to return, although for some Americans intercity light-rail lines will be part of their travel experiences.[41]

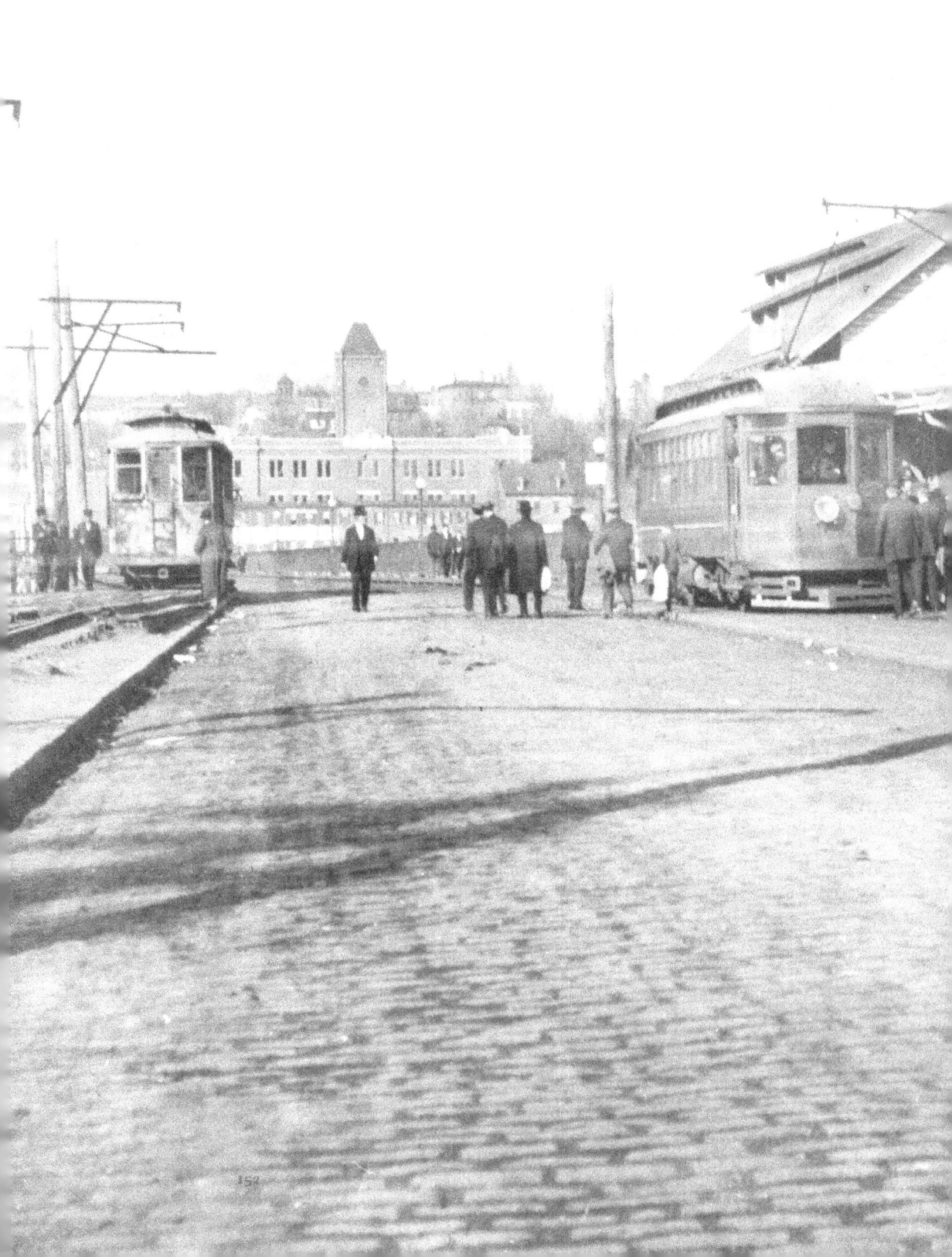

NOTES

1. Enthusiasm

1. William D. Middleton, *The Interurban Era* (Milwaukee: Kalmbach Publishing, 1961), 12; George W. Hilton and John F. Due, *The Electric Interurban Railways in America* (Stanford, Calif.: Stanford University Press, 1960), 4; *Street and Electric Railways, 1902* (Washington, D.C.: Government Printing Office, 1905), 160.

2. William D. Middleton and William D. Middleton III, *Frank Julian Sprague: Electrical Inventor and Engineer* (Bloomington: Indiana University Press, 2009), 65–71; Carl W. Condit, "The Pioneer State of Railroad Electrification," *Transaction of the American Philosophical Society* 67 (November 1977): 3–7; Frederick Rice Jr., "Urbanizing Rural New England," *New England Magazine* 5 (January 1906): 535; Fred H. Whipple, *The Electric Railway* (Detroit, 1889), 111; Michael C. Duffy, *Electric Railways, 1880–1990* (Stevenage, England: Institution of Electric Engineers, 2003), 27.

The "broomstick" moniker is found in a popular Oliver Wendell Holmes poem, "The Broomstick Train; or the Return of the Witches." (*The Complete Poetical Works of Oliver Wendell Holmes* [Boston: Houghton, Mifflin, 1895], 303–304). This lengthy composition closes with these words:

Often you've looked on a rushing train,
But just what moved it was not so plain.
It couldn't be those wires above,
For they could neither pull nor shove;
Where was the motor that made it go?
You couldn't guess, *but now you know.*

Remember my rhymes when you ride again
On the rattling rail by the broomstick train!

3. Middleton and Middleton, *Frank Julian Sprague*, 73–85.

4. "Historical Interurban Roads," *Electric Railway Journal* 34 (October 2, 1909): 593.

5. Hilton and Due, *Electric Interurban Railways*, 53–65; William D. Middleton, *South Shore: The Last Interurban*, rev. 2nd ed. (Bloomington: Indiana University Press, 1999), 15–16; C. Francis Harding and Dressel D. Ewing, *Electric Railway Engineering*, 2nd ed. (New York: McGraw-Hill, 1916), 11, 106–14; "Westinghouse Electric Railway Equipments and Locomotives," *Electric Railway Historical Society Bulletin* 39 (1962): n.p.

6. John F. Due, *The Intercity Electric Railway Industry in Canada* (Toronto: University of Toronto Press, 1966), 16–17; Harre W. Demoro, *Electric Railway Pioneer: Commuting on the Northwestern Pacific, 1903–1941* (Glendale, Calif.: Interurban Press, 1983), 18, 22–23.

7. Hilton and Due, *Electric Interurban Railways*, 70–83; "The Niles Car and Manufacturing Co., 1910," *Electric Railway Historical Society Bulletin* 29 (February 1958): n.p.; Scott D. Trostel, *The Barney and Smith Car Company: Car Builders* (Fletcher, Ohio: Cam-Tech Publishing, 1993), 169–70; "Modern Lightweight Cars," *Electric Railway Historical Society Bulletin* 33 (February 1959).

8. Hilton and Due, *Electric Interurban Railways*, 83–86; "The Story of the Cedar Valley Road Electric Freight Haulage," *Westinghouse Electric Railway Transportation* (Chicago: Central Electric Railfans' Association Bulletin 118 (1979): n.p.

9. Middleton, *South Shore*, 142; Hilton and Due, *Electric Interurbans in America*, 134–36; Herbert H. Harwood Jr. and Robert S. Korach, *The Lake Shore Electric Railway Story* (Bloomington: Indiana University Press, 2000), 261–63.

10. Hilton and Due, *Electric Interurban Railways*, 26; Fred B. Hiatt, "Development of Interurbans in Indiana," *Indiana Magazine of History* 5 (September 1909): 122; Roy M. Bates, *Interurban Railways of Allen County, Indiana* (Fort Wayne, Ind.: Allen County-Fort Wayne Historical Society, 1958), 3; Clifton J. Phillips, *Indiana in Transition: The Emergence of an Industrial Commonwealth, 1880–1920* (Indianapolis: Indiana Historical Bureau and Indiana Historical Society, 1968), 252–53.

11. Hilton and Due, *Electric Interurban Railways*, 8; Edgar Van Deusen, "Electric Interurban Railway Bonds as Investments," *Annals of the American Academy of Political and Social Science* 30 (September 1907): 144.

12. *Electric Railways: Census of Electrical Industries: 1917* (Washington, D.C.: Government Printing Office, 1920), 9; William D. Middleton and George M. Smerk, eds., *Encyclopedia of North American Railroads* (Bloomington:

Indiana University Press, 2007), 420–21; Chuck Crouse, "Amtrak and PennDOT's Keystone Corridor," *Passenger Train Journal* 37 (2014): 16.

13. George H. Gibson, "High-Speed Electric Interurban Railways," *Annual Report of the Board of Regents of the Smithsonian Institution* (Washington, D.C.: Government Printing Office, 1904), 311; *Chicago Daily Tribune*, September 9, 1907; Philip L. Keister, "The Lee County Central Electric Railway," *Bulletin of the Electric Railway Historical Society* 48 (March 1967): 4; interview with Richard (Dick) George, June 9, 2014.

14. Hilton and Due, *Electric Interurban Railways*, 7–8; Kansas City, Clay County and St. Joseph Railway public timetable, ca. 1913; "The Railroad and the Farmer," *Air Line News* 1 (August 1907): 8; *Street Railway Journal* 29 (April 13, 1907): 637–39; Albert Bigelow Paine, "Short Vacations by Trolley," *World's Work* 6 (July 1903): 3678; Clay McShane and Joel A. Tarr, *The Horse in the City: Living Machines in the Nineteenth Century* (Baltimore: Johns Hopkins University Press, 2007), 167; George interview; interview with Norman Carlson, May 29, 2014, hereafter cited as Carlson interview (with date); *Official Railway Guide of New England* (Boston: New England Street Railway Club, 1907), 45; H. Roger Grant, "Electric Traction Promotion in Oklahoma," in Donovan L. Hofsommer, ed., *Railroads in Oklahoma* (Oklahoma City: Oklahoma Historical Society, 1977), 97–98; Middleton, *The Interurban Era*, 32–33; Edmund Henkhe, *Trolley Trips around Scranton and Hazleton* (privately printed, 1915), 1.

Early in the twentieth century the Delaware, Lackawanna & Western Railroad promoted the cleanliness of its steam-powered passenger trains by popularizing the mythical Phoebe Snow. This beautiful young woman, who wore white linen, selected the road because its anthracite-burning locomotives never showered her clothing with soot and ashes:

Says Phoebe Snow
About to go
Upon a trip to Buffalo
"My gown stays white
from morn till night
Upon the Road of Anthracite."

But an employee of the Illinois Traction System thought that Phoebe Snow would surely prefer the cars of his interurban.

After a ride of a day and night
Over the "Road of Anthracite,"
Phoebe Snow and her five sisters
Rubbed and scrubbed till they had blisters.
"Steam roads are out of date," said they,
"We'll have to travel some other way;
Tomorrow to Springfield we will go,
Dressed all in white from head to toe."
So they boarded a car on the I.T.S.,
When Phoebe said, "I must confess,
I've heard of this road its service fine;
It's hard to beat an electric line."
The car was clean, the woodwork bright,
The tipless porter treated them right,
"No dust, no dirt," all of which shows.
There wasn't a speck on the sisters' clothes.
They arrived in Springfield, white and clean,
Not feeling tired, dirty and mean.
Said Phoebe Snow, retiring that night,
"This beats the 'Road of Anthracite'!"

15. *Air Line News* 2 (June 1908): 12; *Long Beach [California] Tribune*, August 17, 1901.

16. George interview; Lake Shore Electric Railway public timetable, September 1909; *Chicago Daily Tribune*, September 4, 1907.

17. Ernest L. Bogart, "Economic and Social Effects of the Interurban Electric Railway in Ohio," *Journal of Political Economy* (December 1906): 588; *New York Times*, December 30, 1901; March 25, 1905; "Progress of Electric Railways," *Brotherhood of Locomotive Firemen's Magazine* 36 (October 1903): 532; H. Roger Grant, "Interurbans!" *Timeline* 3 (April–May 1986): 18.

18. *Chicago Daily Tribune*, September 3, 1907.

19. Max E. Wilcox, *The Cleveland Southwestern and Columbus Railway Story* (privately printed, n.d.), n.p.

20. Donald L. van Reken, *The Interurban Era in Holland, Michigan* (privately printed, 1981), 54.

21. George interview; *La Grange [Indiana] Standard*, August 27, 1908; Hilton and Due, *Electric Interurban Railways*, 124–33; Roy G. Benedict and James R. McFarlane, *Not Only Passengers: How the Electric Railways Carried Freight, Express and Baggage* (Chicago: Central Electric Railfans' Association, 1992).

22. *Chicago Daily Tribune*, September 3, 1907; George M. Smerk, "The Streetcar: Shaper of American Cities," *Traffic Quarterly* 21 (1967): 579; *Street and Electric Railway*, 1902.

23. *Chicago Daily Tribune*, September 4, 1907.

24. *New York Times*, December 30, 1901.

Promoters and operators of interurbans and the public, too, knew that this transportation alternative to steam had some drawbacks. The most obvious was that a snow, ice, sleet, wind or electrical storm could pull down trackside poles and overhead wires or knock out a substation or other sources of electric power. See *Chicago Daily Tribune*, September 4, 1907.

25. *Chicago Daily Tribune*, September 4, 1907.

26. H. Roger Grant, *The Louisville, Cincinnati and Charleston Rail Road: Dreams of Linking North and South* (Bloomington: Indiana University Press, 2014), 1–10; William H. Thompson, *Transportation in Iowa: A Historical Summary* (Ames: Iowa Department of Transportation, 1989), 93; M. Worth Colwell, "The Worst Roads in America," *Outing* 51 (November 1907): 247; Wayne E. Fuller, *RFD: The Changing Face of Rural America* (Bloomington: Indiana University Press, 1964), 178; Albert Bigelow Paine, "Short Vacation by Trolley," *World's Work* 6 (July

1903): 3673; *Red Oak [Iowa] Express*, December 10, 1909.

27. *Hutchinson [Minnesota] Leader*, March 21, 1913; "Interurbans Boost Farm Values," *Electric Traction Weekly* 3 (April 11, 1907): 350; *Liberty [Missouri] Advance*, January 10, 1913; *40 Reasons Why the Iowa Railroad Is Needed and Ought to Be Built* (n.p., ca. 1908).

28. Joseph A. McGowan, "What Interurban Railways Do for the Public," *Proceedings of the American Street and Interurban Railway Association* (New York: American Street and Interurban Railway Association, 1910), 272; Whipple, *The Electric Railway*, 121.

29. George interview; Clive Carter, *Inland Empire Electric Line: Spokane to Coeur d'Alene and the Palouse* (Coeur d'Alene, Id.: Museum of North Idaho, 2009), 8; Mildred M. Walmsley, "The Bygone Electric Interurban Railway System," *Professional Geographer* 17 (May 1965): 2.

30. "Interurban Railway Operation," *Air Line News* 2 (February 1908): 3; McGowan, "What Interurban Railways Do for the Public," 271.

31. H. Roger Grant, *The Corn Belt Route: A History of the Chicago Great Western Railroad Company* (DeKalb: Northern Illinois University Press, 1984), 37; *Pittsburg [Kansas] Headlight*, January 3, 1911.

32. Craig R. Semsel, *Built to Move Millions: Streetcar Building in Ohio* (Bloomington: Indiana University Press, 2008), 11, 14–39.

33. Bogart, "Economic and Social Effects of the Interurban Electric Railway in Ohio," 589–90.

34. *Air Line News* 2 (February 1908): 3–4.

35. *Chicago Sunday Tribune*, September 8, 1907.

36. *Los Angeles Times*, June 22, 1902.

37. Hilton and Due, *Electric Interurban Railways*, 13, 25–41, 186–87; Middleton, *Interurban Era*, 17.

38. H. Roger Grant, "'Interurbans Are the Wave of the Future': Electric Railway Promotion in Texas," *Southwestern Historical Quarterly* 23 (Fall 1980): 30.

39. Ibid., 29, 32.

40. Ibid., 32.

41. Ibid., 35–36; Louis C. Hennick and E. Harper Charlton, *Louisiana: Its Street and Interurban Railways* (privately printed, 1962), 142.

Texans who longed for the "hub" concept might make their dreams come true with intercity buses. In 1929 the secretary of the Jasper Chamber of Commerce made these remarks: "We can depend upon the Bus service for more frequent means of getting about than the [steam] Railroad. [It] is made possible by six Highways radiating out of our little town. Each of these Highways accommodate from one to three Buses each way every day. The Buses assist the surrounding communities in reaching our little city for shopping and other business purposes." He closed with these thoughts: "This manner of service could not be rendered by any other means of transportation." The Interurban Era, of course, had passed. Jack Rhodes, *Intercity Bus Lines of the Southwest* (College Station: Texas A&M University Press, 1988), 38.

42. Grant, "'Interurbans Are the Wave of the Future,'" 36.

At least one circle routing scheme appeared. At an extremely late date–1950–a consulting engineer in Charleston, South Carolina, proposed a state-owned electric road that would utilize the existing Piedmont & Northern interurban between Greenwood and Spartanburg and would build from Greenwood to Columbia via Newberry and from Spartanburg to Columbia via Union, Chester and Winnsboro. No construction ever occurred.

43. Grant, "'Interurbans Are the Wave of the Future,'" 36–37; *Minneapolis Journal*, June 23, 1907.

44. Grant, "'Interurbans Are the Wave of the Future,'" 37–38; *Semi-Weekly Courier-Times* (Tyler, Texas), October 30, 1909.

45. Grant, "'Interurbans Are the Wave of the Future,'" 41–42.

46. H. Roger Grant, "The Unbuilt Interurbans of Nevada," *Nevada Historical Society Quarterly* 24 (Fall 1980): 150–51.

Remarkably, interest in electric traction appeared early on in Nevada. In 1892 the *Street Railway Journal* reported the incorporation of the Reno Electric Railway & Land Company. Capitalized at $200,000, this firm sought to "build and operate electric railroads and street railways and purchase land in Nevada and California."

47. Grant, "The Unbuilt Interurbans in Nevada," 151.

48. Ibid., 151–52.

49. Ibid., 152.

50. Ibid.; Hilton and Due, *Electric Interurban Railways*, 255, 311, 328–29, 379, 405.

51. Grant, "The Unbuilt Interurbans in Nevada," 152.

52. Ibid.

53. Ibid., 154.

54. Ibid.

55. Ibid.

56. H. Roger Grant, *Self-Help in the 1890s Depression* (Ames: Iowa State University Press, 1983), 74–100.

57. Grant, "The Unbuilt Interurbans in Nevada," 155–56.

58. Hilton and Due, *Electric Interurban Railways*, 69–70.

59. William H. Wilson, *The City Beautiful Movement in Kansas City* (Columbia: University of Missouri Press, 1964), 100–19; *Kansas City Star*, January 18, 1918; Edward A. Conrad, *Heartland Traction: The Interurban Lines of Kansas City* (Blue Springs, Mo.: HeartlandRails Publishing, 2006), Appendix D.

60. H. Roger Grant, *Ohio's Railway Age in Postcards* (Akron, Ohio: University of Akron Press, 1996), 26; Hilton and Due, *Electric Interurban Railways*, 13, 42.

61. Grant, "'Interurbans Are the Wave of the Future,'" 45–46.

62. Aaron Isaacs, *Twin Ports by Trolley: The Streetcar Era in Duluth-Superior* (Minneapolis: University of Minnesota Press, 2014), 295.

63. H. Roger Grant, "The Des Moines & Red Oak Railway: A Stillborn Interurban," *Railroad History* 206 (Spring–Summer 2012), 67–69.

64. Ibid., 67, 69.

65. Ibid., 69.

66. Ibid.

67. Ibid., 70.

Even before the proposal for a Red Oak to Des Moines interurban, Burlington officials realized that their Creston–Greenfield–Cumberland branch was merely a lightly traveled appendage, prompting the company to survey a line that would run between Des Moines, Greenfield, Cumberland, and Omaha. *New York Times*, April 12, 1903.

68. Grant, "The Des Moines & Red Oak Railway," 70; Maury Klein, *Union Pacific: The Rebirth, 1894–1969* (New York: Doubleday, 1989), 296–98; *Electric Railway Journal* 39 (June 3, 1911): 94.

69. Grant, "The Des Moines & Red Oak Railway," 70.

70. Ibid.

71. John W. Ripley, "Topeka to Eskridge or Bust!" *Bulletin of the Shawnee County Historical Society* 46 (December 1969): 89.

72. Grant, "The Des Moines & Red Oak Railway," 72.

73. Ibid., 71.

74. Ibid., 72.

75. Ibid., 72–73.

76. Ibid., 73–74.

77. Hilton and Due, *Electric Interurban Railways*, 264, 271, 273.

78. Carlson interview, April 18, 2015.

79. William C. Redfield, *Sketch of the Geographical Rout of a Great Railway* (New York: Carvill, 1830); *American Rail-Road Journal*, March 17, 1832; David Haward Bain, *Empire Express: Building the First Transcontinental Railroad* (New York: Penguin Putnam, 1999), 3–10, 16.

80. *St. Louis Republic*, January 24, 1892; "High Speed Electric Railway between Chicago and St. Louis," *Street Railway Journal* 8 (March 1892): 174.

81. *New York Times*, August 15, 1906; January 26, 1907; *Hastings [Nebraska] Daily Tribune*, December 20, 1907; *Air Line News* 1 (April 1907): 11; Conrad, *Heartland Traction*, Appendix C.

82. *Minneapolis Journal*, June 23, 1907.

The concept of constructing a railroad in sections was not unique to interurbans. There were steam road promoters who embraced the same strategy. A contemporary project to the Minneapolis, Kansas City & Gulf was the Midland Continental Railroad that sought to build between Winnipeg, Manitoba, and the Gulf of Mexico. This road succeeded in completing only its first section, the 72 miles between the North Dakota communities of Wimbledon, Jamestown, and Edgeley.

83. Hilton and Due, *Electric Interurban Railways*, 38–41, 48, 275.

84. *New York Times*, August 21, 1906.

85. Thomas R. Bullard, *Faster Than the Limiteds: The Chicago–New York Electric Air Line Railroad and Its Subsidiaries* (Oak Park, Ill.: privately printed, 1991), 4–5.

86. A. C. Miller, "Chicago–New York Electric Air Line," *Progress Magazine* (September 1909): 53–54.

87. *Prospectus of the Chicago–New York Electric Air Line Railroad* (Chicago: Co-operative Construction Company 1906); Bullard, *Faster Than the Limiteds*, 6.

88. *Chicago Sunday Tribune*, June 8, 1906; *Prospectus of the Chicago–New York Electric Air Line Railroad*.

89. Bullard, *Faster Than the Limiteds*, 8; Thomas R. Bullard and William M. Shapotkin, *Faster Than the Limiteds: The Story of the Chicago–New York Electric Air Line Railroad and Its Transformation into Gary Railways* (Chicago: Central Electric Railfans' Association, 2004), 31.

90. "Construction Work Begun," *Air Line News* 1 (October 1, 1906): 1; *New York Times*, September 2, 1906.

91. Bullard and Shapotkin, *Faster Than the Limiteds*, 33.

92. Ibid.

93. "Graft Has Been Capitalized," *Air Line News* 3 (October 1908): 11; Middleton, *The Interurban Era*, 27; Frederick H. Wood, "The Air Line–The People's Road," *Air Line News*, 3 (November 1908): 9, 13; *The Book of Opportunity* (Chicago: Chicago–New York Electric Air Line Railroad, n.d), i.

94. Blake A. Mapledoram, "750 Miles in 10 Hours!" *Railroad Magazine* 68 (December 1956): 42.

95. *Prospectus of the Chicago–New York Electric Air Line Railroad*.

96. Hilton and Due, *Electric Interurban Railways*, 358; M. W. Savage to Charles F. Wells, May 2, 1911, in possession of author.

97. Richard S. Prosser, *Rails to the North Star: A Minnesota Railroad Atlas* (Minneapolis: University of Minnesota Press, 2007), 47–48; William D. Middleton, "The Strange, Successful Story of the Railroad That Was Once Named for a Race Horse," *Trains* 19 (June 1959): 16–22.

98. "The Kankakee Idea," *Air Line News* 3 (February 1909): 15.

99. Ibid.; Miller, "Chicago–New York Electric Air Line," 56.

100. "Air Line Excursion," *Air Line News* 4 (May 1910): 5.

101. "Good Will and Enthusiasm," *Air Line News* 3 (November 1908): 4; "Holds the Golden Key," *Air Line News* 2 (September 1909): 8.

102. Mapledoram, "750 Miles in 10 Hours!" 43.

103. Ibid., 44.

104. Bullard, *Faster Than the Limiteds*, 19, 23; Bullard and Shapotkin, *Faster Than the Limiteds*, 51.

105. Bullard, *Faster Than the Limiteds*, 32–37.

106. "The Great Steel City of Gary," *Air Line News* 1 (September 1907): 12–13; Miller, "Chicago–New York Air Line," 60; Bullard and Shapotkin, *Faster Than the Limiteds*, 67–68; Raymond A. Mohl and Neil Betten, "The Failure of Industrial City Planning: Gary, Indiana, 1906–1910," *Journal of the American Institute of Planners* 38 (July 1972): 203–204.

107. Bullard and Shapotkin, *Faster Than the Limiteds*, 72–73, 81–83; "To the Stockholders of the Chicago–New York Electric Air Line Railroad Company," July 20, 1911, 1–2.

108. Bullard and Shapotkin, *Faster Than the Limiteds*, 131–38; L. E. Woodward to John O. Armann, August 6, 1915, Gary & Interurban Railroad Company papers, Indiana Historical Society, Indianapolis.

109. Hilton and Due, *Electric Interurban Railways*, 40; Mapledoram, "750 Miles in Ten Hours!" 45.

As for the physical remains of the Air Line, traction enthusiast W. E. Robertson made these comments: "I explored the 'Air Line' area in 1946 and well remember the impressive Coffee Creek fill before it was pulled down to make way for the Indiana Toll Road. I made numerous field trips after 1946 as I was really hooked. Standing atop the Coffee Creek fill was really a treat, one could see for miles around." W. E. Robertson to Arthur D. Dubin, May 21, 1985.

110. Hilton and Due, *Electric Interurban Railways*, 41.

111. Miller, "Chicago–New York Electric Air Line," 62.

112. Herbert H. Harwood Jr., *Blue Ridge Trolley: The Hagerstown and Frederic Railway* (San Marino, Calif.: Golden West Books, 1970), 9.

113. Hilton and Due, *Electric Interurban Railways*, 265–66, 287.

114. Middleton, *South Shore*, 159–74.

115. Hilton and Due, *Electric Interurban Railways*, 270.

116. H. Roger Grant, "Electric Traction Promotion in the South Iowa Coalfields," *Palimpsest* 58 (January–February 1977): 22, 29.

117. Peter Weller and Charles Franzen, *Remembering the Southern Iowa Railway* (privately printed, 1992), 14; *Monroe County News* (Albia, Iowa), September 9, 2014.

118. Weller and Franzen, *Remembering the Southern Iowa Railway*, 8; Edward L. Shutts and H. L. Mann, "History of Traction in Southern Iowa," (privately printed, 1963), 4; *Centerville [Iowa] Iowegian*, April 22, 1910.

119. Weller and Franzen, *Remembering the Southern Iowa Railway*, 15, 17, 19, 22; *Albia [Iowa] Republican*, February 26, 1914; Frank P. Donovan Jr., "The Southern Iowa Railway," *Palimpsest* 35 (May 1954): 206.

120. Shutts and Mann, "History of Traction in Southern Iowa," 8; Weller and Franzen, *Remembering the Southern Iowa Railway*, 19, 23–24.

121. Weller and Franzen, *Remembering the Southern Iowa Railway*, 34, 44–50; interview with Don L. Hofsommer, October 1, 2014; Shutts and Mann, "History of Traction in Southern Iowa," 5, 10–11.

122. Weller and Franzen, *Remembering the Southern Iowa Railway*, 40–41, 66–67.

2. Interurbans in Daily Life

1. Harry Christiansen, *Northern Ohio's Interurbans and Rapid Transit Railways* (privately printed, 1965), 7; George W. Hilton and John F. Due, *The Electric Interurban Railways in America* (Stanford, Calif.: Stanford University Press, 1960), 91; Carl C. Taylor, *Rural Sociology: A Study of Rural Problems* (New York: Harper & Brothers, 1926), 136–37.

2. *Annual Reports of the Department of Agriculture, 1912* (Washington, D.C.: Government Printing Office, 1913), 11–12, 258; Clayton S. Ellsworth, "Theodore Roosevelt's Country Life Commission," *Agricultural History* 34 (October 1960): 155–72.

3. Wayne E. Fuller, *RFD: The Changing Face of Rural America* (Bloomington: Indiana University Press, 1964), 181; *Cincinnati [Ohio] Post*, July 22, 1903; Frederick Rice Jr., "Urbanizing Rural New England," *New England Magazine* 53 (January 1906): 531–32; Harriet C. Brown, *Grandmother Brown's Hundred Years* (Boston: Little, Brown, 1929), 113–14; William A. Kittinger to Albert D. Ogborn, March 19, 1901, Albert D. Ogborn papers, Indiana Historical Society, Indianapolis, hereafter cited as Ogborn papers; Carl Van Doren, *An Illinois Boyhood* (New York: Viking Press, 1939), 54.

4. John Keller, "Findlay's Interurban Golden Spike Ceremony," *Northwest Ohio Quarterly* (July–October 1944): 138.

5. *Cincinnati [Ohio] Commercial Tribune*, January 8, 1903; E. Bryant Phillips, "Interurban Projects in and around Omaha," *Nebraska History* 30 (September 1949): 271.

6. *Coopersville [Michigan] Observer*, April 17, 1896.

7. "Farmers and Inter-Urbans," *Air Line News* 1 (January 1907): 7; *Through the Heart of Ohio: The Columbus, Delaware and Marion Electric Railroad Company* (Columbus, Ohio: Columbus, Delaware & Marion Electric Railroad, 1903); *American Railroad Journal*, November 9, 1850.

8. "Puget Sound Electric Railway," *Interurban News Letter* Special No. 2 (1945): 3.

9. Samuel E. Moffett, "The War on the Locomotive: The Marvelous Development of the Trolley Car System," *McClure's Magazine* 20 (March 1903): 458–59; Ernest L. Bogart, "Economic and Social Effects of the Interurban Electric Railway in Ohio," *Journal of Political Economy* 14 (December 1906): 596.

10. *Chicago Sunday Tribune*, September 8, 1907; interview with Richard (Dick) George, June 12, 2014, hereafter cited as George interview; interview with Norman Carlson, November 10, 2014, hereafter cited as Carlson interview (with date).

11. "The Railroad and the Farmer," *Air Line News* 1 (August 1907): 8–9; *40 Reasons Why the Iowa Railroad Is Needed and Ought to Be Built* (n.p., ca. 1908).

12. Bogart, "Economic and Social Effects of the Interurban Electric Railway in Ohio," 599; *40 Reasons Why the Iowa Railroad Is Needed and Ought to Be Built*.

13. William D. Middleton, *The Interurban Era* (Milwaukee: Kalmbach Publishing, 1961), 32–33.

14. *40 Reasons Why the Iowa Railroad Is Needed and Ought to Be Built*.

15. *State Farmers' Institute Session of 1913–1914* (East Lansing, Michigan: Agricultural College, 1914), 6; Wayne A. De John, "The Interurban Years," *Palimpset* 62 (March–April, 1981): 40.

16. *40 Reasons Why the Iowa Railroad Is Needed and Ought to Be Built*.

17. "The Electric Interurban Railroad," *Yale Review* (August 1904): 191–92.

18. *Street and Electric Railways, 1902, Special Reports* (Washington D.C.: Government Printing Office, 1905), 111; Christiansen, *Northern Ohio's Interurbans and Rapid Transit Railways*, 33.

19. *Chicago Tribune*, September 3, 1907; John W. Brookwalter, "The Farmer's Isolation and the Remedy," *Forum* 12 (September 1891): 54–55.

20. *Chicago Tribune*, September 3, 1907; Carl Hamilton, ed., *Pure Nostalgia: Memories of Early Iowa* (Ames: Iowa State University Press, 1979), 162; Rice, "Urbanizing Rural New England," 534–35; Middleton, *The Interurban Era*, 16.

21. "Interurbans Boost Farm Values," *Electric Traction Weekly* 3 (April 11, 1907): 350; Rice, "Urbanizing Rural New England," 529; Liberty Hyde Bailey, *The Country-Life Movement in the United States* (New York: Macmillan Company, 1913), 13; Hilton and Due, *Electric Interurban Railways*, 117; Robert E. Ireland, *Entering the Auto Age: The Early Automobile in North Carolina, 1900–1930* (Raleigh: North Carolina Department of Cultural Resources, 1990), 64.

22. Lewis Atherton, *Main Street on the Middle Border* (Bloomington: Indiana University Press, 1954),

33–216; Henry M. Sletten, *Growing Up on Bald Hill Creek* (Ames: Iowa State University Press, 1977), ix.

23. H. Roger Grant, *Ohio on the Move: Transportation in the Buckeye State* (Athens: Ohio University Press, 2000), 120.

24. *Street and Electric Railways, 1902, Special Reports*, 114–15.

25. Atherton, *Main Street on the Middle Border*, 260.

26. Bogart, "Economic and Social Effects of the Interurban Electric Railway in Ohio," 589.

27. William L. McGuire and Charles Teed, *The Fruit Belt Route: The Railways of Grand Junction, Colorado, 1890–1935* (Grand Junction, Colo.: National Railway Historical Society, Rio Grande Chapter, 1981), 32.

28. David F. Nestle, *The Leatherstocking Route: A History of the Southern New York Railway Company and Its Predecessors* (privately printed, 1959), 13.

29. Fox & Illinois Union Railroad Company public timetable, January 1, 1915.

30. Ray Morris, "Trolley Competition with the Railroads," *Atlantic Monthly* 93 (1904): 732.

31. Atherton, *Main Street on the Middle Border*, 231.

32. *Trolley Talk*, November 1908, 5; *Chicago Sunday Tribune*, September 8, 1907.

33. *Street and Electric Railways, 1902, Special Reports*, 114–15; H. Roger Grant, *Twilight Rails: The Final Era of Railroad Building in the Midwest* (Minneapolis: University of Minnesota Press, 2010), 6; Walter D. Moody, *Men Who Sell Things* (Chicago: A. C. McClung, 1912), 20; *Chicago Daily Tribune*, September 3, 1907.

34. *Street and Electric Railways, 1902, Special Reports*, 112.

35. *Through the Heart of Ohio*, n.p.

36. Timothy B. Spears, *100 Years on the Road: The Traveling Salesman in American Culture* (New Haven, Conn.: Yale University Press, 1995), 23–49; Frank J. Arkins, "The Merchant Who Cannot Travel," *Harper's Weekly* 37 (April 5, 1893): 18.

37. Loren Reid, *Hurry Home Wednesday: Growing Up in a Small Missouri Town, 1905–1921* (Columbia: University of Missouri Press, 1978), 122.

38. Moody, *Men Who Sell Things*, 89.

39. William J. Petersen, ed., "Kendrick W. Brown Memories of a Commercial Traveler," *Palimpsest* 52 (May 1971): 238; Gerald Carson, *The Old Country Store* (New York: Oxford University Press, 1954), 190; Fred B. Hiatt, "Development of Interurbans in Indiana," *Indiana Magazine of History* 5 (September 1909): 125.

40. "New York to Chicago by Trolley," *Air Line News* 4 (September 1909): 7; Herb Woods, *Galveston-Houston Electric Railway* (Glendale, Calif.: Interurbans, 1959), 17; *Chicago Daily Tribune*, September 4, 1907; Hiatt, "Development of Interurbans in Indiana," 129; Ruth Cavin, *Trolleys: Riding and Remembering the Electric Interurban Railways* (New York: Hawthorn Books, 1976), 46; Moffett, "The War on the Locomotive," 453; *Long Beach [Calif.] Press*, August 12, 1902; J. Annan, "From the Diary of a Traveling Man," *Outlook* 122 (August 20, 1919): 608; Joint Time Table No. 5, Northern Texas Traction Company and Tarrant County Traction Company, n.d.; "Sources of Interurban Patronage," *Electric Railway Journal* 34 (November 6, 1909): 963.

41. *Street Railway Journal*, 30 (March 25, 1905): 538.

42. Hilton and Due, *Electric Interurban Railways*, 109–11, 132–33.

43. Morris, "Trolley Competition with the Railroads," 733–34; "Growth of Leading American Electric Railways: New York State Railways," *Brill Magazine* 13 (May 1927).

44. Hilton and Due, *Electric Interurban Railways*, 100–02; Frank P. Donovan Jr., "Interurbans in Iowa," *Palimpsest* 35 (May 1954): 191; Chicago, North Shore & Milwuakee Railroad public timetable, April 26, 1925, 11; Morris, "Trolley Competition with the Railroads," 735; "Progress of Electric Railways," *Brotherhood of Locomotive Firemen's Magazine* 36 (October 1903): 534–35.

45. H. Roger Grant, *Getting Around: Exploring Transportation History* (Malabar, Fl.: Krieger Publishing, 2003), 129.

46. Forest Crissey, "Experiences of a Salesman," *World's Work* 10 (August 1905): 6570; *Kansas City Star*, January 29, 1918; Spears, *100 Years on the Road*, 193, 221; Don Marquis, "My Memories of the Old-Fashioned Drummer," *American Magazine* 107 (February 1927): 20.

47. Interview with Barbara Lamphier, November 21, 2014.

48. Ernst Gonzenbach, "How Can the Small Road Best Promote Traffic and Increase Its Revenues?" *Proceedings of the American Street and Interurban Railway Association* (New York: Federal Printing, 1908), 49.

49. Guy Morrison Walker, *The Why and How of Interurban Railways* (Chicago: Kenfield Publishing, 1904), 4; William C. Jones and Noel T. Holley, *The Kite Route: Story of the Denver and Interurban Railroad* (Boulder, Colo.: Pruett Publishing, 1986), 20; "Rails to Suburbia: The Strang Line & Overland Park," DVD produced by the Overland Park Historical Society, 2010; "Riverside Lots," Gary & Interurban Railroad papers, Indiana Historical Society, Indianapolis; Charles H. Jones, "The Rehabilitation of the Chicago, South Shore & South Bend Railroad," *Baldwin Locomotives* 8 (July 1929): 60; Carlson interview, May 29, 2014; Albany Southern Railroad Company public timetable, October 12, 1911.

50. William B. Friedricks, *Henry E. Huntington and the Creation of Southern California* (Columbus: Ohio State University Press, 1992), 6–10, 12; Michael F. Sheehan, "Land Speculation in Southern California: The Role of Railroads, Trolley Lines and Autos," *American Journal of Economics and Sociology* 41 (April 1982): 206–207.

51. Christiansen, *Northern Ohio's Interurbans and Rapid Transit Railways*, 15.

52. "Making a Suburb of Chesterton," *Air Line News*, 4 (May 1910): 9; *St. Louis Globe-Democrat*, July 30, 1957; Hilton and Due, *Electric Interurban Railways*, 335–38, 406–13; Herbert H. Harwood Jr., *The New York, Westchester and Boston Railway: J. P. Morgan's Magnificent Mistake* (Bloomington: Indiana University Press, 2008), 68, 98–99; William D. Middleton, *South Shore: The Last Interurban* (Bloomington: Indiana University Press, 1999), 31.

53. Herbert H. Harwood Jr., and Robert S. Korach, *The Lake Shore Electric Story* (Bloomington: Indiana

University Press, 2000), 45, 75; Herbert H. Harwood Jr., *Rails to the Blue Ridge* (Falls Church, Va.: Pioneer America Society, 1969), 21, 25–26, 37.

54. Charles F. Price, "The Promotion of Traffic," *Electric Railway Review* 19 (January 25, 1908): 115; Harwood, *Rails to the Blue Ridge*, 26; Herbert H. Harwood Jr. to author, November 24, 2014.

55. Iain Gately, *Rush Hour: How 500 Million Commuters Survive the Daily Journey to Work* (London: Head of Zeus, 2014); Cavin, *Trolleys*, 45.

56. Davitt McAteer, *Monongah: The Tragic Story of the 1907 Monongah Mine Disaster* (Morgantown: West Virginia University Press, 2014), 227.

57. Edward S. Mason, *The Street Railway in Massachusetts: The Rise and Decline of an Industry* (Cambridge, Mass.: Harvard University Press, 1932), 193.

58. *York [Maine] Current*, September 24, 1897; Bogart, "Economic and Social Effects of the Interurban Electric Railway in Ohio," 600.

59. A. P. Butts, *Walter Willson and His Crooked Creek Railroad* (Webster City, Iowa: Fred Hahne Printing Company, 1976), 112.

60. Hilton and Due, *Electric Interurban Railways*, photograph at end of chapter 4, 116–17; Carlson interview, April 29, 2015.

Norman Carlson made these comments on "Going to School on the North Shore Line":

> Between Evanston and Waukegan along its Shore Line Route the North Shore Line was the "school bus" of its time in the affluent suburbs along the western shore of Lake Michigan. Service was provided to public, private, and parochial schools from the grammar to the university level. There was even a stop on Westleigh Road in Lake Forest named Sacred Heart for the adjacent Sacred Heart Academy, today's Woodland Academy.
>
> Catholic girls travelled to Waukegan while Catholic boys travelled to Wilmette.
>
> Until 1936 there was no high school in Lake Forest. All students rode the trains to Highland Park to attend its public high school. Northwestern University was steps away in Evanston while Lake Forest College a bit of a longer walk. A considerable traffic source was New Trier High School adjacent to the Indian Hill station in Winnetka. There was even a set out track for the school "trippers."
>
> The school business was so great that the North Shore Line converted two former dining cars to school "trippers." All interior bulkheads were removed so the crews could see the entire car in one glance. Seats were obtained from the Chicago Rapid Transit Company to maximize capacity. These two cars' only assignment was transporting school children.
>
> There was a "conspiracy" between the railroad and New Trier to maintain discipline that is best illustrated by this example. One morning a high school girl missed the "school train." So she started walking down the railroad right-of-way toward school. The following train pulled up behind her whereupon the motorman inquired what she was doing. Invited to board the train she was carried to the Indian Hill stop.
>
> Well, here is the "conspiracy." The conductor calls the dispatcher to report the incident. The dispatcher calls the Principal's Office, the office calls the parents and a "counseling session" is held with the student and parents. Problem solved–no muss–no fuss–no attorney's. Things were easily solved in the Interurban Era.

Carlson to author, May 4, 2015.

61. Harwood, *The New York, Westchester and Boston Railway*, 58.

62. *Through the Heart of Ohio*, n.p.; "On the Move Since 1904: The Crandic Route," Special Edition Centennial DVD (Cedar Rapids, Iowa: Alliant Energy Transportation, 2004).

63. Lamphier interview.

64. Butts, *Walter Willson and His Crooked Creek Railroad*, 112.

65. Jones and Holley, *The Kite Route*, 33–34; interview with Linda Graybeal, June 26, 2015.

66. *Bethel College Monthly* (December 1913): 10; Peter J. Wedel, *The Story of Bethel College* (North Newton, Kans.: Bethel College, 1954), 214.

67. Malcolm D. Isely, *Arkansas Valley Interurban* (Los Angeles: Interurbans, 1956), 16; *Bethel College Monthly*, 11.

68. *Bethel College Monthly*, 10–11.

69. G. Wallace Chessman and Wyndham M. Southgate, *Heritage and Promise: Denison, 1831–1981* (Granville, Ohio: Denison University, 1981), 39.

70. William H. Henning, ed., *Detroit: Its Trolleys and Interurbans* (Mt. Clemons, Mich.: Michigan Transit Museum, 1976), 26.

71. Donovan, "Interurbans in Iowa," 200–201; H. Roger Grant and Don L. Hofsommer, *Iowa's Railroads: An Album* (Bloomington: Indiana University Press, 2009), 113, 116.

72. John E. Merriken, *Every Hour–On the Hour: A Chronicle of the Washington, Baltimore and Annapolis Electric Railroad*, Bulletin No. 130 (Chicago: Central Electric Railfans's Association, 1993), 59; North Shore Line public timetable, December 1, 1942.

73. George interview; Robert H. Derrah, *Derrah's Street Railway Guide for Eastern Massachusetts* (Boston: Keeden Press, 1898), 3.

74. George interview; *By Trolley through Western New England* (Boston: Robert H. Derrah, 1904), n.p.; Moffett, "The War on the Locomotive," 460; Beth L. Bailey, *From Front Porch to Back Seat: Courtship in Twentieth-Century America* (Baltimore: Johns Hopkins University Press, 1988); Randall V. Mills, "Early Electric Interurbans in Oregon: Forming the Portland Railway, Light and Power System," *Oregon Historical Quarterly* 44 (March 1943): 94; William Dean Howells, *Confessions of a Summer Colonist (from Literature and Life)*, available at http://www.amazon.com/Confessions-Summer-Colonist-Literature-Life-ebook/dp/B00847AME0/ref=tmm_kin_swatch_0?_encoding=UTF8&qid=1455036771&sr=8-1; "Open Cars and Pleasure Riding," *Electric Railway Journal* 34 (July 10, 1909): 62.

75. Pittsburgh, Harmony, Butler & New Castle and Pittsburgh, Mars

& Butler Railway Company public timetable, November 11, 1917.

76. Albert Bigelow Paine, "Short Vacations by Trolley," *World's Work* 6 (July 1903): 3673, 3676, 3678; Richard Le Gallienne, "Jitneying in the Berkshires," *Harper's Magazine* 139 (September 1919): 540.

77. H. Roger Grant, *Visionary Railroader: Jervis Langdon Jr. and the Transportation Revolution* (Bloomington: Indiana University Press, 2008), 12; Shelden S. King, "The Elmira, Corning & Waverly Railway," *Chemung County Historical Journal* 11 (June 1966): 1488; Harre W. Demoro, *Electric Railway Pioneer: Commuting on the Northwestern Pacific, 1903–1941* (Glendale, Calif.: Interurban Press, 1983), 30.

78. Roy G. Benedict and James R. McFarlane, *Not Only Passengers: How the Electric Railways Carried Freight, Express and Baggage* (Chicago: Central Electric Railfans' Association, 1992), 50; *Electric Railways of Northeastern Ohio* (Chicago: Central Electric Railfans' Association, 1965), 149.

79. Jack Keenan, *The Uncertain Trolley: A History of the Dayton, Springfield and Urbana Electric Railway* (Fletcher, Ohio: Cam-Tech Publishing, 1992), 56; *Along the Line* (Cincinnati, Ohio: Cincinnati, Lawrenceburg & Aurora Street Railroad Company, n.d.), 27.

80. Phillip L. Keister, "The Sterling, Dixon and Eastern Electric Railway," *Electric Railway Historical Society* 40 (March 1963): 6.

81. Clinton W. Lucus, *A Trolley Honeymoon from Delaware to Maine* (New York: M. W. Hazen Company, 1904), 43.

82. H. Roger Grant, ed., "A Traction Odyssey: New York to Chicago in 1909," *Electric Traction Special* (Summer 1979–1980): 7–12; "New York to Chicago by Electric Railway," *Electric Railway Journal* 34 (August 28, 1909): 321–22.

83. "Progress of Utica Trolley Tour," *Electric Railway Journal* 35 (May 21, 1910): 908; "Successful Completion of the Utica Electric Railway Trip," *Electric Railway Journal* 35 (May 28, 1910): 950; *Utica [New York] Observer*, May 24, 1910. A detailed account of the Utica trip is found in Larry Plachno, *The Longest Interurban Charter* (Palo, Ill.: Transportation Trails, 1988).

84. "The Trolley Way into and out of Detroit," Detroit United Lines, Summer 1916.

85. Price, "The Promotion of Traffic," 115.

86. George W. Hilton, *The Toledo, Port Clinton and Lakeside Railway* (Montevallo, Ala.: Montevallo Historical Press, 1997), 12.

87. Douglas V. Shaw, "Making Leisure Pay: Street Railway Owned Amusement Parks in the United States, 1900–1925," *Journal of Cultural Economics* 10 (December 1986): 68–69; Albert D. Ogburn to R. M. Barbour, September 14, 1901, Ogborn papers; *Monroe County [Albia, Iowa] News*, January 7, 1915; James N. J. Henwood and John G. Muncie, *Laurel Line, An Anthracite Region Railway* (Glendale, Calif.: Interurban Press, 1986), 39, 41–42; Dale Samuelson, *American Amusement Park* (St. Paul, Minn.: MBI Publishing, 2001), 53; *McGraw Electric Railway List* (New York: McGraw-Hill Company, 1918), 51, 161.

88. Samuelson, *American Amusement Park*, 50–52; David W. Francis and Diane D. Francis, *Cedar Point: The Queen of American Watering Places* (Canton, Ohio: Daring Books, 1988), 40; Harwood and Korach, *The Lake Shore Electric Story*, 62–65; Hilton, *The Toledo, Port Clinton and Lakeside Railway*, 12.

89. Harry Christiansen, *Lake Shore Electric* (Cleveland: privately printed, 1963), 21; David Francis and Diana Francis, *Cedar Point: The Queen of American Watering Places* (Fairview Park, Ohio: Amusement Park Books, 1995).

90. Charles S. McCaleb, *Tracks, Tires and Wires: Public Transportation in California's Santa Clara Valley* (Glendale, Calif.: Interurban Press, 1981), 64.

91. O. R. Cummins, "A Granite State Interurban," *Electric Railway Historical Society* 12 (March 1954): 8; *Trolley Trips, Great Blue Hill and Reservation, Ponkapoag and Houghton's Ponds* (Boston: Blue Hill Street Railway Company, 1906); George V. Campbell, *North Shore Line Memories* (Northbrook, Ill.: Domus Books 1980), 47.

For years Ravinia Park was the summer home of the Chicago Symphony Orchestra. A guest conductor once stormed off the stage at the sound of a North Shore air horn, declaring emphatically that Ravinia was the only railroad station in the world with a resident symphony orchestra.

92. Theodore Morrison, *Chautauqua: A Center of Education, Religion, and the Arts in America* (Chicago: University of Chicago Press, 1974), 93; Hilton, *The Port Clinton and Lakeside Railway*, 5–12.

93. Edward A. Conrad, *Tri-State Traction: The Interurban Trolleys of Southwest Missouri, Southeast Kansas and Northeast Oklahoma* (Blue Springs, Mo.: Heartland Rails Publishing, 2004), 49.

94. Hilton and Due, *Electric Interurban Railways*, 277; "Winona Interurban Railway Co.," in *American Street Railway Investments* (New York: McGraw Hill, 1909), 92.

95. *Intelligencer* [Anderson, S.C.], April 18, 1916; Thomas T. Fetters and Peter W. Swanson Jr., *Piedmont and Northern: The Great Electric System of the South* (San Marino, Calif.: Golden West Books, 1974), 28.

96. William D. Middleton, "Goodbye to the Interurban," *American Heritage* 17 (April 1966): 69; Nick Casner and Valeri Kiesig, *Trolley: Boise's Valley's Electric Road, 1891–1928* (Boise, Id.: Black Canyon Communications, 2002), 35.

97. D. D. Hatfield, *Dominguez Air Meet: Eleven Days in January* (Inglewood, Calif.: Northrop University Press, 1976), 4; *Electric Railway Journal* 37 (June 10, 1911): 55; *Los Angeles Times*, January 10, 2010.

98. McAteer, *Monongah*, 144.

99. George interview.

100. "Violations of Rules on Interurban Railways," *Electric Railway Journal* 34 (July 17, 1909): 101; Casper Jackson to A. D. Ogborn, February 23, 1901, Ogborn papers; Rodger Burns, *How to Become a Motorman* (n.p., n.d.).

101. Bob Sell and Jim Findlay, *The Teeter and Wobble: Tales of the Toledo and Western RY Co.* (Blissfield, Mich.: Blissfield Advance, 1993), 74; Harwood, *Rails to the Blue Ridge*, 40.

102. George interview.

103. Philip L. Keister, "The Rockford and Interurban Railway," *Electric Railway Journal* 22 (November

1956): 30–31; *Bulletin of the National Railway Historical Society* 49 (1984): n.p.; *Don'ts for Motormen* (Waverly, Sayre & Athens Traction Company, ca. 1910); Russell L. Olson, *The Electric Railways of Minnesota* (Hopkins, Minn.: Minnesota Transportation Museum, 1976), 460.

104. Fred A. Rozum, *Streetcars in Kewanee and Galva, Illinois* (Kewanee, Ill.: Kewanee Historical Society, 2008), 30–31.

105. Harre W. Demoro, *The Key Route: Transbay Commuting by Train and Ferry: Part 1* (Glendale, Calif.: Interurban Press, 1985), 56–58.

106. Colin J. Davis, *Power at Odds: The 1922 National Railroad Shopmen's Strike* (Urbana: University of Illinois Press, 1997).

107. Carl Bajema, Dave Kindem, and Jim Budzynski, *The Lake Line: The Grand Rapids, Grand Haven and Muskegon Railway* (Chicago: Central Electric Railfans' Association, 2010), 188–90.

108. Conrad, *Tri-State Traction*, 32, 52.

109. Nestle, *The Leatherstocking Route*, 10.

110. C. D. Emons, "The Relations of the Electric Railway Company with Its Employes," *Annals of the American Academy of Political and Social Science* 37 (January 1911): 90.

111. Nestle, *The Leatherstocking Route*, 5.

112. King, "The Elmira, Corning & Waverly Railway," 1483.

113. Dennis White, "Pacific Electric Fullerton Branch," *Hot Rail! Newsletter* 5 (Summer 2007): 5.

114. Lawrence A. Brough and James H. Graebner, *From Small Town to Downtown: A History of the Jewett Car Company, 1893–1919* (Bloomington: Indiana University Press, 2004), 27.

115. *Electric Railway Journal* 37 (June 10, 1911): 40.

116. For an analysis of the origins of the progressive movement, especially as a consumer response to acts of corporate arrogance, see David P. Thelen, *The New Citizenship: Origins of Progressivism in Wisconsin, 1885–1900* (Columbia: University of Missouri Press, 1972).

117. Clay McShane and Joel A. Tarr, *The Horse in the City: Living Machines in the Nineteenth Century* (Baltimore: Johns Hopkins University Press, 2007), 71; *York Courant*, June 11, 1897.

118. B. J. T. Jeup to Board of Public Works, City of Indianapolis, October 7, 1904, Ogborn papers.

119. Joseph M. Canfield, *TM: The Milwaukee Electric Railway and Light Company* (Chicago: Central Electric Railfans' Assocation, 1972), 235; Thelen, *The New Citizenship*, 277.

120. Robert Eastman Hickman, "A History of the Joplin & Pittsburg Electric Railway Company, 1890–1929," unpublished M.A. thesis, Kansas State Teachers College at Pittsburg, 1948, 21.

121. Donald L. van Reken, *The Interurban Era in Holland, Michigan* (privately printed, 1981), 56.

122. *Bulletin of the National Railway Historical Society* 49, n.p.; Middleton, *The Interurban Era*, 234.

123. Benedict and McFarlane, *Not Only Passengers*, 64.

124. *Chicago Daily Tribune*, September 22, 1910.

125. *New York Times*, September 23, 1910; Roy M. Bates, *Interurban Railways of Allen County, Indiana* (Fort Wayne, Ind.: Allen County–Fort Wayne Historical Society, 1958), 33; Larry W. Owen, *The Kingsland Wreck: A Memorial* (n.p.: CreateSpace Independent Publishing Platform, 2013).

126. George K. Bradley, *Fort Wayne Valley Trolleys* (Chicago: Central Electric Railfans' Association, 1983), 63–66; Hilton and Due, *Electric Interurban Railways*, 89; *Kansas City [Mo.] Independent*, n.d., in possession of author.

127. Bates, *Interurban Railways of Allen County, Indiana*, 33; *Lincoln [Neb.] Evening News*, September 9, 1910; Larry W. Owen, *The Kingsland Wreck* (privately printed, 2011), 46–47.

128. Clifton J. Phillips, *Indiana in Transition: The Emergence of an Industrial Commonwealth, 1880–1920* (Indianapolis: Indiana Historical Bureau and Indiana Historical Society, 1968), 261.

129. *Chicago Daily Times*, December 15, 1936; *Sarasota [Fl.] Herald-Tribune*, November 17, 1944.

130. Carlson interview, December 15, 2014.

131. *Electric Railways of Northeastern Ohio*, 143; *Report of the Railroad Commission of Ohio for the Year 1907* (Springfield, Ohio: State Printers, 1907), 102–106.

132. *Report of the Railroad Commission of Ohio for the Year 1908* (Springfield, Ohio: State Printer, 1908), 124–29.

133. *Albia [Iowa] Union*, February 5, 1909.

134. Hilton and Due, *Electric Interurban Railways*, 334; Louis C. Hennick and E. Harper Charlton, *Louisiana: Its Street and Interurban Railways* (privately printed, 1962), 116–17, 121.

135. Toledo and Chicago Interurban Railway Co. public timetable, January 21, 1912; Buffalo & Erie Railway Co. public timetable, February 1, 1925; Cleveland, Southwestern & Columbus Ry. public timetable, May 16, 1916; H. Roger Grant, "The Public Be Damned! Setting the Record Straight about a Famous Remark," *Locomotive and Railway Preservation* 62 (November–December 1995): 24–25.

136. Canfield, *TM*, 173, 175–76.

3. Saying Goodbye

1. George W. Hilton and John F. Due, *The Electric Interurban Railway in America* (Stanford, Calif.: Stanford University Press, 1960), 186–87, 208–209.

It can be argued that no device, not even the railroad or the interurban, experienced a more rapid rise than the magnetic telegraph.

2. *A Deluxe Electric Line Chair Car Service* (Akron: Northern Ohio Power & Light Co., 1927); *Crimson Limited Trains* (Dallas: Northern Texas Traction Co., 1927).

3. Hilton and Due, *Electric Interurban Railways*, 266; Jack Keenan, *Cincinnati and Lake Erie Railroad: Ohio's Great Interurban System* (San Marino, Calif.: Golden West Books, 1974), 53–54, 70; *Deshler [Ohio] Flag*, July 3, 1930.

4. Keenan, *Cincinnati and Lake Erie Railroad*, 70–74.

Before creating the Cincinnati & Lake Erie, Dr. Conway had revitalized one of its core units, the Cincinnati, Hamilton & Dayton Railway. At the Moraine, Ohio, shops in June 1927 this master publicist showed off to an audience, estimated at 25,000, the equipment betterments that recently had been made. What everyone remembered was "a mammoth bonfire" when seven obsolete interurban cars were torched. As the cars burned, a band played "There'll Be A Hot Time in the Old Town Tonight." When the flames died down, "floodlights were turned on, revealing the ranks of the new cars, manned by crews in carefully groomed and pressed uniforms. Sirens and bells on the cars created a cacophony while a brilliant fireworks display of rockets and bombs exploded above the crowd, accompanied by a 'flyover' of airplanes from nearby Wright Field." William D. Middleton, "When the 'Red Devil' Went Out in Style," *Timeline* 24 (October–December 2007): 29–30.

5. Sylvia Nichols Allen, *The People Will Be Served: A History of the Vermont Transit Bus Company* (privately printed, 2011), 28–29.

6. Jeffrey R. Brashares, *The Southwestern Lines* (Cleveland: Ohio Interurban Memories, 1982), 76; Hilton and Due, *Electric Interurban Railways*, 336.

7. Toledo & Indiana Railroad public timetables, March 14, 1926, April 3, 1927, June 8, 1930; Burton B. Crandall, *The Growth of the Intercity Bus Industry* (Syracuse, N.Y.: Syracuse College of Business Administration, 1954), 24, 29; Albert E. Meier and John P. Hoschek, *Over the Road: A History of Intercity Bus Transportation in the United States* (Upper Montclair, N.J.: Motor Bus Society, 1975), 21; Hilton and Due, *Electric Interurbans Railways*, 177, 231–33.

8. Hilton and Due, *Electric Interurbans Railways*, 266, 273, 377; James J. Flink, *The Automobile Age* (Cambridge, Mass.: MIT Press, 1988), 132; Robert S. Lynd and Helen Merrell Lynd, *Middletown: A Study in American Culture* (New York: Harcourt, Brace, 1929), 255–56.

9. U. S. Bureau of the Census, *Historical Statistics of the United States, Colonial Times to 1957* (Washington, D.C.: Government Printing Office, 1960), 462.

If an abandoned interurban had handled carload freight in standard, interline cars, a steam railroad might acquire the profitable remnants, or a nonelectrified short-line might take over operations.

10. Hilton and Due, *Electric Interurban Railways*, 130, 134–35; Joseph Brinker, "Making Freight Trains Do More Work," *Popular Science Monthly* 95 (September 1919): 20; Herbert H. Harwood Jr. and Robert S. Korach, *The Lake Shore Electric Railway Story* (Bloomington: Indiana University Press, 2000), 122–23, 261–62; Harry Christiansen, *Northern Ohio's Interurbans and Rapid Transit Railways* (Cleveland: Transit Data, 1965), 38–39; James Greene and Stephen D. Maguire, "Lake Shore Electric," *Railroad Magazine* 56 (November 1951): 76–90; Lake Shore Electric Railway public timetable, February 22, 1931; "Vignettes of the Road of Service," *First and Fastest* 29 (Spring 2013): 29; H. Roger Grant, *The Corn Belt Route: A History of the Chicago Great Western Railroad Company* (DeKalb: Northern Illinois University Press, 1984), 120–21; William D. Middleton, "Electric Railway Freight," *Railroad History* 151 (Autumn 1984): 34–35.

11. Interview with Richard (Dick) George, June 9, 2014, hereafter cited as George interview.

12. David M. Kennedy, *Freedom from Fear: The American People in Depression and War, 1929–1945* (New York: Oxford University Press, 1999), 160–89.

13. Robert C. Post, "Renaissance Man: An Interview with George Krambles," *Railroad History* 175 (Autumn 1996): 72.

14. George interview.

15. Interview with H. K. Ferrell, April 12, 1970; George interview; *St. Louis Globe-Democrat*, July 21, 1958.

16. Interview with James Andrew, November 3, 1989.

17. Quotation in Hilton and Due, *Electric Interurban Railways*, 250–51.

18. Edward A. Conrad, *Heartland Traction: The Interurban Lines of Kansas City* (Blue Springs, Mo.: Heartland Rails Publishing Company, 2006), 41.

19. Hilton and Due, *Electric Interurban Railways*, 366; Conrad, *Heartland Traction*, 181; *Excelsior Springs [Missouri] Daily Standard*, March 1, 1933.

20. *Excelsior Springs Daily Standard*, March 11, March 24, May 10, October 17, 1933, April 25, 1934; Conrad, *Heartland Traction*, 181.

21. *Excelsior Springs Daily Standard*, April 24, May 10, July 5, July 9, 1934.

22. *Excelsior Springs Daily Standard*, August 17, August 23, 1934; September 11, 1934; Conrad, *Heartland Traction*, 183.

23. William D. Middleton, "Reflections on the Interurban Era," paper presented at Indiana Historical Society, n.d., 1, in possession of author.

24. *Cleveland Plain Dealer*, March 1, 1931.

25. H. Roger Grant, *Railroads and the American People* (Bloomington: Indiana University Press, 2012), 257–58.

26. *Remember When–Trolley Wires Spanned the Country* (Chicago: Central Electric Railfans' Association, 1980), 6.

27. *Remember When*, 6.

E. Jay Quinby, founder of the Electric Railroaders' Association, did not favor the name choice of Central Electric Railfans' Association, and he made his feeling clear to CERA member George Krambles. But Krambles pointed out that the inspiration for the appellation came from an industry trade association, Central Electric Railway Association (CERA), formed in 1906, and the Chicago organization was not about to change its name. Interview with Norman Carlson, January 2, 2015, hereafter cited as Carlson interview (with date).

28. Mark Effle, *I.N.L.: The Early Interurban Newsletters, 1943–1944* (n.p.: Interurban Publications, 1978); Electric Railway Historical Society, video, 2014; interview with Donald Duke, May 4, 1991.

29. Interview with Gary Dillon, November 4, 2014; Carlson interview, January 2, 2015; John D. Denney, "York Railways Revised," *NRHS Bulletin* 72 (Spring 2007): 15.

30. Harre W. Demoro, "Ira L. Swett" (essay), Electric Railway Historical Association, n.p., n.d.

31. Conrad, *Heartland Traction*, 144.

32. *St. Louis Globe-Democrat*, March 4, 1956.

33. *St. Louis Globe-Democrat*, July 25, 1942; July 24, 1948; Illinois Terminal Railroad public timetable,

February 27, 1949; James D. Johnson, compiler, *The Lincoln Land Traction* (Wheaton, Ill.: Traction Orange Company, 1965), 59–60, 113–14.

Those interurbans that still provided passenger service during World War II, including several in Iowa, experienced a spike in their ridership. See Don L. Hofsommer, "Demise Postponed: Iowa Electric Interurban Railways and World War II," *Railroad History* 212 (Spring–Summer 2015): 48–65.

34. *St. Louis Globe-Democrat*, February 26, 1956; Carlson interview, April 18, 2015.

35. *St. Louis Globe-Democrat*, March 4, 1956; Johnson, *The Lincoln Land Traction*, 18.

36. Larry A. Sakar, *Speedrail: Milwaukee's Last Rapid Transit?* (Glendale, Calif.: Interurban Press, 1991), 49–50.

37. Stephen B. Smalley, *The Cincinnati, Georgetown and Portsmouth Railroad* (Wyoming, Ohio: Trolley Talk, 1975): 15.

38. Byron Olsen to author, January 9, 2015.

39. William D. Middleton, *South Shore: The Last Interurban*, rev. 2nd ed. (Bloomington: Indiana University Press, 1999), 159–74; NICTD press release, 2015, in possession of author.

40. Paul Grether, "A Streetcar Named Revival: North American Cities Experiment Anew with Century Old Concept," *Trains* 74 (July 2014): 24–33; Carlson interview, April 18, 2015.

41. *New York Times*, March 17, 2015.

INDEX

Page numbers in *italics* indicate illustrations

Achtenberg, Benjamin M., 138–39
Ade, George, 68
Adrian, Michigan, 39
Air Line News, 43–44, 46
Air Line Stockholders' Association of the World, 45–46
Akron, Ohio, 20, 26, 38
Akron Street Railway Company, 20
Albany, New York, 41, 83
Albany Southern Railroad, 83
Albia, Iowa, 22, 52–55, *53*
Albia & Centerville Railroad, 52
Albia Commercial Club, 52
Albia Interurban Railway, 22, 52, 100, 123, *123*
Alden, John, 143
Alhambra, California, 23
Allen, Horatio, 3, 39
Alum Park, California, 103–104
Amalgamated Association of Street and Electric Railway Employees of America, 111–13
American Car Company, 54
American Railway Union, 108
Ames, Iowa, 149
Anderson, Indiana, 9, 58
Anderson, South Carolina, 105
Annapolis, Maryland, 91
Appleyard, William, 129
Arkansas Valley Interurban Railway, 89–90, *89*
Athens, Ohio, 38
Atlanta, Georgia, 151
Atlantic Shore Line Railway, 148
Auburn, New York, 70
Auburn & Syracuse Electric Railroad, 71
Aurora, Illinois, 41
Aurora Trust and Savings Bank, 41
Austin, Texas, 24
automobile usage, 130
Ayers, O. K, 132

Bailey, Liberty Hyde, 67
Baldwin, Mathias, 3
Baltimore, Maryland, 4, 91
Bamberger Electric Railroad, 28
Banger Railway & Light Company, 67
Barnes, Elizabeth, 143
baseball, 105–106
Bay Area Rapid Transit, 151
Beaumont, Texas, 26
Berkshire Street Railway, 95
Berlin, Germany, 4
Berlin Industrial Exhibition, 4
Bethel, Ohio, 147
Bethel College, 89–90
Biddleford & Saco Railroad, 147, 148
Bill Cotton's Canoe Livery (Elmira, New York), 95
Bi-State Development Agency, 151
Bladensburg, Maryland, 3
Bluemont, Virginia, 71, 85
Bluffton, Indiana, 120–21
Boise, Idaho, 27, 106
Boise Valley Traction Company, 106
Bonham, Texas, 26
Bonner, Joseph, 131
Bonner Railwagon, 131–33, *133*
Boone, Iowa, 149
Boston, Massachusetts, 3, 40
Bradley, D. C., 52
Brenham, Texas, 24
Broomstick Train, The (poem), 153n2
Brotherhood of Locomotive Firemen, 14
Bryan, Ohio, 130
Bucyrus, Ohio, 106
Buffalo, New York, 98
Buffalo & Erie Railway, 124
Burkeville, Texas, 25
Burkeville Railway, 25
Burlington, Vermont, 129
Burlington Railroad. *See* Chicago, Burlington & Quincy Railroad
Burton, Charles, 43

Caldwell, Idaho, 106
Cambridge Springs, Pennsylvania, 102
Campbell and Phelan Company (Morris, Illinois), 70
Camp Dodge, Iowa, 91
Camp Green, Ohio, 72–73
Canton, Ohio, 38
Carlson, Norman, 159n60
Carson, California, 106
Carson City, Nevada, 28
Carter, Boake, 121–22
Carter-Waters Company, 55
Carthage (Missouri) Chautauqua Assembly, 104
Cedar Point Park, Ohio, 101–104
Cedar Rapids, Iowa, 88, *131*
Cedar Rapids & Iowa City Railway, 10, 88, 130, 131
Centerville, Albia & Southern Railway, 50, 52–53, *53*
Centerville, Iowa, 52–54
Centerville, Moravia & Albia Railroad, 52
Centerville Light & Traction Company, 52–54
Central Electric Railfans' Association, 140, 141–42, 162n27
Central Electric Railway Association, 76–77, 162n27
Chagrin Falls, Ohio, 122
Chappell Hill, Texas, 24
Charleston, South Carolina, 39
Charlotte, North Carolina, 105
Chautauqua, New York, 104
Chautauquas, 104
Chautauqua Traction Company, 104
Chemung River, 95
Chester, South Carolina, 155n42
Chesterfield, Indiana, 72
Chesterton, Indiana, 48
Chicago, Anamosa & Northern Railroad, 32

165

Chicago, Aurora & Elgin Railroad, 50, 84, 122, 144
Chicago, Burlington & Quincy Railroad, 33–34, 41, 52, 155n67
Chicago, Illinois, 39–43, 48, 50, 75, 77, 84, 92, 97, 104, 118, 121, 129–30, 134, 140, 142, 150
Chicago, Milwaukee, St. Paul & Pacific Railroad, 11, 52
Chicago, North Shore & Milwaukee Railroad, 50, 77, 80, 84, 88, 91, 91–92, 104, 115, 121–22, 130, 133–34, 144, 159n60, 160n91
Chicago, Ottawa & Peoria Railway, 101
Chicago, Rock Island & Pacific Railroad, 52
Chicago, South Shore & South Bend Railroad, 50, 82–84, 121–22, 133, 150
Chicago & Alton Railroad, 39–40
Chicago & Milwaukee Railroad, 104
Chicago & North Western Railway, 36, 88, 121, 149
Chicago & St. Louis Electric Railway, 39–40
Chicago City Railway, 40
Chicago Great Western Railway, 21, 133
Chicago–New York Air Line Railroad, 41–49, 43, 141, 156n109. See also Miller, Alexander C.
Chicago Rapid Transit Company, 159n60
Chillicothe, Ohio, 38
Chippewa-on-the-Lake, Ohio, 146
Cincinnati, Georgetown & Portsmouth Railroad, 28, 146–47
Cincinnati, Hamilton & Dayton Railway, 162n1
Cincinnati, Lawrenceburg & Aurora Electric Street Railroad, 96
Cincinnati, Ohio, 59, 96, 128
Cincinnati & Lake Erie Railroad, 128–30, 129
Cincinnati Car Company, 128
Circleville, Ohio, 38
Civil Works Administration, 136
Clark, B. B., 33
Clarke, George E., 43
Clarksburg, West Virginia, 86
Cleburne, Texas, 26
Cleveland, Ohio, 5, 14–15, 38, 42, 66, 84, 98, 106, 129, 132, 139
Cleveland, Painesville & Eastern Railroad, 84
Cleveland, Southwestern & Columbus Railway, 15, 20, 106, 124
Cleveland, Southwestern Railway & Light Company, 129–30, 139, 146

Cleveland & Chagrin Falls Electric Railway, 5
Cleveland & Eastern Traction Company, 66
Cleveland Provision Company, 134
Clinton, Davenport & Muscatine Railway, 63, 73
Clinton, Iowa, 62
Coeur d'Alene, Idaho, 20
Coffee Creek, Indiana, 47, 49, 156n109
Coggan, Iowa, 32
Colman Selling Company, 81
Colorado Springs & Cripple Creek District Railway, 11
Columbia, Missouri, 40
Columbia, South Carolina, 155n42
Columbus, Delaware & Marion Electric Railroad, 60, 72, 88, 132
Columbus, Kansas, 118
Columbus, Magnetic Springs & Northern Railway, 51–52
Columbus, Ohio, 38, 77, 98, 123, 128
commercial travelers, 73–81
commuters, 81, 84–92
Concord, California, 87
Connecticut Trolley Museum, 147
Conway, Thomas, Jr., 128–29, 161n4
Cooper, Peter, 3
Co-Operative Construction Company, 44
Cooperstown, New York, 69, 99
Coopersville, Michigan, 59
Corning, New York, 95
Coshocton, Ohio, 32
Country Life Commission, 58
crime, 107
Crimson Limited (interurban train), 127–28
Crooked Creek Railroad, 86
Curtiss, Glenn H., 106
Curtiss Exhibition Company, 106–107
Cuyahoga Falls, Ohio, 101, 122

Daft, Leo, 3–4
Dallas, Texas, 24–26, 40
dangers and wrecks, 6–7, 107, 119–20, 120
Dan Patch Line, 45
Davenport, Iowa, 62–63, 73
Davenport, Thomas, 3
Davidson, Robert, 3
Dayton, Ohio, 77, 98
Dayton, Springfield & Urbana Electric Railway–Urbana, Bellefontaine & Northern Railway, 95–96
Decatur, Illinois, 80, 141, 144
Deemer, Horace, 33
Delaware, Lackawanna & Western Railroad, 154n14

Delaware, Ohio, 50
Denison University, 90
Denver, Colorado, 40, 81
Denver & Interurban Railroad, 81, 89
Derrah's Street Railway Guide, 92
Des Moines, Iowa, 33–34, 35–38, 40, 91, 148–49
Des Moines & Red Oak Railway, 37–38, 37. See also Red Oak & North Eastern Interurban Promotion Company
Des Moines River, 149
Detroit, Jackson & Chicago Railway, 90
Detroit, Michigan, 20, 98, 118, 129
Detroit United Railway, 50, 98–99
D. H. Burnham and Company, 31
disease, 107
Dixie Flyer (interurban train), 136
Dixon, Illinois, 96
Dominguez Air Field, California, 106
DON'Ts *for Motormen* (booklet), 111
Due, John, 67–68, 127
Duke, Donal, 142
Duluth, Minnesota, 33
Dunellen, New Jersey, 96–97

Easley, George, 33
Eastern Michigan Normal College, 88
Eastern Ohio Traction Company, 95, 122
East Haven, Connecticut, 147
Easton, Pennsylvania, 4
East Windsor, Connecticut, 147
Edgeley, North Dakota, 156n82
Edinburgh, Scotland, 3
El Cajon, California, 151
Elder, Bowman, 135
Electric Railroaders' Association, 140–41, 162n27
Electric Railway Club, 113
Electric Railway Historical Society, 142
Electric Railway Journal, 116
Electric Railways Freight Company, 131
Elmira, Corning & Waverly Railway, 95, 114
El Paso, Texas, 26
Elway Transit Company, 131
Elyria (Ohio) High School, 86
Elyria, Ohio, 68, 86
employees, 107–16, 102, 134–36; conductors, 110–11; Italian laborers, 114; Mexican laborers, 115; motormen, 109–11; "Rule G," 108; strikes, 111–13
Employees Mutual Benefit Association, 113
Erie, Pennsylvania, 98
Estellville, Virginia, 39

Evanston, Illinois, 159n60
Everett, Henry, 83
Excelsior Springs, Missouri, 137

Fairmont, West Virginia, 86
Fairmont & Clarksburg Electric Railroad, 107
Fairmont Coal Company, 85
Fallon, Nevada, 28
Fallon Electric Railway, 28, 30–31
Falls Rivet and Machine Company of Ohio, 122
farmers, 57–65, 67–68; children of, 66–67; wives of, 63–66
Farmers' railroad movement, 30
Farnham Third Rail System, 47
Farwell, Texas, 24
Ferrell, H. K., 136
Fonda, Johnstown & Gloversville Railroad, 11
Fort Dodge, Des Moines & Southern Railway, 61, 86, 88, 98, 141, 148–50
Fort Dodge, Iowa, 86, 149
Fort George G. Meade, 91
Fort Sheridan, Illinois, 92
Fort Wayne, Indiana, 98, 120–21, 130
Fort Wayne & Wabash Valley Traction Company, 119–20
Fort Worth, Texas, 25–26
Foster, Ross and Company (Auburn, New York), 70–71
Fox & Illinois Union Railroad, 70
Fraser, Iowa, 149
Frederick & Middletown Railway, 49–50
Friedricks, William B., 83
Fruita, Colorado, 69
Fullerton, Ohio, 66

Gainesville, Texas, 33
Gainesville, Whitesboro & Sherman Electric Railway, 33
Gainesville & Sherman Traction Company, 33
Galva, Illinois, 111–12
Galveston, Texas, 26, 40
Garrettsville, Ohio, 66
Gary, Indiana, 48
Gary & Interurban Railway, 48, 82
Gary Connecting Railways, 48
Gary Land Company, 48
Gary Street Railway, 48–49, 141
Gastonia, North Carolina, 105
Gay Hill, Texas, 24
G. C. Kuhlman Car Company, 127
General Electric Company, 5
George, Dick, 135–36
Georgetown, Ohio, 25
Giant's Causeway Portrush & Bush Valley Railway & Tramway, 4
Gillman City, Missouri, 74

Glasgow, Scotland, 3
Glens Park, The (Ohio), 101
Goerz, Rudolf, 90
Golden West Books, 142
Goodrum, Indiana, 47–48
Goshen, Indiana, 42, 105
Goshen, South Bend & Chicago Railway, 44
Grand Junction, Colorado, 69
Grand Rapids, Grand Haven & Muskegon Railway, 113
Grand Rapids, Holland & Lake Michigan Rapid Railway, 15, 118
Grand Rapids, Michigan, 15, 63
Grand River Valley Railroad, 69
Grand View College, 148
Granite City, Illinois, 145
Granville, Ohio, 90
Greater Cleveland Regional Transit Authority, 150
Great Falls & Old Dominion Railway, 83, 84–85
Great Lakes Naval Station, Illinois, 91, 92
Great Northern Railway, 11
Greenfield, Iowa, 33–34, 36–37
Greenwood, South Carolina, 105, 155n42

Hammond, Indiana, 48
Harrigan, Nevada, 28
Hartford & Springfield Street Railway, 96
Hartford City, Indiana, 118
Hartwick, New York, 113
Harwood, Herbert H., Jr., 85
Hascall, C. A., 28, 31
Haskell, Texas, 26
Haskell Traction Company, 26
Hazen, Nevada, 28
Hedley, William, 3
Heinz, H. J., 105
Hemphill, M. R., 26
Henry, Charles, 9
Herkimer, New York, 69
Highland Park, Illinois, 104, 159n60
Hilton, George, 67–68, 127
Hiram, Ohio, 122
Hiteman, Iowa, 22, 123, 123
Hocking, Iowa, 22
Holland, Michigan, 15, 118
Holland Palace Car Company, 77
Holmes, Oliver Wendell, 154n2
Hope, Illinois, 59
Horachek, John, 144
Houston, Texas, 24–25, 40
Howells, William Dean, 93
How to Become a Motorman (pamphlet), 109
Hudson, New York, 83
Huntington, Henry E., 83

Huron, Ohio, 74
Hutchinson, Kansas, 89

Idaho & Nevada Southern Railway, 27
Illini Railroad Club, 141, 145
Illinois Central Railroad, 32, 36, 136–37
Illinois Railroad Museum, 147
Illinois State Board of Arbitration, 111–12
Illinois Terminal Railroad, 50, 136, 141, 144–45, 149
Illinois Traction System, 15, 61, 77, 80, 84, 115
Imogene, Iowa, 37
Independence, Texas, 24
Independent Order of Odd Fellows, 98
Indiana General Assembly, 121
Indianapolis, Crawfordsville & Western Railway, 108
Indianapolis, Indiana, 12, 61, 75, 77, 92, 98, 117, 136
Indianapolis, New Castle & Winchester Traction Company, 117
Indianapolis & Southeastern Bus Company, 136
Indianapolis Traction Terminal, 20, 31, 125
Indiana Railroad, 72, 118, 126, 127, 134–36, 140
Indiana State Board of Railway Commissioners, 120–21
Indiana Steel Company, 48
Indiana University Press, 142
Interborough Rapid Transit Company, 97, 144
Interstate Public Service System, 77
Interstate Trolley Club, 140
Interurban Central Station Company (Kansas City, Missouri), 31
Interurban Films, 142
Interurban Press, 142
Interurban Railroad Museum, 147
Inter-Urban Railway (of Iowa), 91
Interurbans, 8–11; "Big Schemes," 39–49; bus affiliates, 130; collapse and abandonment, 127, 134–38, 145, 162n9; completed projects, 49–55; container freight service, 133–34; development, 3–9; drawbacks, 107, 154n24; enthusiasts, 140–47; funeral cars, 15; mileage, 23; Nevada interurban promotion, 26–28, 30–31; opposition, 59–60, 68–69; partially built, 32–38; popularity, 11–23; public concerns, 116–24; refrigerator cars, 134; remembrances, 139–45, 147–49; revival, 150–51; service commitments and betterments, 124–34, 126; service complaints, 122–24;

sleeping cars, 77–80; Texas interurban promotion, 24–26; unbuilt schemes, 23–28, 30–31; unbuilt terminals, 31–32; World War II traffic, 162n33
Interurbans News-Letter, 142
Iowa & Illinois Railway, 62
Iowa Central Railway, 52
Iowa Chapter, National Railway Historical Society, 141
Iowa City, Iowa, 88

Jackson, Casper, 108, 110
Jamestown, North Dakota, 156n82
Jamestown, Westfield & Northwestern Railway, 28
Jasper, Texas, 155n41
Jefferson, Texas, 25
Jim Crow laws, 105
Johns Hopkins University Press, 144
Jones, Bob, 105
Joplin & Pittsburg Electric Railway, 21, 118

Kalamazoo, Michigan, 63
Kankakee, Illinois, 45–46, 137
Kankakee & Urbana Traction Company, 136–37
Kansas City, Clay County & St. Joseph Auto Transit Company, 139
Kansas City, Clay County & St. Joseph Railway, 12, 19, 31, 121, 135–38
Kansas City, Kansas, 137
Kansas City, Missouri, 31–32, 40, 137–38, 143
Kansas City, Leavenworth & Western Railway, 137
Kansas City, St. Joseph, Liberty & Excelsior Springs Railway, 138
Kansas City Car Dealers Association, 79–80
Kansas City Interurban Terminal Company, 31
Kansas City Kaw Valley Railroad, 10
Kansas State School for the Blind, 137
Kell, Frank, 26
Kemp, Joseph, 26
Kempfer, C. J., 136
Kendallville, Indiana, 124
Kennebunkport, Maine, 147
Kenner, Louisiana, 124
Kennywood Park, Pennsylvania, 101
Kent, Ohio, 122
Kewaunee, Illinois, 110–11
Kewaunee & Galva Railway, 19, 111
Key System, 112
Kingsland, Indiana, 119–20, 140
Kingsland Wreck, The (sheet music), 121

Kirkland Realty Company, 79
Kirksville, Missouri, 74
Klebolt, Maurice, 144, 145
Knightstown, Indiana, 58
Kobush-Wagenhalls Steam Motor Car, 35
Krambles, George, 135, 141, 162n27

"L" (Chicago Transit Authority), 88, 121
Lackawanna & Wyoming Valley Railroad, 100
Lake Forest, Illinois, 159n60
Lake Forest College, 159n60
Lake Shore & Michigan Southern Railway, 14, 41, 68
Lake Shore Electric Railway, 13–14, 14, 74, 78–79, 84–85, 100, 101, 103, 131–32, 103, 138
Lakeside Chautauqua, Ohio, 104
Lakeview Valley, Colorado, 81
Lakeville, Minnesota, 45
Lakewood, Ohio, 84
La Mesa, California, 150
Lancaster, Ohio, 38
Lancaster Railroad & Locomotive Society, 140
La Porte, Indiana, 43, 47
Lebanon, Ohio, 59
Lee Center, Illinois, 12
Leesburg, Virginia, 85
Le Gallienne, Richard, 95
Liberty, Missouri, 19, 79, 137
Lima, Ohio, 69, 77
Lima Merchants' Trading Association, 69
Linnsburg, Indiana, 108
Lippincott, Henry, 59–60
London, Ohio, 123
Long Beach, California, 13
Longview, Texas, 25
Los Angeles, California, 20, 23, 83
Los Angeles International Air Meet (1911), 106–107
Los Angeles Inter-Urban Railway, 82
Los Angeles Pacific Railroad, 61
Louisville, Kentucky, 20, 61, 98, 136
Loveland, Roelif, 139
Lucas, Clinton, 96
Lucas, Louisa, 96
Lynd, Helen, 130
Lynd, Robert, 130
Lyon, C. P., 47

Madison, Wisconsin, 39
Magnetic Springs, Ohio, 51
magnetic telegraph, 161n1
Manhattan Limited (passenger train), 97
Mapledoram, Blake, 44, 47, 49
Marblehead, Ohio, 103

Marshall, Texas, 25
Mason, Edward, 86
Masonic Order, 98
Massachusetts Institute of Technology, 115
Massachusetts Street Railway Association, 92
McGowan, Hugh J., 21–23
McKeen, W. R., Jr., 35
McKeen Motor Car Company, 35, 36
McKinley, William B., 13–15
McKinney (Texas) Commercial Club, 26
McKinney, Texas, 26
McLean, Virginia, 84
Memphis, Tennessee, 119, 151
Mesaba Railway, 111
MetroLink (St. Louis, Missouri), 151
Meyers Lake Park, Ohio, 101
Michiana Regional Airport, 150
Michigan Agricultural College, 63
Michigan Central Railroad, 11
Michigan United Railway, 61
Middleton, William D., 139
Middletown (book), 130
Middletown, Maryland, 49
Midland Continental Railroad, 156n82
Midway Airport (Chicago, Illinois), 130
military personnel, 90–92
Miller, Alexander C., 41–43, 46
Millersville, Texas, 24
Miller Train Control Corporation, 41
Mill Valley, California, 95
Milwaukee, Wisconsin, 77, 92, 119, 125, 145
Milwaukee Electric Railway & Light Company, 39, 125, 130
Milwaukee Light & Heat Company, 117–18
Milwaukee Rapid Transit & Speedrail Company, 145
Milwaukee Road. *See* Chicago, Milwaukee, St. Paul & Pacific Railroad
Minden, Nebraska, 28
Minneapolis, Kansas City & Gulf Electric Railway, 25, 40–42
Minneapolis, Minnesota, 33, 40, 45, 147
Minneapolis, Northfield & Southern Railway, 45
Minneapolis, St. Paul & Sault Ste. Marie Railroad, 33, 117
Minneapolis, St. Paul, Rochester & Dubuque Electric Traction Company, 45
Minneapolis Streetcar Museum, 147
Missouri & Kansas Interurban Railway, 80–82, 143

Missouri Central Railway, 40
Missouri Pacific Railway, 17
Missouri Public Service Commission, 138–39
Moana Hot Springs, Nevada, 27
Mohawk, New York, 69, 114
Monongah, West Virginia, 85, 107
Monongahela Valley Traction Company, 85–86
Montgomery Ward and Company, 70
Moore, Edward, 84
Moraine, Ohio, 162n4
Moravia, Iowa, 52, 55
Morris, Illinois, 70
Moulton, J. S., 97, 97
Mount Etna, Iowa, 34
Muncie, Indiana, 75, 118, 160
Mystic, Iowa, 52–55

Nampa, Idaho, 106
Nashville, Chattanooga & St. Louis Railway, 119
Nashville, Tennessee, 119
National City, California, 151
National Railway Historical Society, 55, 140
Nevada Cooperative Colony, 30
Nevada Interurban Railway, 27
New Albany Street Railway, 108
Newark, Ohio, 32, 90, 106
Newark & Granville Street Railway, 90
Newberry, South Carolina, 155n42
Newcastle, Indiana, 58
New England Electric Railway Historical Society, 148
New England Street Railway Club, 94
New Orleans, Louisiana, 124, 151
New Orleans Public Service Company, 124
New Philadelphia, Ohio, 38
Newton, Kansas, 89–90
New Trier High School (Winnetka, Illinois), 87, 159n60
New York, New Haven & Hartford Railroad, 11, 133
New York, New York, 41, 46, 84, 87, 96–97, 140, 144
New York, Westchester & Boston Railway, 84, 87
New York Central Railroad, 41–42, 77, 124
New York State Railways, 77, 98
Niagara Gorge Electric Railway, 93
Northern Indiana Commuter Transportation District, 150
Northern Ohio Light & Traction Company, 8
Northern Ohio Power & Light Company, 127, 130–31
Northern Ohio Railway Museum, 147

Northern Ohio Traction & Light Company, 38, 101, 109, 122, 134
Northern Texas Traction Company, 127–28, 130
Northfield, Minnesota, 45
North Shore Line. *See* Chicago, North Shore & Milwaukee Railroad
North Shore Railroad (Northwestern Pacific Railroad), 7
Northwestern Pacific Railroad, 95
Northwestern Pennsylvania Railway, 102
Northwestern University, 88, 159n60
Norwalk, Ohio, 78

Oakland, California, 87
Oberlin, Ohio, 68
Oelwein, Iowa, 20
Ohio Electric Railway, 50, 90, 97, 123, 128
Ohio Interurban Railway Association, 76
Ohio Public Service Company, 131
Ohio Wesleyan University, 88
Oklahoma City, Oklahoma, 40
Oklahoma Railway, 87
Olathe, Kansas, 143
Olsen, Bryon, 148–49
Omaha, Nebraska, 40
Omaha & Nebraska Central Railway, 59
Oneonta, Cooperstown & Richmond Springs Railway, 99, 114
Oneonta, New York, 69–70
Oneonta & Mohawk Valley Railway, 7
Orange Empire Railroad Museum, 147
Order of United Commercial Travelers, 77
Oregon Electric Railway, 77, 115
Orem Line, 143
Orleans-Kenner Electric Railway, 124
Otsego (interurban car), 99
Overland Park, Kansas, 81, 143

Pacific Coast Railway, 28
Pacific Electric Railway (book), 142
Pacific Electric Railway, 23, 50, 61, 75–76, 82, 83–84, 92, 101, 106, 115
Pacific Northwest Traction Company, 130
Page, Charles, 3
Paine, Albert Bigelow, 95
P&N Park, South Carolina, 105
Paoli, Pennsylvania, 11
Pathé News Weekly, 128–29
Paul Smith's Electric Railway, 100
Paxton, Illinois, 137
Payne, Frank, 52, 54
Payson, Utah, 143
Penn-Ohio Public Service Company, 130

Pennsylvania Motor Company, 4
Pennsylvania Railroad, 11, 41, 42, 97
Peoria, Illinois, 144
Perris, California, 147
Peru, Indiana, 105
Philadelphia, Pennsylvania, 11, 116, 140
Philadelphia & Eastern Electric Railway, 119
Piedmont & Northern Railway, 50, 105, 106, 155n42
Pioneer, Ohio, 39
Pittsburg, Kansas, 21
Pittsburgh, Butler & New Castle and Pittsburgh, Mars & Butler Railways, 93–94
Pittsburgh, Pennsylvania, 42
Pittsburgh Railway, 101
Plano, Texas, 147
pleasure seekers, 92–107
Pontiac, Michigan, 63
Port Arthur, Texas, 26
Port Chester, New York, 84
Port Clinton, Ohio, 24
Portland, Maine, 96
Portsmouth, Kittery & York Electric Railway, 86, 93, 116
Portsmouth, Ohio, 38
Post, Robert C., 135
Price, Charles F., 85
Provo, Utah, 143
Puget South Electric Railway, 60
Pullman strike, 108
Purdue University, 115
P. W. Brook and Company (New York City), 11

Quanah (Texas) Chamber of Commerce, 26
Quanah & Medicine Mound Traction Company, 26
Quinby, E. Jay, 162n27
Quincy, Illinois, 74
Quincy, Omaha & Kansas City Railroad, 74

Railroad Enthusiasts (organization), 140
Railroadians of America (organization), 140
Railroad Magazine, 141
Railway & Locomotive Historical Society, 140
"Railway Riot" (Waukesha, Wisconsin), 117–18
Ralston, Samuel, 121
Rambling Club (Elmira, New York), 95
Rapid Railway, 59
Ravinia Park, Illinois, 104, 160n91
Reconstruction Finance Corporation, 138

INDEX **169**

Red Arrow Lines, 150
Redfield, William, 39
Red Oak, Iowa, 33–34, 36–38
Red Oak & North Eastern Interurban Promotion Company, 33–36. *See also* Des Moines & Red Oak Railway Company
Redondo Beach Park, California, 101
Reno, Nevada, 27–28
Reno Electric Railway & Land Company, 155n46
Reno Traction Company, 27
Rhyolite, Nevada, 27
Richfield Springs, New York, 114
Richmond Union Passenger Railway, 4
Richwood, Ohio, 51
Riverside Park, Idaho, 106
Roberts and Abbott (engineering firm), 34
Robertson, W. E., 156n109
Roby & Northern Railway, 28, 29
Rochester, New York, 98
Rochester & Sodus Bay Railway, 77
Rochester & Syracuse Railroad, 110
Rockford & Interurban Railway, 133–34
Rock Island, Texico, Farwell & Southern Railway, 24
Rock Island Railroad, 52
Rocky Glen Park, Pennsylvania, 100–101, 104
Rocky River, Ohio, 84
Rome, Watertown & Ogdensburg Railroad, 77
Roosevelt, Franklin, 134
Rosslyn, Virginia, 84
rowdyism, 107
Rule, Texas, 26
Rural Electrification Administration, 62
Rye Beach Park, Ohio, 100

Sacramento Northern Railway, 87, 130
"Safety First" campaigns, 121
Saginaw, Michigan, 63
Saltair Park, Utah, 101
Saltana (steamboat), 119
Salt Lake, Garfield & Western Railroad, 101
Salt Lake & Utah Railroad, 143
Salt Lake City, Utah, 143
San Antonio, Texas, 24–25
San Diego, California, 151
San Diego Metropolitan Transit System, 151
San Diego Trolley, 151
Sandusky, Milan & Norwalk Electric Railway, 6
Sandusky, Ohio, 24, 78, 101, 103, 103

San Francisco, California, 40, 151
San Francisco–Oakland Terminal Railway, 112
San Gabriel, California, 23
San Pedro, Los Angeles & Salt Lake Railroad, 75
Santa Clara & San Jose Electric Railway, 103
San Ysidro, California, 151
Sausalito, California, 95
Savage, Marion Willis (Will), 45
Scioto Valley Traction Company, 38
Sears, Roebuck, 70
Seashore Trolley Museum, 147–48, 148
Seattle, Washington, 151
Seiberling, Frank A., 26
Seventh Ward Civic Improvement League of Jefferson Parish, Louisiana, 124
Seville, Ohio, 147
Shaker Heights Rapid Line, 150
Shopmen's Strike of 1922, 112–13
Shore Line Trolley Museum, 147
Shreveport, Louisiana, 24
Silver Lake Junction, Ohio, 109
Sir Knight's Excursion, 102
Smith, Frank, 120
Smith, Frederick E., 26
Snow, Phoebe, 154n14
Soo Line Railroad. *See* Minneapolis, St. Paul & Sault Ste. Marie Railroad
South Bend, Indiana, 150
South Carolina Canal & Rail Road Company, 39
Southeastern Pennsylvania Transportation Authority (SEPTA), 150
Southern Iowa Industrial Railroad, 55
Southern Iowa Railway, 55
Southern Iowa Traction Company, 52
Southern New York Power & Railway Company, 113–14
Southern New York Railway, 69
Southern Ohio Public Service Company, 135
Southern Pacific Railroad, 28
South Goldfrog, Nevada, 27
South La Porte, Indiana, 47–48
South Omaha, Nebraska, 59
South Shore Railroad. *See* Chicago, South Shore & South Bend Railroad
Southwest Missouri Electric Railway, 17, 104, 113
Sparks, Nevada, 27
Sparta, Illinois, 136
Spartanburg, South Carolina, 105, 155n42
Spokane, Washington, 20
Spokane & Inland Empire Railroad, 20

Sprague, Frank Julian, 3–5
Sprague Electric Railway and Motor Company, 4
Springfield, Illinois, 144–45
Springfield, Massachusetts, 3
Springfield, Ohio, 123, 128, 130
SS *Eastland* (lake steamer), 119
Stark County Electric Railroad, 132
Starved Rock State Park, Illinois, 101
station architecture and structures, 78, 125
Stephenson, George, 3
Sterling, Dixon & Eastern Traction Company, 95
Sterling, Illinois, 95
Sterro-Photo Company, 93
Stickney, A. B., 21
Stillwater, Nevada, 28
St. Joseph, Missouri, 137–38
St. Louis, Missouri, 39–40, 84, 144–45, 151
St. Louis Car Company, 144
Stone and Webster Company, 26
Stout Airlines, 129
St. Paul, Minnesota, 147
Strong, William B., Jr., 81
Studebaker, J. M., 105
students, 86–90, 159n60
suburban development, 81–84, 86
Suisun City, California, 147
Summerford, Ohio, 122
Sunday, Billy, 105
Swett, Ira, 142–43
Symington, William, 3

Terre Haute, Indiana, 87
Terre Haute, Indianapolis & Eastern Traction Company, 21, 87, 134
Texas-Louisiana Traction Company, 24–25
Texico, New Mexico, 24
Tiffin, Fostoria & Eastern Electric Railway, 23
Tiffin, Ohio, 23–24
Toledo, Bowling Green & Southern Traction Company, 9
Toledo, Ohio, 14, 39, 44, 98, 128, 129, 130, 132
Toledo, Port Clinton & Lakeside Railway, 100, 103–104, 140–41
Toledo & Chicago Interurban Railway, 64, 124
Toledo & Indiana Railroad, 130–31
Toledo & Western Railway, 38–39, 109
Tomlinson, Birdie, 121
Tonopah, Divide & Goldfield Electric Railroad, 27
Topeka, Eskridge & Council Grove Railroad, 36–37
Topeka, Kansas, 37

Transcontinental Electric Railroad, 40
Travelers' Protective Association of America, 77
Trolley Honeymoon from Delaware to Maine, A (book), 96–97
Trolley Wayfinder (guide book), 94
Truckee-Carson Water Project, 27
Truck Ferry Service (Trailer-on-Flatcar), 133
trucks, 130–34
Twin City & Lake Superior Railway, 33
Twin City Lines, 149
Twin Falls, Idaho, 27

Uhrichville, Ohio, 38
Union, Illinois, 147
Union, Ohio, 25
Union, South Carolina, 155n42
Union Pacific Railroad, 35, 139
Union Traction Company of Indiana, 9, 75
Union Trust Company of Spokane, 20–21
United States Naval Academy, 91
United States Post Office, 70
United States Steel Corporation, 48
University of Illinois, 115, 137
University of Iowa, 88
University of Michigan, 88, 90
University of Minnesota, 149
University of Pennsylvania, 128
Urbana, Illinois, 136
Utica (New York) Boosters, 98
Utica, New York, 97–98
Utica Electric Railway Tour, 97–98

Valparaiso, Indiana, 48–49
Valparaiso & Northern Railway, 48
Van Depoele, Charles, 3–4
Vanderbilt, William Henry, 124
Van Deusen, Edgar, 10–11
Van Doren, C. A., 136–37
Van Doren, Carl, 58–59, 136–37
Van Wert, Ohio, 97
Vermont Transit Company, 129
Versailles, Ohio, 25
villagers, 68–73
Virginia & Truckee Railroad, 28

Wabash Railroad, 37–38, 52
Warsaw, Indiana, 105
Washington, Arlington & Falls Church Railway, 83
Washington, Baltimore & Annapolis Electric Railway, 91, 140
Washington, D.C., 3, 85, 91, 151
Washington, Texas, 24
Washington & Old Dominion Railway, 10, 28, 65, 71, 85, 109–10
Waterloo, Cedar Falls & Northern Railway, 77
Watertown, Wisconsin, 39
Waukegan, Illinois, 88, 159n60
Waukesha, Wisconsin, 117–18, 145
Waverly, Sayre & Athens Traction Company, 111
Webb City, Missouri, 113
Webster City, Iowa, 86
Webster Crossing, Ohio, 66
Wells, Nevada, 27
Werner von Siemens, Ernst, 3–4
West Coast Interurbans: California (book), 142
Western Ohio Railway, 69, 85
Western Railroad Museum, 147
Westinghouse Electric and Manufacturing Company, 5, 11
Westminster, Colorado, 89
Westminister University, 88–89
Westville, Indiana, 47
Wheeling, West Virginia, 38
White Plains, New York, 84
Whitney, Asa, 39
Wichita, Kansas, 40, 89
Wichita Falls, Texas, 26
Wichita Falls & Northwestern Railway, 26
Wichita Falls Traction Company, 26
Wiergate, Texas, 25
Wiley High School (Terre Haute, Indiana), 87
Willdred Flats, Ohio (apartment house), 78–79, 78
William Penn, Texas, 24
Wilmette, Illinois, 159n60
Wilmington, Delaware, 96
Wimbledon, North Dakota, 156n82
Winnetka, Illinois, 87, 159n60
Winnipeg, Manitoba, 156n82
Winnsboro, South Carolina, 155n42
Winona Interurban Railway, 105
Winona Lake Assembly and Summer Assembly, Indiana, 105
Winterset, Iowa, 33–34, 37
Wofford College, 88
Works Progress Administration, 136

Yolande (interurban car), 98–99
York, Maine, 116–17
York Corner, Maine, 86
York Railway, 143
Ypsilanti, Michigan, 90

Zanesville, Ohio, 32, 135
Zion, Illinois, 88

BOOKS IN THE RAILROADS PAST & PRESENT SERIES

Landmarks on the Iron Road:
Two Centuries of North
American Railroad Engineering
William D. Middleton

South Shore: The Last Interurban
(revised second edition)
William D. Middleton

Katy Northwest: The Story of a
Branch Line Railroad
Don L. Hofsommer

"Yet there isn't a train I wouldn't
take": Railway Journeys
by William D. Middleton
William D. Middleton

The Pennsylvania Railroad
in Indiana
William J. Watt

In the Traces:
Railroad Paintings of Ted Rose
Ted Rose

A Sampling of Penn Central:
Southern Region on Display
Jerry Taylor

The Lake Shore
Electric Railway Story
Herbert H. Harwood Jr. &
Robert S. Korach

The Pennsylvania Railroad at Bay:
William Riley McKeen and the
Terre Haute & Indianapolis Railroad
Richard T. Wallis

The Bridge at Québec
William D. Middleton

History of the J. G. Brill Company
Debra Brill

Uncle Sam's Locomotives: The
USRA and the Nation's Railroads
Eugene L. Huddleston

Metropolitan Railways:
Rapid Transit in America
William D. Middleton

Perfecting the American
Steam Locomotive
J. Parker Lamb

From Small Town to Downtown:
A History of the Jewett Car
Company, 1893–1919
Lawrence A. Brough &
James H. Graebner

Limiteds, Locals, and Expresses
in Indiana, 1838–1971
Craig Sanders

Steel Trails of Hawkeyeland:
Iowa's Railroad Experience
Don L. Hofsommer

Amtrak in the Heartland
Craig Sanders

When the Steam
Railroads Electrified
(revised second edition)
William D. Middleton

"The GrandLuxe Express:"
Traveling in High Style
Karl Zimmermann

Still Standing: A Century of
Urban Train Station Design
Christopher Brown

The Indiana Rail Road Company:
America's New Regional Railroad
Christopher Rund

Evolution of the American
Diesel Locomotive
J. Parker Lamb

The Men Who Loved Trains:
The Story of Men Who Battled
Greed to Save an Ailing Industry
Rush Loving Jr.

The Train of Tomorrow
Ric Morgan

Built to Move Millions:
Streetcar Building in Ohio
Craig R. Semsel

The CSX Clinchfield Route
in the 21st Century
Jerry Taylor & Ray Poteat

The New York, Westchester &
Boston Railway: J. P. Morgan's
Magnificent Mistake
Herbert H. Harwood Jr.

Iron Rails in the Garden State:
Tales of New Jersey Railroading
Anthony J. Bianculli

Visionary Railroader:
Jervis Langdon Jr. and the
Transportation Revolution
H. Roger Grant

The Duluth South Shore & Atlantic Railway: A History of the Lake Superior District's Pioneer Iron Ore Hauler
John Gaertner

Iowa's Railroads: An Album
H. Roger Grant &
Don L. Hofsommer

Frank Julian Sprague: Electrical Inventor and Engineer
William D. Middleton &
William D. Middleton III

Twilight of the Great Trains
(expanded edition)
Fred W. Frailey

Little Trains to Faraway Places
Karl Zimmermann

Railroad Noir: The American West at the End of the Twentieth Century
Linda Grant Niemann

From Telegrapher to Titan: The Life of William C. Van Horne
Valerie Knowles

The Railroad That Never Was: Vanderbilt, Morgan, and the South Pennsylvania Railroad
Herbert H. Harwood Jr.

Boomer: Railroad Memoirs
Linda Grant Niemann

Indiana Railroad Lines
Graydon M. Meints

The Indiana Rail Road Company: America's New Regional Railroad
(revised & expanded edition)
Christopher Rund, Fred W. Frailey, & Eric Powell

The CSX Clinchfield Route in the 21st Century
(now in paperback)
Jerry Taylor & Ray Poteat

Wet Britches and Muddy Boots: A History of Travel in Victorian America
John H. White Jr.

Landmarks on the Iron Road: Two Centuries of North American Railroad Engineering
(now in paperback)
William D. Middleton

On Railways Far Away
William D. Middleton

Railroads of Meridian
J. Parker Lamb, with contributions
David H. Bridges & David S. Price

Railroads and the American People
H. Roger Grant

The Electric Pullman: A History of the Niles Car and Manufacturing Company
Lawrence A. Brough

John Frank Stevens: Civil Engineer
Clifford Foust

Off the Main Lines: A Photographic Odyssey
Don L. Hofsommer

The Rock Island Line
Bill Marvel

The Railroad That Never Was: Vanderbilt, Morgan, and the South Pennsylvania Railroad
(now in paperback)
Herbert H. Harwood Jr.

The Louisville, Cincinnati & Charleston Rail Road: Dreams of Linking North and South
H. Roger Grant

The Iowa Route: A History of the Burlington, Cedar Rapids & Northern Railway
Don L. Hofsommer

The Railroad Photography of Jack Delano
Tony Reevy

Railroaders without Borders: A History of the Railroad Development Corporation
H. Roger Grant

The Lake Shore Electric Railway Story
(now in paperback)
Herbert H. Harwood Jr. &
Robert S. Korach

Electric Interurbans and the American People
H. Roger Grant

H. ROGER GRANT is Kathryn and Calhoun Lemon Professor of History at Clemson University. He is author of more than thirty books, including *Visionary Railroader* (IUP, 2008), *Iowa's Railroads* (with Don L. Hofsommer) (IUP, 2009), *Railroads and the American People* (IUP, 2012), *The Louisville, Cincinnati & Charleston Rail Road: Dreams of Linking North and South* (IUP, 2014) and *Railroaders without Borders: A History of the Railroad Development Corporation* (IUP, 2015).

This book was designed by Jamison Cockerham and
set in type by Tony Brewer at Indiana University
Press, and printed at Thompson Shore, Inc.

The typefaces are Arno, designed by Robert Slimbach in 2007;
Caecilia, designed by Peter Matthias Noordzij in 1990; Rosewood,
designed by Kim Buker Chansler, Carl Crossgrove, and Carol
Twombly in 1994; and Stempel Schneidler, designed by F. H. Ernst
Schneidler in 1982. All are issued by Adobe Systems, Inc.

www.ingramcontent.com/pod-product-compliance
Lightning Source LLC
Chambersburg PA
CBHW080925100426
42812CB00007B/2377